Design 9661

EASY-LIVING HOMES

200 Exciting Plans for Active Adults, Professional Couples & Empty-Nesters

HOME PLANNERS
TUCSON, ARIZONA

TABLE OF CONTENTS

CONTINUE THE TRADITION—
Comfortable Cottages Sized Perfectly for You 3

THIS IS THE FUTURE—
Contemporary Plans With All the Comforts of Home 45

OLD-WORLD ACCENTS—
Revisit a European Heritage 75

TIME TO RELAX—
Porches That Welcome Easy Times 109

LIVE THE SUNSHINE DREAM—
Sun-Kissed Homes to Romance the Soul 151

YOU EARNED IT!—
Luxury Homes With a Casual Elegance 183

OUTSIDE POSSIBILITIES—
Garages, Potting Sheds and More..199

When You're Ready to Order 212
Price Schedule and Plans Index..218
Additional Plans Books 222
About the Designers 224

Published by Home Planners
Editorial and Corporate Offices:
3275 West Ina Road, Suite 110
Tucson, Arizona 85741

Distribution Center:
29333 Lorie Lane
Wixom, Michigan 48393

Rickard D. Bailey, CEO and Publisher
Cindy Coatsworth Lewis, Publications Manager
Paulette Mulvin, Senior Editor
Lorie Anderson, Project Editor
Paul D. Fitzgerald, Senior Graphic Designer
Karen L. Leanio, Graphic Designer
Mike Shanahan, Graphic Designer
Jay C. Walsh, Production Artist

Photo Credits
Front & Back Covers: ° Jon Riley

First Printing, June, 1997

10 9 8 7 6 5 4 3 2 1

Printed in the United States of America.

Library of Congress Catalog Card Number: 97-071441

ISBN: 1-881955-38-9

On the front and back cover: Design 9661 from Donald A. Gardner, Architects, Inc., has all the amenities of a luxury home in a manageable square footage that's perfect for a couple. For more information about this design, see page 44.

CONTINUE THE TRADITION

Comfortable Cottages Sized Perfectly for You

While larger homes speak volumes on the subject of high style and opulence, it takes a very special design to incorporate those special "creature comforts" into a more manageable square footage. So created was the design concept of Easy-Living homes. Specially catering to the needs and desires of active adults, these plans focus on the ebbs and tides of a lifestyle that values easy times. Increasingly active adult lifestyles—that may or may not involve children (or grandchildren!)—require a home that can wear all the hats of a busy couple. You'll want your new home to act in a variety of roles: a gracious setting for entertaining, a casual place to kick up your heels, a welcome retreat from your busy schedule— all without having that "tied down" feeling of a larger, more maintenance-intensive home.

The homes we've selected for this section span the breadth of our favorite traditional designs—in moderate square footages that a seasoned homeowner will surely appreciate. The easy style and understated elegance of Design 9728 (on page 19) is evident at every turn. With a fine division of the formal dining room with the great room, stylish features such as the soaring cathedral ceiling and decorative columns continue the casually elegant look of the home. All of the homes we present to you are designed with the highest standards of architectural integrity and ingenuity—and each has a personality as individual as you!

Design 8956

First Floor: 845 square feet
Second Floor: 845 square feet
Total: 1,690 square feet

Design by
Larry W. Garnett
& Associates, Inc.

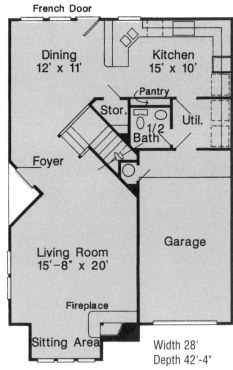

French Door

Dining
12' x 11'

Kitchen
15' x 10'

Pantry

Stor.

Util.

1/2
Bath

Foyer

Garage

Living Room
15'-8" x 20'

Fireplace

Sitting Area

Width 28'
Depth 42'-4"

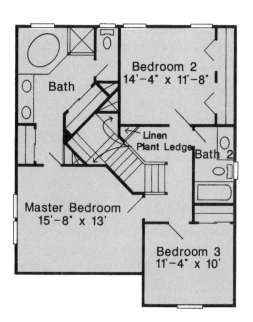

Bath

Bedroom 2
14'-4" x 11'-8"

Linen
Plant Ledge

Bath 2

Master Bedroom
15'-8" x 13'

Bedroom 3
11'-4" x 10'

A n angled staircase lends diversity to this cozy, three-bedroom plan. The large living room affords amenities such as a fireplace and a quaint sitting area. The roomy kitchen features a corner sink and bar that services the dining room. Here you'll find a French door opening to the rear yard. A storage closet accommodates odds and ends. With a powder room and a utility area accessing the garage, the first floor functions with convenience in mind. The second floor features a master suite with an oversized bath offering a twin vanity, spa tub and a compartmented toilet. Two secondary bedrooms and a full hall bath complete this level.

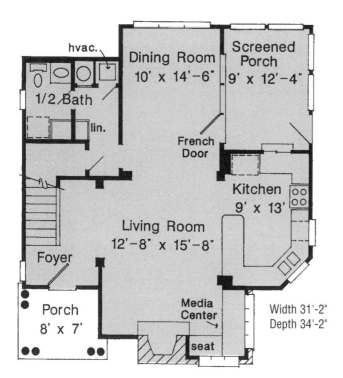

hvac.

1/2 Bath

lin.

Dining Room
10' x 14'-6"

Screened Porch
9' x 12'-4"

French Door

Kitchen
9' x 13'

Living Room
12'-8" x 15'-8"

Foyer

Porch
8' x 7'

Media Center

seat

Width 31'-2"
Depth 34'-2"

Design 9164

First Floor: 771 square feet
Second Floor: 632 square feet
Total: 1,403 square feet

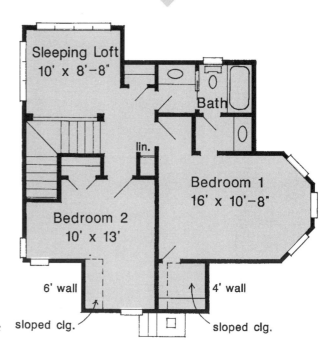

Sleeping Loft
10' x 8'-8"

Bath

lin.

Bedroom 1
16' x 10'-8"

Bedroom 2
10' x 13'

6' wall

4' wall

sloped clg.

sloped clg.

Come home to this delightful shingle-style cottage. A stone chimney adds appealing texture to the exterior. The first floor boasts open spaces and a delightful screened porch. A built-in media center and window seat in the living room cut down on clutter. A fireplace here provides a cozy atmosphere. The wrap-around kitchen features plenty of cabinet space. The larger bedroom has a bay window and private access to the compartmented bath. One other bedroom plus a sleeping loft—perfect for guests or as a studio—finish the second floor.

Design by
**Larry W. Garnett
& Associates, Inc.**

Design 9186

First Floor: 1,340 square feet
Second Floor: 514 square feet
Total: 1,854 square feet

This quaint brick home excels in livability. The front porch gives way to a multi-faceted living area emphasized by a fireplace. The kitchen serves this area through a pass-through, making entertaining a breeze. Defined by columns, the dining room presents a simply elegant atmosphere for meals. The rear of the house is made up of the master bedroom suite. A full private bath with dual lavatories, a compartmented toilet and a separate tub and shower enhance this retreat. Upstairs, two bedrooms each sport walk-in closets and share a full bath. A detached two-car garage rests to the rear of the plan.

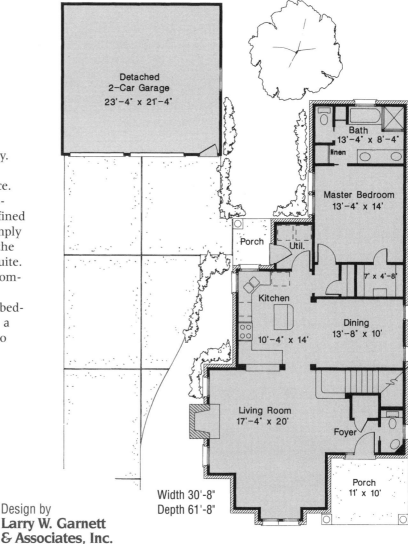

Detached
2-Car Garage
23'-4" x 21'-4"

Bath
13'-4" x 8'-4"

Linen

Master Bedroom
13'-4" x 14'

Porch

Util.

7' x 4'-8"

Kitchen
10'-4" x 14'

Dining
13'-8" x 10'

Living Room
17'-4" x 20'

Foyer

Porch
11' x 10'

Width 30'-8"
Depth 61'-8"

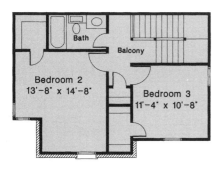

Bath

Balcony

Bedroom 2
13'-8" x 14'-8"

Bedroom 3
11'-4" x 10'-8"

Design by
**Larry W. Garnett
& Associates, Inc.**

Design by
Larry W. Garnett & Associates, Inc.

Width 35'-8"
Depth 44'-8"

Screened Porch
10' x 10'

Bedroom 1
15' x 12'

sliding French doors

Bath

linen

Dining
10' x 10'

Kitchen
11' x 8'

cabinets

Util.

sliding French doors

Living Area
17'-4" x 14'

Foyer

Veranda
(8' depth)

Bedroom 3
11'-4" x 11'-6"
10' clg.

raised clg.

Bath

Balcony

seat

Bedroom 2
11'-4" x 10'
10' clg.

Design 9131

First Floor: 978 square feet
Second Floor: 464 square feet
Total: 1,442 square feet

QUOTE ONE®

Cost to build? See page 214
to order complete cost estimate
to build this house in your area!

Rear Elevation

From the covered front veranda to the second-story Palladian window, this home exudes warmth and grace. Though smaller in square footage, the floor plan offers plenty of room. The living area is complemented by a cozy corner fireplace and is attached to a dining area with French doors to a screened porch and the front veranda. The galley-style kitchen is the central hub of the first floor. A large bedroom on this floor has an attached full bath and serves equally well as a guest bedroom or the master suite. The second floor holds two bedrooms and another full bath. An open balcony area here overlooks the foyer below.

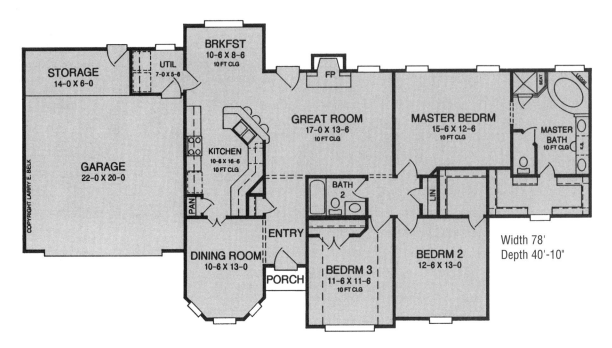

STORAGE
14-0 X 6-0

UTIL
7-0 X 5-6

BRKFST
10-6 X 8-6
10 FT CLG

FP

GARAGE
22-0 X 20-0

KITCHEN
10-6 X 16-6
10 FT CLG

GREAT ROOM
17-0 X 13-6
10 FT CLG

MASTER BEDRM
15-6 X 12-6
10 FT CLG

MASTER
BATH
10 FT CLG

COPYRIGHT LARRY E. BELK

PAN

BATH
2

LIN

ENTRY

DINING ROOM
10-6 X 13-0

PORCH

BEDRM 3
11-6 X 11-6
10 FT CLG

BEDRM 2
12-6 X 13-0

Width 78'
Depth 40'-10"

**Design by
Larry E. Belk
Designs**

This traditional elevation fronts a compact layout with all the frills normally found in a larger home. Ten-foot ceilings in all major living areas give the home an open, spacious feel. The kitchen features an angled eating bar, a pantry and lots of cabinet and counter space. The master suite is highlighted by a luxury bath. Standard features include His and Hers vanities with knee space, a corner whirlpool tub and a separate shower with a seat. An enormous walk-in closet with a window for natural light completes this owner's retreat. Bedrooms 2 and 3 and a large linen closet are nearby. Bedroom 2 is notable for its oversized walk-in closet. Please specify basement or crawlspace foundation when ordering.

Design 8064

Square Footage: 1,742

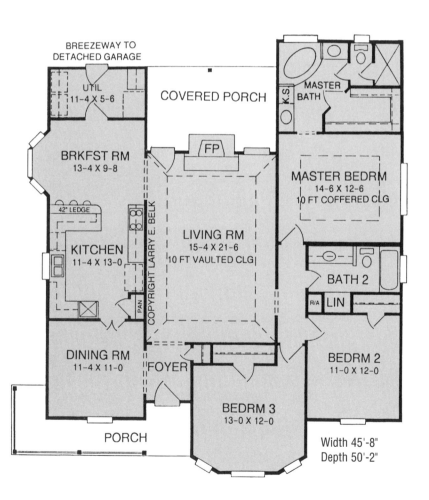

BREEZEWAY TO
DETACHED GARAGE

UTIL
11-4 X 5-6

COVERED PORCH

MASTER
BATH

K.S.

BRKFST RM
13-4 X 9-8

FP

MASTER BEDRM
14-6 X 12-6
10 FT COFFERED CLG

42" LEDGE

KITCHEN
11-4 X 13-0

LIVING RM
15-4 X 21-6
10 FT VAULTED CLG

COPYRIGHT LARRY E. BELK

BATH 2

PAN

R/A   LIN

DINING RM
11-4 X 11-0

FOYER

BEDRM 2
11-0 X 12-6

PORCH

BEDRM 3
13-0 X 12-0

Width 45'-8"
Depth 50'-2"

Design 8165

Square Footage: 1,772

A Victorian flair gives this cottage its curb
appeal. Inside, a large living room boasts
a centerpiece fireplace and coffered ceiling.
The spacious kitchen is joined to the breakfast room with a convenient snack bar. The
master suite includes a ten-foot coffered ceiling and a luxury bath complete with a corner
whirlpool tub, a separate shower, His and
Hers vanities and a roomy walk-in closet.
Two additional bedrooms share a hall bath.
A two-car garage plan is included with this
design and can be connected to the home
with a breezeway. Please specify crawlspace
or slab foundation when ordering.

Design by
**Larry E. Belk
Designs**

Design 9238

First Floor: 1,421 square feet
Second Floor: 448 square feet
Total: 1,869 square feet

Always a welcome site, the covered front porch of this home invites entry to its delightful floor plan. Living areas to the back of the house include the great room with a stylish see-through fireplace to the hearth kitchen with bayed dinette, planning desk, and large corner walk-in pantry. The formal dining room is traditionally placed at the front of the plan and is updated with a built-in hutch. A split-bedroom sleeping plan puts the master suite with whirlpool tub, walk-in closet, and double vanity on the first floor away from two second-floor bedrooms and shared full bath.

Design by
Design Basics, Inc.

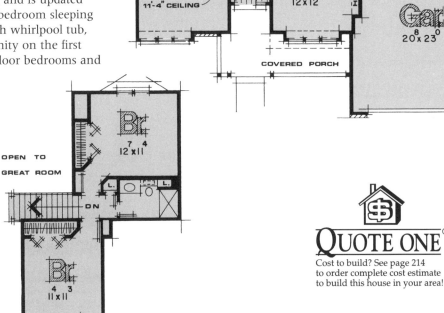

Width 52'
Depth 47'-4"

Width 52'
Depth 45'-4"

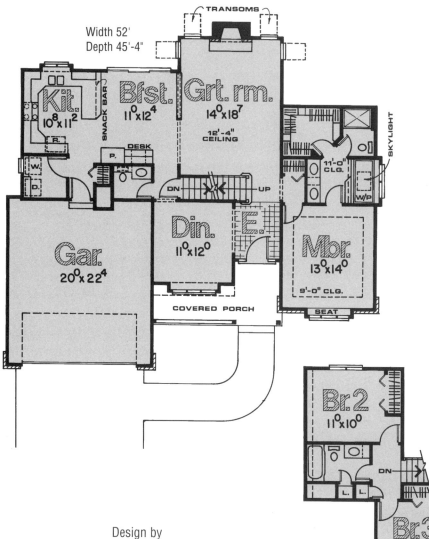

Kit. 10⁸x11²

Bfst. 11⁰x12⁴

Grt. rm. 14⁰x18⁷

12'-4" CEILING

SNACK BAR

DESK

P.

DN   UP

11'-0" CLG.

SKYLIGHT

W/P

Gar. 20⁰x22⁴

Din. 11⁰x12⁰

Mbr. 13⁰x14⁰

9'-0" CLG.

COVERED PORCH

SEAT

TRANSOMS

Design by
Design Basics, Inc.

Br.2 11⁰x10⁰

Br.3 11⁰x10⁰

DN

L. L.

Design 9265

First Floor: 1,297 square feet
Second Floor: 388 square feet
Total: 1,685 square feet

A lovely covered porch welcomes family and guests to this delightful 1½-story home. From the entry, the formal dining room with boxed windows and the great room with fireplace are visible. A powder room for guests is located just beyond the dining room. An open kitchen/dinette features a pantry, planning desk, and a snack-bar counter. The elegant master suite is appointed with formal ceiling detail and a window seat. A skylight above the whirlpool, a decorator plant shelf and double sinks all dress up the master bath. Secondary bedrooms on the second floor share a centrally located bath.

QUOTE ONE®
Cost to build? See page 214
to order complete cost estimate
to build this house in your area!

Design 8166

Square Footage: 1,955

Design by
Larry E. Belk Designs

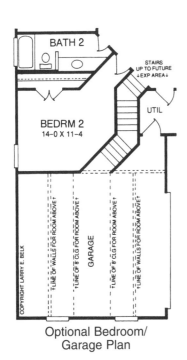

Optional Bedroom/ Garage Plan

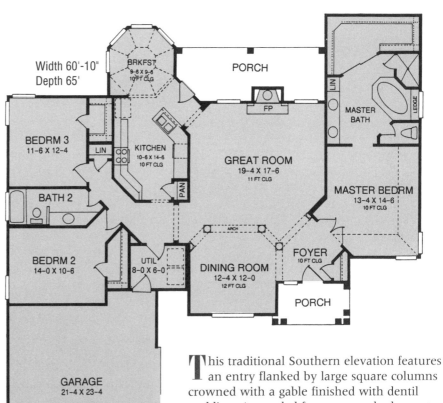

Width 60'-10"
Depth 65'

This traditional Southern elevation features an entry flanked by large square columns crowned with a gable finished with dentil molding. An angled foyer opens the home to a large great room accented with a fireplace. A formal dining room is defined with a series of columns that give this cottage an elegant, gracious feel. The master suite is entered through double doors and is privately located away from the secondary bedrooms. A future expandable area is located above the garage. Please specify crawlspace or slab foundation when ordering.

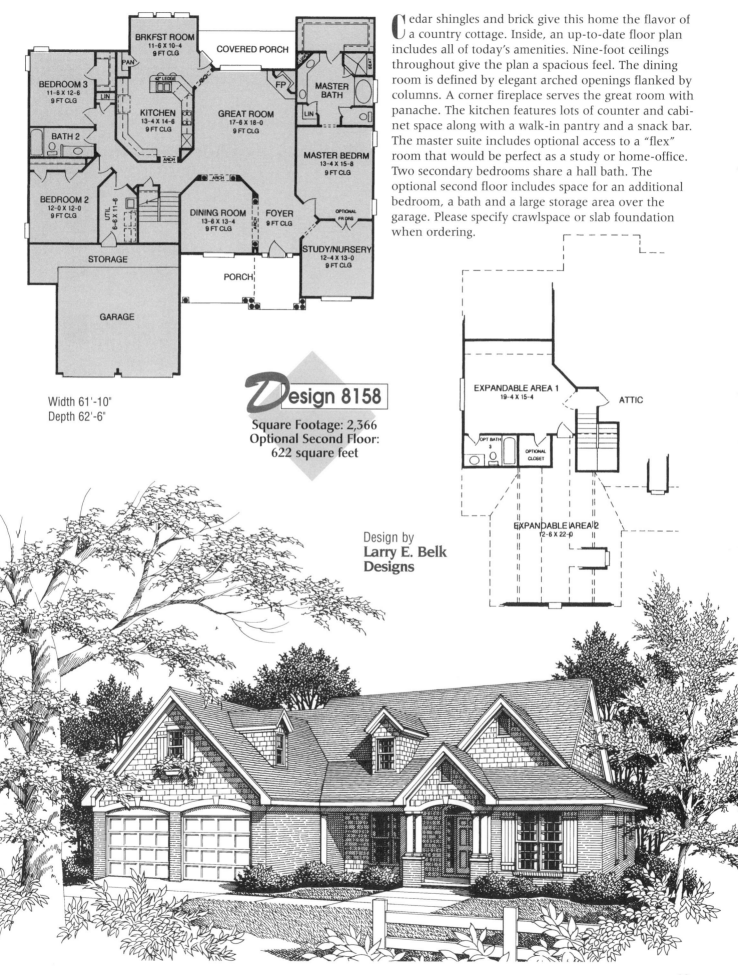

BRKFST ROOM
11-6 X 10-4
9 FT CLG

COVERED PORCH

BEDROOM 3
11-6 X 12-6
9 FT CLG

PAN

42" LEDGE

MASTER
BATH

FP

KITCHEN
13-4 X 14-6
9 FT CLG

GREAT ROOM
17-6 X 18-0
9 FT CLG

BATH 2

LIN

MASTER BEDRM
13-4 X 15-8
9 FT CLG

ARCH

BEDROOM 2
12-0 X 12-0
9 FT CLG

UTIL
6-6 X 11-6

ARCH

DINING ROOM
13-6 X 13-4
9 FT CLG

FOYER
9 FT CLG

ARCH

OPTIONAL
FR DRS

STORAGE

PORCH

STUDY/NURSERY
12-4 X 13-0
9 FT CLG

GARAGE

Width 61'-10"
Depth 62'-6"

Design 8158

Square Footage: 2,366
Optional Second Floor:
622 square feet

Design by
**Larry E. Belk
Designs**

EXPANDABLE AREA 1
19-4 X 15-4

ATTIC

OPT BATH
3

OPTIONAL
CLOSET

EXPANDABLE AREA 2
12-6 X 22-0

Cedar shingles and brick give this home the flavor of a country cottage. Inside, an up-to-date floor plan includes all of today's amenities. Nine-foot ceilings throughout give the plan a spacious feel. The dining room is defined by elegant arched openings flanked by columns. A corner fireplace serves the great room with panache. The kitchen features lots of counter and cabinet space along with a walk-in pantry and a snack bar. The master suite includes optional access to a "flex" room that would be perfect as a study or home-office. Two secondary bedrooms share a hall bath. The optional second floor includes space for an additional bedroom, a bath and a large storage area over the garage. Please specify crawlspace or slab foundation when ordering.

Design 8174

Square Footage: 1,136

This cozy cottage is dressed up with stately corner quoins, multi-pane windows and a hipped roof with front gables. The central family room offers a spacious gathering place with easy access to the rear yard. A graceful arch separates the country kitchen, complete with a bay window eating nook. The master bedroom has a large walk-in closet and a twin-vanity bath. Two secondary bedrooms share a full hall bath. The front-load, two-car garage has extra room for storage. Please specify slab or crawlspace foundation when ordering.

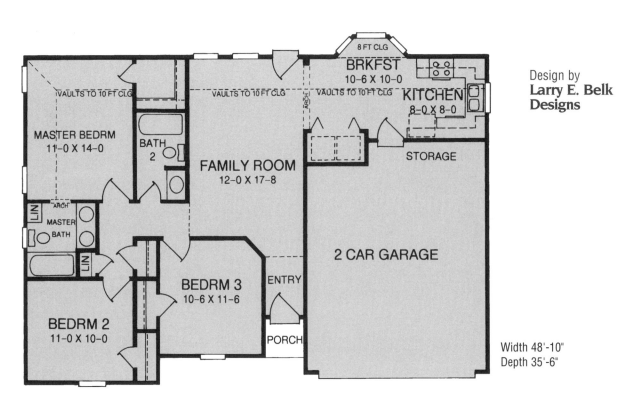

Design by
Larry E. Belk Designs

Width 48'-10"
Depth 35'-6"

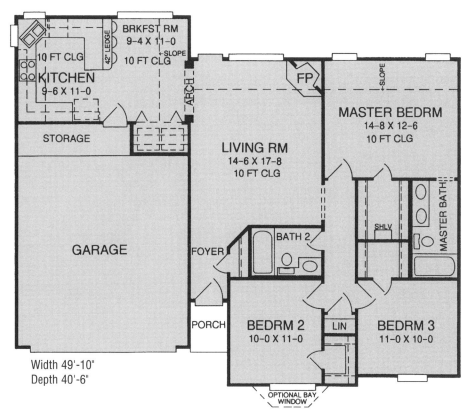

KITCHEN
9-6 X 11-0

10 FT CLG

BRKFST RM
9-4 X 11-0
42" LEDGE
SLOPE
10 FT CLG

STORAGE

GARAGE

FOYER

PORCH

LIVING RM
14-6 X 17-8
10 FT CLG

ARCH

FP

SLOPE

MASTER BEDRM
14-8 X 12-6
10 FT CLG

MASTER BATH

SHLV

BATH 2

BEDRM 2
10-0 X 11-0

LIN

BEDRM 3
11-0 X 10-0

OPTIONAL BAY WINDOW

Width 49'-10"
Depth 40'-6"

Design by
**Larry E. Belk
Designs**

Design 8169
Square Footage: 1,310

This beautiful, brick one-story has so much charm, you'll fall in love with it at first sight. The foyer opens right into the large living room which is accented by a corner fireplace and backyard access. Through an arch is the sunny breakfast room and a wonderful kitchen—conveniently located to avoid cross-room traffic. In the sleeping zone, two family bedrooms share a full hall bath and each has a walk-in closet. The large master suite also offers a walk-in closet along with a pri-vate bath with a dual-bowl vanity. A two-car garage completes this compact yet cozy plan. Please specify slab or crawlspace foundation when ordering.

Design 8168

Square Footage: 1,628

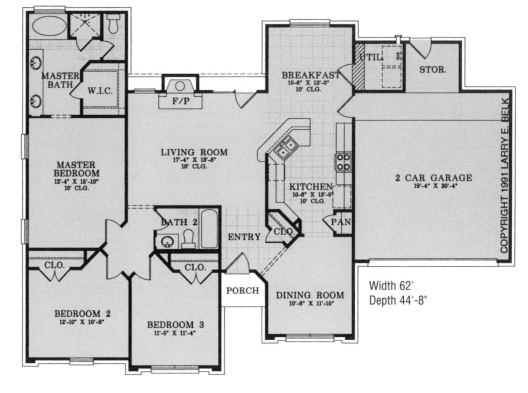

MASTER BATH

W.I.C.

F/P

BREAKFAST
10'-6" X 12'-0"
10' CLG.

UTIL

STOR.

MASTER BEDROOM
12'-4" X 15'-10"
10' CLG.

LIVING ROOM
17'-4" X 18'-8"
10' CLG.

KITCHEN
10'-6" X 13'-0"
10' CLG.

2 CAR GARAGE
19'-4" X 20'-4"

CLO.

BATH 2

ENTRY

CLO.

PAN

CLO.

CLO.

PORCH

DINING ROOM
10'-6" X 11'-10"

BEDROOM 2
12'-10" X 10'-8"

BEDROOM 3
11'-0" X 11'-4"

COPYRIGHT 1991 LARRY E. BELK

Width 62'
Depth 44'-8"

Design by
**Larry E. Belk
Designs**

A lovely traditional facade complements this up-to-date floor plan. Inside, the open angled breakfast bar connects the kitchen and breakfast room to the main living area. The living room is graced by a centered fireplace and access to the rear yard. The master suite features a roomy walk-in closet, double vanities and a separate shower and whirlpool tub. Two secondary bedrooms have stylish angled entries and share a full hall bath. A two-car garage has an additional storage room with a separate door. Please specify crawl-space or slab foundation when ordering.

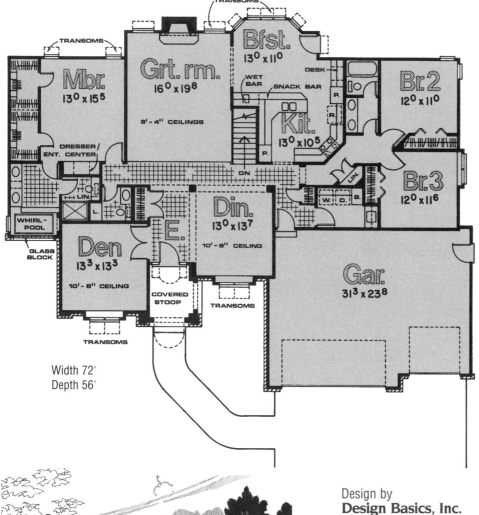

Mbr.
13⁰ x 15⁵

Grt. rm.
16⁰ x 19⁸

9'-4" CEILINGS

TRANSOMS

Bfst.
13⁰ x 11⁰

DESK

WET BAR

SNACK BAR

Kit.
13⁰ x 10⁵

Br.2
12⁰ x 11⁰

Br.3
12⁰ x 11⁶

DRESSER / ENT. CENTER

LIN.

WHIRL-POOL

GLASS BLOCK

Den
13³ x 13³

10'-8" CEILING

Din.
13⁰ x 13⁷

10'-8" CEILING

COVERED STOOP

Gar.
31³ x 23⁸

TRANSOMS

TRANSOMS

Width 72'
Depth 56'

Design by
Design Basics, Inc.

Design 9323

Square Footage: 2,276

Drama and harmony are expressed by utilizing a variety of elegant exterior materials. An expansive entry views the private den with French doors and an open dining room (both rooms have extra-high ceilings). The great room with a window-framed fireplace is conveniently located next to the eat-in kitchen with bayed breakfast area. Special amenities include a wet bar/servery, two pantries, planning desk, and snack bar. Two secluded secondary bedrooms enjoy easy access to a compartmented bath with a twin vanity. His and Hers closets and a built-in armoire that could be an entertainment center or a dresser, grace the master bedroom. A luxurious master bath features glass blocks over the whirlpool, double sinks and an extra linen storage cabinet. An alternate elevation is provided at no extra cost.

Design 7226

Square Footage: 1,479

A covered porch and interesting window treatments add charisma to this cheerful ranch home. The entry opens onto a sunny great room warmed by a center fireplace framed with transom windows. Nearby, an efficient kitchen is highlighted by an island snack bar, a corner sink flanked with windows and access to the back yard. The spacious master suite features a walk-in closet and a pampering master bath with a whirlpool tub and compartmented toilet and shower area. Two secondary bedrooms—one an optional den designed with French doors—share a full hall bath.

Design by
Design Basics, Inc.

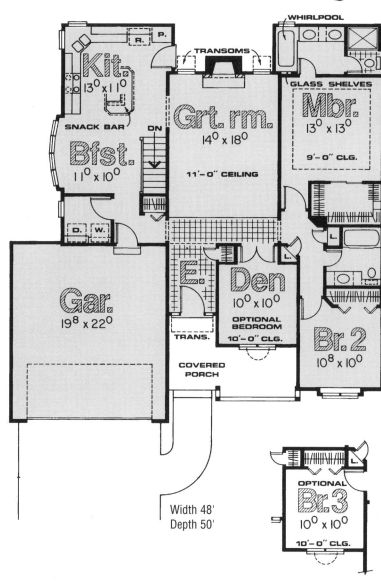

Width 48'
Depth 50'

B. NATHAN.

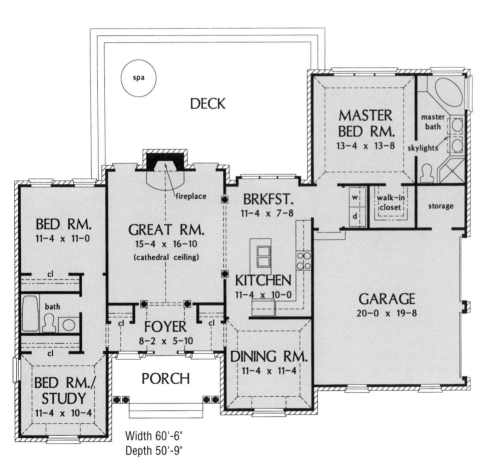

spa

DECK

BED RM.
11-4 x 11-0

cl

bath

cl

BED RM./
STUDY
11-4 x 10-4

GREAT RM.
15-4 x 16-10
(cathedral ceiling)

fireplace

cl

FOYER
8-2 x 5-10

cl

PORCH

BRKFST.
11-4 x 7-8

KITCHEN
11-4 x 10-0

DINING RM.
11-4 x 11-4

MASTER
BED RM.
13-4 x 13-8

master
bath

skylights

w
d

walk-in
closet

storage

GARAGE
20-0 x 19-8

Width 60'-6"
Depth 50'-9"

Design 9728

Square Footage: 1,576

This stately one-story home exhibits sheer elegance with its large, arched windows, round columns, covered porch, and brick veneer. In the foyer, natural light enters through arched windows in clerestory dormers. In the great room, a dramatic cathedral ceiling and a fireplace set a mood of casual elegance. Through gracious, round columns, the kitchen and breakfast room open for comfortable entertaining. The master bedroom is fashioned with a large, walk-in closet and a well-planned master bath with a double-bowl vanity, a garden tub, and a corner shower. Two additional bedrooms and a full bath are located at the opposite end of the house for privacy.

Design by
**Donald A. Gardner,
Architects, Inc.**

19

Design 2682

First Floor (Basic Plan): 976 square feet
First Floor (Expanded Plan): 1,230 square feet
Second Floor (Both Plans): 744 square feet
Total (Basic Plan): 1,720 square feet
Total (Expanded Plan): 1,974 square feet

L D

Here is an expandable Colonial with a full measure of Cape Cod Charm. For those who wish to build the basic house, there is an abundance of livability. Twin fireplaces serve the formal living room and the country kitchen. Both areas are spacious and have plenty of windows. The formal dining room is accented with a bay window. The expanded plan has an additional study, covered rear porch and a garage. Upstairs, the master bedroom has a private bath, and two family bedrooms share a hall bath. The expanded plan includes an additional attic room for storage.

QUOTE ONE®

Cost to build? See page 214 to order complete cost estimate to build this house in your area!

Design by
Home Planners

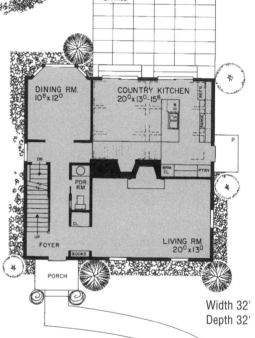

Width 32'
Depth 32'

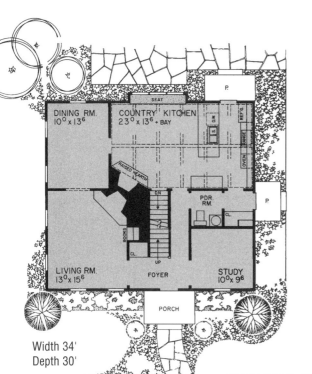

DINING RM.
10⁰ x 13⁶

COUNTRY KITCHEN
23⁰ x 13⁶ + BAY

SEAT

RAISED HEARTH

DN

PDR. RM.

LIVING RM.
13⁰ x 15⁶

FOYER

UP

STUDY
10⁰ x 9⁶

PORCH

Width 34'
Depth 30'

Design by
Home Planners

QUOTE ONE®

Cost to build? See page 214
to order complete cost estimate
to build this house in your area!

ROOF

BATH

BATH

BEDROOM
12⁴ x 11⁰

LINEN

MASTER
BEDROOM
13⁰ x 15⁸

WALK-IN
CLOSET

DN

SHELVES

CEILING CLIP

BEDROOM
11⁰ x 12⁰

ROOF

First Floor: **1,020 square feet**
Second Floor: **777 square feet**
Total: **1,797 square feet**

L **D**

This charming plan is designed to be the perfect starter or retirement home thanks to its ideal blend of comfort and easy style. Inside, it contains a very livable floor plan. An outstanding first floor centers around the huge country kitchen which includes a beam ceiling, a raised-hearth fireplace, a window seat and rear-yard access. The living room with its warming corner fireplace and private study are to the front of the plan. Upstairs are three bedrooms and two full baths. Built-in shelves and a linen closet in the upstairs hallway provide excellent storage.

California Engineered Plans and California Stock Plans are available for this home. Call 1-800-521-6797 for more information.

Design 2597

Square Footage: 1,515

L **D**

Whether it's a starter house you are after, or one in which to spend your retirement years, this pleasing farmhouse will provide a full measure of pride in ownership. The contrast of vertical and horizontal lines, the double front doors and the coach lamppost at the garage create an inviting exterior. The floor plan functions in an orderly and efficient manner. The spacious gathering room and dining room have a delightful view of the rear yard and make entertaining, both family and friends, a joy. The master bedroom has a private bath and a walk-in closet. Two additional bedrooms share a full hall bath. Extra amenities include plenty of storage facilities, two sets of glass doors to the terraces, a fireplace in the gathering room, a basement and an attached two-car garage.

Design by
Home Planners

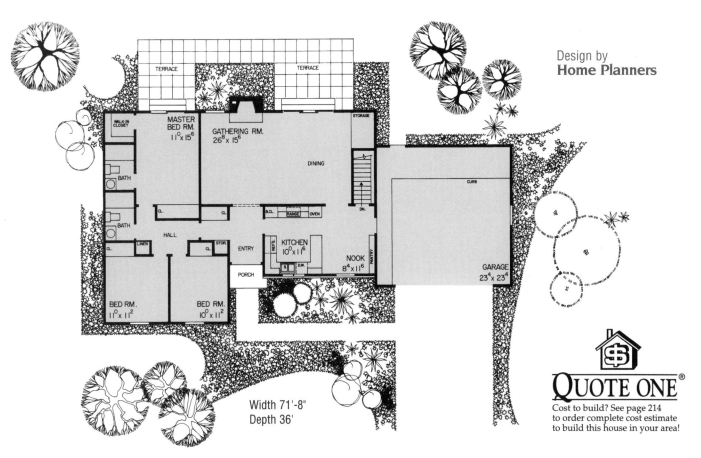

Width 71'-8"
Depth 36'

QUOTE ONE®
Cost to build? See page 214
to order complete cost estimate
to build this house in your area!

This traditional Cape Cod cottage is updated with an open floor plan that invites easy living. True to tradition, the formal living room is located in the front of the plan, just off the foyer. Comfortable living will surely be centered around the fireplace in the family room with the conjoining spacious kitchen. Enjoy casual dining at the snack bar or sit down for a meal in the formal dining room with a bumped-out bay window. A study on the main level would also make a nice guest room thanks to the full hall bath nearby. Up the central stairs, you will find the master bedroom with a private bath and two secondary bedrooms that have private access to a shared bath.

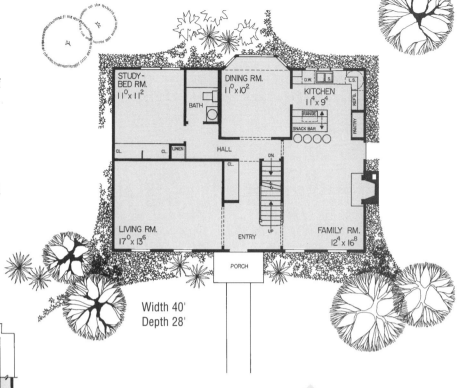

Width 40'
Depth 28'

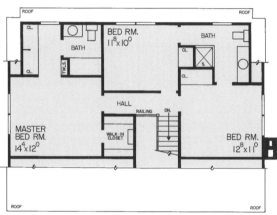

Design by
Home Planners

Design 2571

First Floor: 1,137 square feet
Second Floor: 795 square feet
Total: 1,932 square feet

L **D**

23

Design 2563

First Floor: 1,500 square feet
Second Floor: 690 square feet
Total: 2,190 square feet

L D

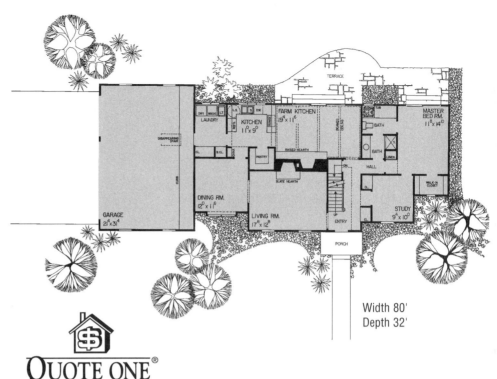

This charming Cape Cod will capture your heart with its warm appeal. From the large living room with a fireplace and adjacent dining room to the farm kitchen with an additional fireplace, the plan works toward livability. The first floor laundry and walk-in pantry further aid in the efficiency of this plan. The master bedroom is located on this level for privacy and is highlighted by a luxurious bath and sliding glass doors to the rear terrace. A front study might be used as a guest bedroom or a library. Upstairs there are two bedrooms and a sitting room plus a full bath to accommodate the needs of family members. Both bedrooms have access to the attic. A three-car garage allows plenty of room for vehicles and storage space.

Design by
Home Planners

Width 80'
Depth 32'

QUOTE ONE®

Cost to build? See page 214 to order complete cost estimate to build this house in your area!

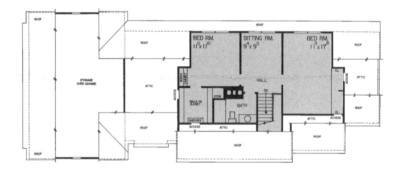

Photo by Laszlo Regos

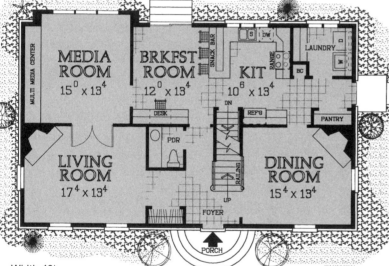

Width 48'
Depth 28'-8"

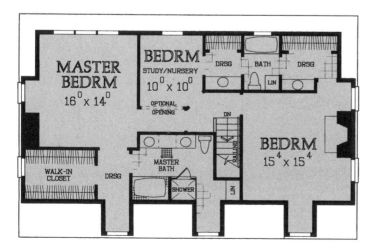

Design 3519

First Floor: 1,396 square feet
Second Floor: 1,169 square feet
Total: 2,565 square feet

L

This stately brick cottage perfectly blends the amenities of a larger home with the coziness of a Colonial cottage. Traditional in design, the split living and dining rooms open off the foyer. Each is detailed with a corner fireplace and large, multi-pane windows. Casual living areas are to the rear of the plan and include a large eat-in country kitchen complete with a snack bar, planning desk and a breakfast nook. A separate media room features a full-wall entertainment center. Upstairs, the master bedroom is highlighted with an expansive walk-in closet with a dressing room and a bath with twin vanities. A gracious room to offer to your guests, the romantic second bedroom suite has a fireplace and private access to a large compartmented bath. A smaller bedroom next to the master suite would make a perfect study and has private access to the compartmented bath.

QUOTE ONE®

Cost to build? See page 214
to order complete cost estimate
to build this house in your area!

Design by
Home Planners

Design 2777

Square Footage: 2,006

L **D**

Many years of delightful living will surely be enjoyed in this one-story traditional. The covered front porch adds charm to the exterior as do the paned windows. Easy living centers around the large gathering room with a raised hearth fireplace and sliding doors to the rear terrace. The dining room is set off just enough to accommodate more formal dinners and is easily accessible from the eat-in kitchen. The kitchen amenities include a cook-top island, an abundance of cabinet and counter space along with an adjoining utility room. The master bedroom has private patio access, a large walk-in closet and a compartmented bath. A study, a secondary bedroom and a full hall bath complete the plan. Extra storage space is available in the two-car garage.

Design by
Home Planners

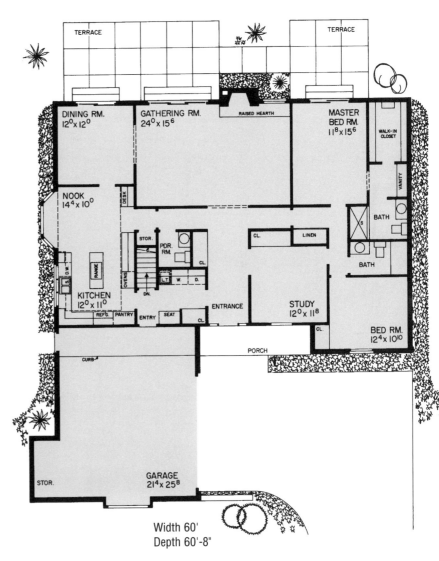

Width 60'
Depth 60'-8"

Design by
Home Planners

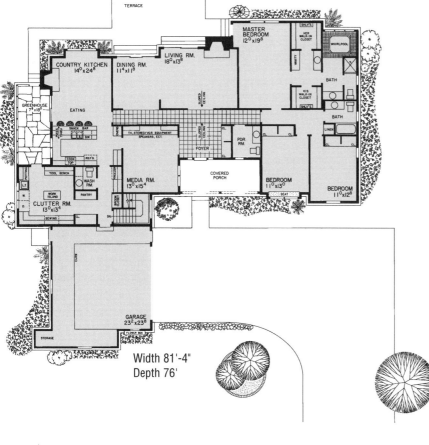

TERRACE

COUNTRY KITCHEN
14⁰x24⁸

DINING RM.
11⁴x11⁸

LIVING RM.
18⁰x13⁸

MASTER BEDROOM
12⁰x19⁶

HER WALK-IN CLOSET

WHIRLPOOL

GREENHOUSE
7⁸x18⁰

EATING

BATH

SNACK BAR

HIS WALK-IN CLOSET

COOK TOP

REF'G.

T.V. STEREO/VCR EQUIPMENT
SPEAKERS, ECT.

SLOPED CEILING

FOYER

PDR. RM.

BATH

LINEN

TOOL BENCH

WASH RM.

WORK ISLAND

PANTRY

MEDIA RM.
13⁰x15⁴

COVERED PORCH

BEDROOM
11⁰x13⁰

BEDROOM
11⁰x12⁸

CLUTTER RM.
13⁰x13⁰

SEWING

STORAGE

GARAGE
23²x23⁸

FLOWER BOX

Width 81'-4"
Depth 76'

Rear Elevation

Design 2880

Square Footage: 2,758
Greenhouse: 149 square feet

L D

This comfortable traditional home offers plenty of modern livability. A clutter room off the two-car garage is an ideal space for a workbench, sewing or hobbies. Across the hall there is a media room, the perfect place for stereo, video and more. A spacious country kitchen to the right of the greenhouse (great for fresh herbs) is an cozy gathering place for family and friends, as well as a convenient work area. Both the formal living room, with its friendly fireplace, and the dining room provide access to the rear grounds. A spacious, amenity-filled master suite features His and Hers walk-in closets, a relaxing whirlpool tub and access to the rear terrace. Two large secondary bedrooms share a full bath.

QUOTE ONE®

Cost to build? See page 214
to order complete cost estimate
to build this house in your area!

Design 8229

Square Footage: 1,955

Design by
Larry E. Belk Designs

A detailed covered porch and arch-topped windows announce a scrupulously designed interior, decked out with amenities. A grand foyer with a 10-foot ceiling and columned archway sets an elegant tone throughout the house. Picture windows flanking a centered fireplace lend plenty of natural light to the great room, which is open through grand, columned archways to the formal dining area and bay windowed breakfast room. The roomy kitchen is conveniently positioned between the dining and breakfast rooms and shares an informal eating counter with the great room. A utility room and walk-in pantry are tucked neatly to the side of the plan. Sleeping quarters are privately set to one side of the house. The master bedroom is delightfully appointed with a large walk-in closet, a dual vanity bath and a corner spa tub. Please specify crawlspace or slab foundation when ordering.

MASTER BEDRM
12-8 X 14-6
10 FT CLG

SLOPE   SLOPE

MASTER BATH
10 FT CLG

BATH 2

FP

BRKFST RM
12-0 X 10-0
10 FT CLG

GREAT ROOM
18-6 X 15-6
10 FT CLG

LIN

BEDRM 2
11-0 X 13-6

ARCH   ARCH

42" LEDGE

ARCH

KITCHEN
12-6 X 14-0
10 FT CLG

UTIL
6-8 X 8-6

PAN

FOYER
10 FT CLG

BEDRM 3
12-6 X 13-4

DINING ROOM
12-2 X 14-0
10 FT CLG

PORCH

GARAGE

COPYRIGHT LARRY E. BELK

Width 65'
Depth 58'-8"

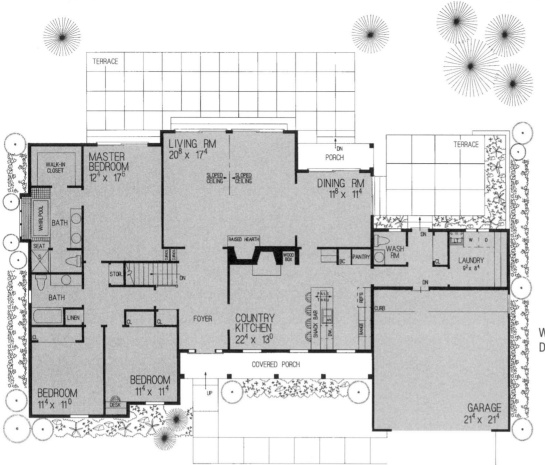

TERRACE

MASTER BEDROOM
12⁴ x 17⁶

WALK-IN CLOSET

LIVING RM
20⁸ x 17⁴

SLOPED CEILING SLOPED CEILING

DN
PORCH

DINING RM
11⁸ x 11⁴

TERRACE

WHIRLPOOL

BATH

SEAT

S

BATH

LINEN

CL

RAISED HEARTH

WOOD BOX

CUPDS CUPDS

STOR.

DN

FOYER

COUNTRY KITCHEN
22⁴ x 13⁰

BC

PANTRY

PASS THRU

SNACK BAR DW S

RANGE

REF'G

CURB

WASH RM

DN

W I D

CL

LAUNDRY
9² x 8⁴

DN

CL CL

BEDROOM
11⁴ x 11⁰

DESK

BEDROOM
11⁴ x 11⁴

UP

COVERED PORCH

GARAGE
21⁴ x 21⁴

Quote One®

Cost to build? See page 214 to order complete cost estimate to build this house in your area!

Width 76'-4"
Depth 46'

Design 3332

Square Footage: 2,168

L

Nothing completes a traditional-style home quite as well as a country kitchen with fireplace and built-in wood box. Notice also the second fireplace (with raised hearth) and the sloped ceiling in the living room. The nearby dining room has an attached porch and separate dining terrace. Besides two family bedrooms with a shared full bath, there is also a marvelous master suite with rear terrace access, walk-in closet, whirlpool tub and double vanities. A handy washroom is near the laundry, just off the two-car garage.

California Engineered Plans and California Stock Plans are available for this home. Call 1-800-521-6797 for more information.

Design by
Home Planners

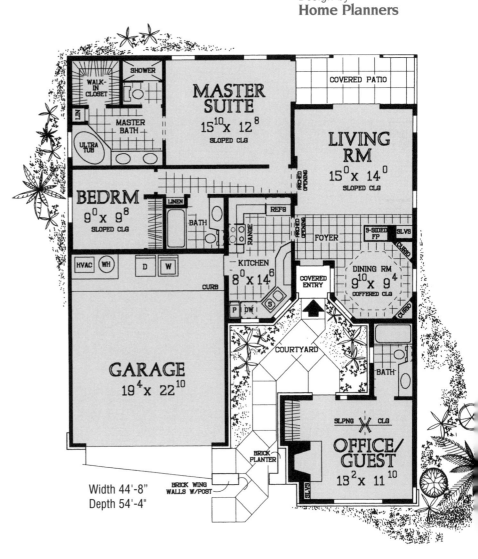

Design 3656

Square Footage: 1,414

L

This cozy cottage contains an abundance of amenities. The front-facing office provides privacy for the entry courtyard. With its separate entrance it offers the perfect haven for an in-home office or for those with live-in parents. Flanking the foyer is a unique dining room with a coffered ceiling and an efficient kitchen with lots of counter space. The corner living room includes a sloping ceiling and access to the covered patio through French doors. The large master suite includes outdoor access and a private bath with a whirlpool, shower, dual sinks and a walk-in closet. An additional bedroom has its own full bath nearby.

Width 44'-8"
Depth 54'-4"

QUOTE ONE®
Cost to build? See page 214
to order complete cost estimate
to build this house in your area!

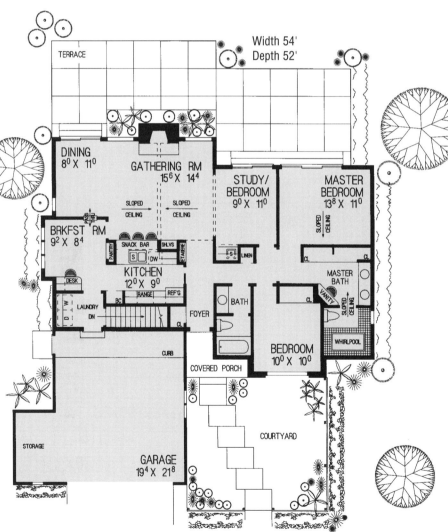

TERRACE

Width 54'
Depth 52'

DINING
8⁰ X 11⁰

GATHERING RM
15⁶ X 14⁴

STUDY/
BEDROOM
9⁰ X 11⁰

MASTER
BEDROOM
13⁸ X 11⁰

SLOPED CEILING — SLOPED CEILING

SLOPED CEILING

BRKFST RM
9² X 8⁴

PANTRY | SNACK BAR | SHLVS

LINEN

PASS THRU

KITCHEN
12⁰ X 9⁰

DESK

RANGE | REF'G

BC

LAUNDRY
DN

FOYER

BATH

MASTER
BATH

VANITY

SLOPED CEILING

WHIRLPOOL

CURB

BEDROOM
10⁰ X 10⁰

COVERED PORCH

COURTYARD

STORAGE

GARAGE
19⁴ X 21⁸

Design by
Home Planners

esign 3355

Square Footage: 1,387

L D

Though modest in size, this fetching one-story home offers a great deal of livability with three bedrooms (or two with study) and a spacious gathering room with a fireplace and a sloped ceiling. The galley kitchen, designed to save steps, provides a pass-through snack bar and has a planning desk and attached breakfast room. In addition to two secondary bedrooms with a full bath, there's a private master bedroom that enjoys views and access to the backyard. The master bath features a large dressing area, a corner vanity and a raised whirlpool tub. Indoor/outdoor living relationships are strengthened by easy access from the dining room, study/bedroom and master bedroom to the rear terrace.

QUOTE ONE®
Cost to build? See page 214
to order complete cost estimate
to build this house in your area!

31

Design 9187

Square Footage (Basic Plan): 1,462

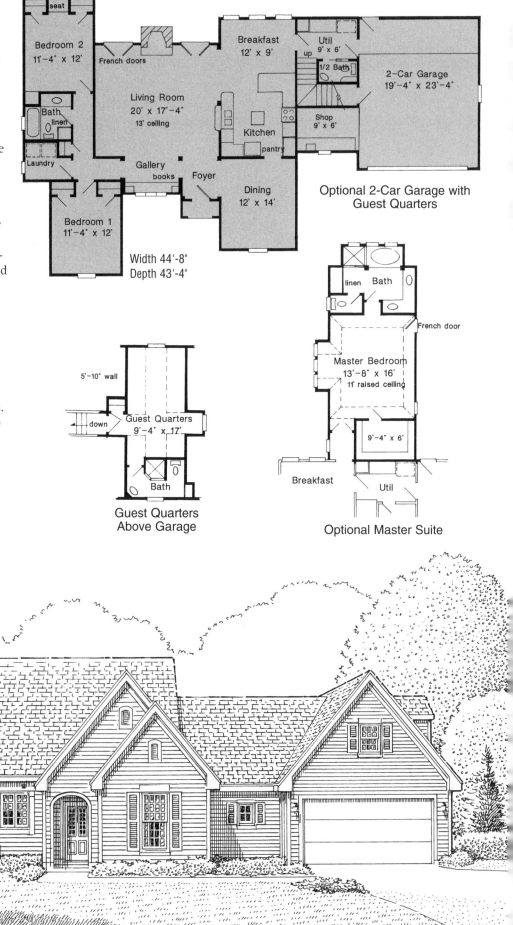

Start small with this charming cottage and grow as you go! The basic design offers amenities often found in homes twice the size. Special features include French doors flanking the charming fireplace in the living room, a window seat bordered by twin closets in Bedroom 2, a laundry room conveniently located to the bedrooms and bath, and an efficient kitchen nestled between the formal dining room and breakfast nook. When you're ready, enlarging the plan is simple, and designed to finish in stages. A sumptuous master suite with a large walk-in closet and pampering bath may be added as the need for additional space arises. A two-car garage with a large shop area, utility room and ½ bath may be completed in the next phase. Completing the expansion of this terrific plan are the guest quarters located above the garage.

Design by
**Larry W. Garnett
& Associates, Inc.**

Bedroom 2
11'-4" x 12'

seat

French doors

Bath
linen

Laundry

Bedroom 1
11'-4" x 12'

Living Room
20' x 17'-4"
13' ceiling

Kitchen
pantry

Gallery
books

Foyer

Dining
12' x 14'

Width 44'-8"
Depth 43'-4"

Breakfast
12' x 9'

Util
9' x 6'
up

½ Bath

Shop
9' x 6'

2-Car Garage
19'-4" x 23'-4"

Optional 2-Car Garage with
Guest Quarters

5'-10" wall

down

Guest Quarters
9'-4" x 17'

Bath

Guest Quarters
Above Garage

linen Bath

French door

Master Bedroom
13'-8" x 16'
11' raised ceiling

9'-4" x 6'

Breakfast

Util

Optional Master Suite

Width 44'-4"
Depth 47'-4"

MASTER SUITE 15¹⁰ x 12⁸ SLOPED CLG

LIVING RM 15⁰ x 14⁰ SLOPED CLG

COVERED PATIO

BEDRM 9⁰ x 9⁸ SLOPED CLG

KITCHEN 8⁰ x 14⁶

DINING RM 9¹⁰ x 9⁴ COFFERED CLG

GARAGE 19⁴ x 22¹⁰

COVERED PORCH

QUOTE ONE®

Cost to build? See page 214
to order complete cost estimate
to build this house in your area!

Design 3659

Square Footage: 1,118

L

Compact yet comfortable, this home has many appealing amenities. From the covered front porch, the entrance foyer opens onto the sunlit, octagonal dining room and the large living room. To the left of the foyer is the efficient kitchen that has the added bonus of no cross-room traffic. The master suite is luxurious and includes a lavish bath complete with a corner tub, a separate shower, a walk-in closet and twin vanities. A secondary bedroom has access to a full hall bath.

Design by
Home Planners

Design by
Home Planners

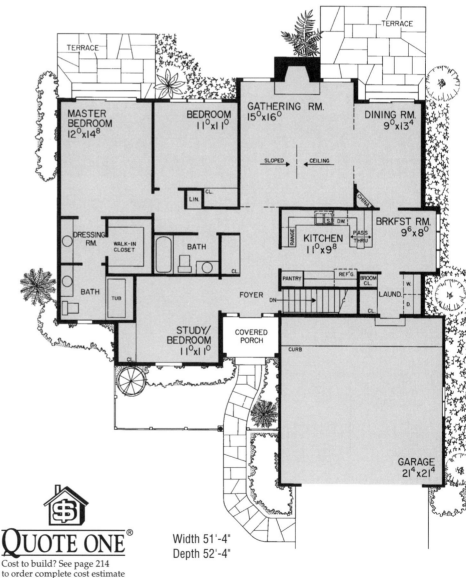

Design 2878

Square Footage: 1,521

L D

This charming one-story traditional design offers plenty of livability in a compact size. Thoughtful zoning puts all sleeping areas to one side of the house apart from household activity in the living and service areas. The home includes a spacious gathering room with a sloped ceiling, in addition to a formal dining room and a separate breakfast room. There's also a handy pass-through between the breakfast room and the large, efficient kitchen. The laundry is strategically located adjacent to the garage and the breakfast/kitchen areas for handy access. A master bedroom enjoys a private bath and a walk-in closet. A third bedroom can double as a sizable study just off the foyer.

California Engineered Plans and California Stock Plans are available for this home. Call 1-800-521-6797 for more information.

QUOTE ONE®

Cost to build? See page 214 to order complete cost estimate to build this house in your area!

Width 51'-4"
Depth 52'-4"

Design by
Home Planners

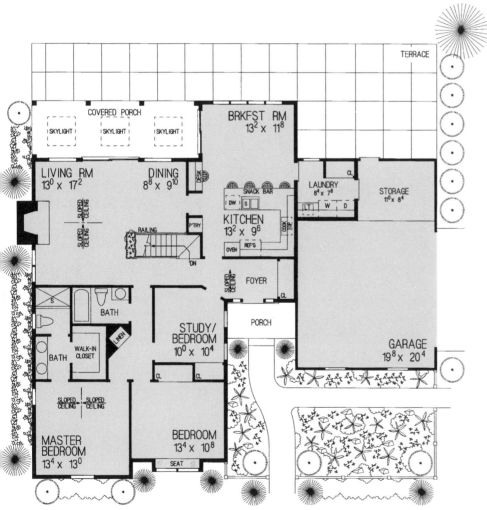

COVERED PORCH

SKYLIGHT   SKYLIGHT   SKYLIGHT

TERRACE

BRKFST RM
13² x 11⁸

LIVING RM
13⁰ x 17²

DINING
8⁸ x 9¹⁰

DESK

SLOPED CEILING   SLOPED CEILING

RAILING

PTRY

SNACK BAR

DW   S

KITCHEN
13² x 9⁶

COOK TOP

OVEN   REF'G

DN

LAUNDRY
8⁴ x 7⁸

LT   W   D

CL

STORAGE
11⁰ x 8⁴

SLOPED CEILING

FOYER

CL

BATH

LINEN

WALK-IN CLOSET

BATH

STUDY/
BEDROOM
10⁰ x 10⁴

CL   CL

PORCH

GARAGE
19⁸ x 20⁴

SLOPED CEILING   SLOPED CEILING

MASTER
BEDROOM
13⁴ x 13⁰

BEDROOM
13⁴ x 10⁸

SEAT

Width 58'
Depth 52'-6"

Design 3340

Square Footage: 1,611

L

A charming cupola over the garage and delightful fan windows set the tone for this cozy cottage. A central fireplace and a sloped ceiling highlight the living room's comfortable design, complete with sliding patio doors and an adjoining dining room. The large eat-in kitchen has a snack bar, planning desk and patio doors from the breakfast room. An angular hallway leads to the master bedroom featuring a large walk-in closet, twin-sink vanity and a compartmented bath. A secondary bedroom features a lovely window seat. A third bedroom is perfectly situated to be a study. The two car garage has a separate storage area with a utility entrance.

QUOTE ONE ®

Cost to build? See page 214
to order complete cost estimate
to build this house in your area!

Design 3487

Square Footage: 1,835

L

Country living is the focus of this charming design. A cozy covered porch invites you into the foyer with the sleeping area on the right and the living area straight ahead. From the windowed front-facing breakfast room, enter the efficient kitchen with its corner laundry room, large pantry, snack-bar pass-through to the gathering room, and passage to the dining room. The massive gathering room and dining room feature sloped ceilings, an impressive fireplace and access to the rear terrace. Terrace access is also available from the master bedroom with its sloped ceiling and a master bath that includes a whirlpool tub, a separate shower and a separate vanity area. A study at the front of the house can also be converted into a third bedroom.

Design by
Home Planners

Width 71'
Depth 43'-5"

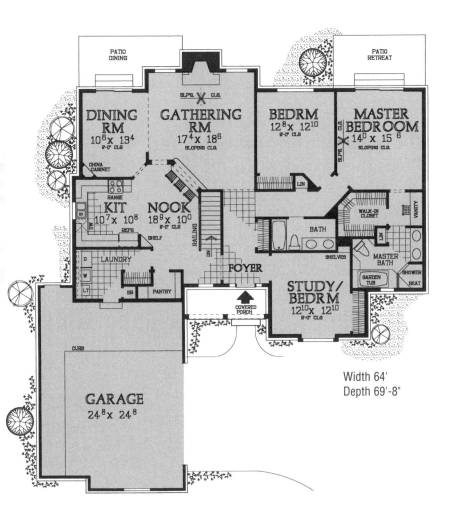

Design 3491

Square Footage: 2,098

L D

PATIO DINING

PATIO RETREAT

DINING RM 10⁸ x 13⁴ 9'-0" CLG

GATHERING RM 17⁴ x 18⁶ SLOPING CLG.

BEDRM 12⁸ x 12¹⁰ 9'-0" CLG

MASTER BEDROOM 14⁰ x 15⁶ SLOPING CLG.

CHINA CABINET

KIT 10⁷ x 10⁸

RANGE

NOOK 18⁹ x 10⁰ 9'-0" CLG.

REFG.

SHELF

RAILING

DN

FOYER

WALK-IN CLOSET

BATH

VANITY

LIN

LIN

MASTER BATH

SHELVES

GARDEN TUB

SHOWER SEAT

LAUNDRY

D

W

LT

BR

PANTRY

COVERED PORCH

STUDY/ BEDRM 12¹⁰ x 12¹⁰ 9'-0" CLG

GARAGE 24⁸ x 24⁸

CURB

Width 64'
Depth 69'-8"

T his is a fine home for a young family or for empty nesters. The versatile bedroom/study offers room for growth or a quiet haven for reading. The U-shaped kitchen includes a handy nook with a snack bar and easy accessibility to the dining room or the gathering room—perfect for entertaining. The master bedroom includes its own private outdoor retreat, a walk-in closet and an amenity-filled bathroom. An additional bedroom and a large laundry room with an adjacent, walk-in pantry complete the plan.

QUOTE ONE®

Cost to build? See page 214
to order complete cost estimate
to build this house in your area!

Design by
Home Planners

Design 9760

Square Footage: 1,475

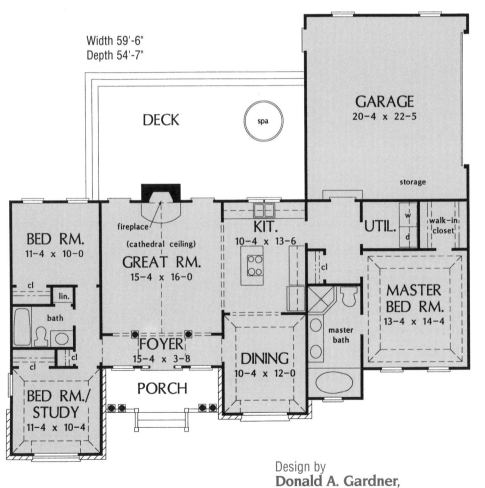

Width 59'-6"
Depth 54'-7"

DECK

spa

GARAGE
20-4 x 22-5

storage

BED RM.
11-4 x 10-0

fireplace
(cathedral ceiling)

GREAT RM.
15-4 x 16-0

KIT.
10-4 x 13-6

UTIL.

walk-in
closet

cl

lin.

bath

cl

FOYER
15-4 x 3-8

master
bath

**MASTER
BED RM.**
13-4 x 14-4

**BED RM./
STUDY**
11-4 x 10-4

PORCH

DINING
10-4 x 12-0

Timeless appeal and gingerbread charm are exhibited in this traditional cottage design. The front porch leads to the columned foyer. A cathedral ceiling in the great room lends height and a feeling of openness, which is further enhanced thanks to a fireplace framed by doors leading to a rear deck. The large kitchen, open to the great room, is equipped with a gourmet cook-top island and is designed to easily serve the dining room. In the quiet master bedroom, a tiered ceiling, a private bath and a walk-in closet are appreciated features. Two secondary bedrooms reside on the left side of the plan and share a full hall bath. The two-car garage is located, out of sight, at the rear of the plan.

Design by
**Donald A. Gardner,
Architects, Inc.**

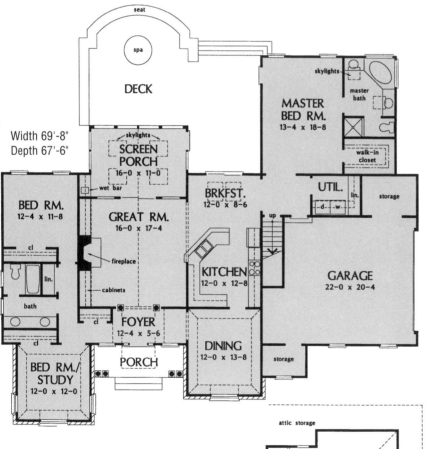

seat

spa

DECK

Width 69'-8"
Depth 67'-6"

SCREEN PORCH
16-0 x 11-0

skylights

wet bar

BED RM.
12-4 x 11-8

GREAT RM.
16-0 x 17-4

cl

fireplace

lin.

cabinets

bath

cl

cl

FOYER
12-4 x 5-6

BRKFST.
12-0 x 8-6

KITCHEN
12-0 x 12-8

DINING
12-0 x 13-8

up

MASTER BED RM.
13-4 x 18-8

skylights

master bath

walk-in closet

UTIL.

lin.

d w

storage

GARAGE
22-0 x 20-4

storage

BED RM./ STUDY
12-0 x 12-0

PORCH

Design by
**Donald A. Gardner,
Architects, Inc.**

attic storage

BONUS RM.
18-0 x 19-0

skylights

down

Design 9734

Square Footage: 1,977
Bonus Room: 430 square feet

A two-story foyer with a Palladian window above sets the tone for this sunlit home. Columns mark the passage from the foyer to the great room, where a centered fireplace and built-in cabinets are found. A screened porch with four skylights above and a wet bar provides a pleasant place to start the day or wind down after work. The kitchen is flanked by the formal dining room and the breakfast room with sliding glass doors to the large, rear deck. Hidden quietly in the rear, the master suite includes a bath with dual vanities and skylights. Two family bedrooms (one an optional study) share a bath with twin sinks. Please specify basement or crawl-space foundation when ordering.

Quote One®

Cost to build? See page 214
to order complete cost estimate
to build this house in your area!

39

This attractive three-bedroom house projects a refined image with its gable and hipped roof, brick veneer and arched windows while offering a touch of country with its covered front porch. The entrance foyer flanked by a dining room and a bedroom/study leads to a spacious great room with sloped ceiling and clerestory above to add impressive vertical volume. The dining room and breakfast room have cathedral ceilings with arched windows flooding the house with natural light. The master bedroom boasts a cathedral ceiling and a bath with a whirlpool tub, a shower and a double-bowl vanity. The second floor allows for two additional bedrooms along with a bonus room. Please specify basement or crawlspace foundation when ordering.

Design by
Donald A. Gardner, Architects, Inc.

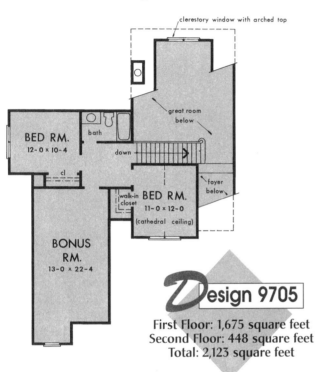

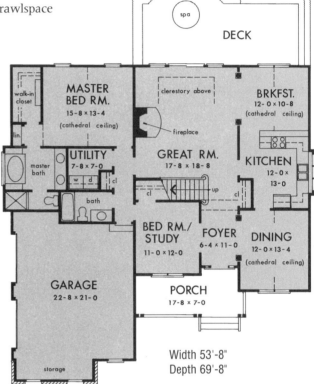

Design 9705

First Floor: 1,675 square feet
Second Floor: 448 square feet
Total: 2,123 square feet

Width 53'-8"
Depth 69'-8"

Photo by Jon Riley

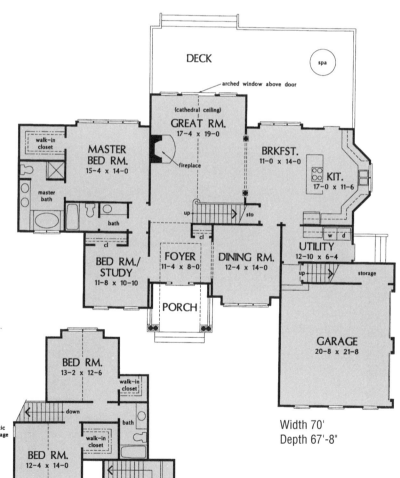

DECK

spa

arched window above door

(cathedral ceiling)

GREAT RM.
17-4 x 19-0

BRKFST.
11-0 x 14-0

KIT.
17-0 x 11-6

walk-in closet

MASTER
BED RM.
15-4 x 14-0

fireplace

master bath

bath

up

sto

cl

w   d

cl

BED RM./
STUDY
11-8 x 10-10

FOYER
11-4 x 8-0

DINING RM.
12-4 x 14-0

UTILITY
12-10 x 6-4

up

storage

PORCH

GARAGE
20-8 x 21-8

BED RM.
13-2 x 12-6

walk-in closet

down

bath

attic storage

walk-in closet

BED RM.
12-4 x 14-0

down

BONUS RM.
12-8 x 21-8

attic storage

attic storage

Width 70'
Depth 67'-8"

Design 9736

First Floor: 1,839 square feet
Second Floor: 527 square feet
Total: 2,366 square feet
Bonus Room: 344 square feet

An arched entrance and windows combine with round columns to give a touch of class to the exterior of this traditional home. The foyer leads to all areas of the house, minimizing corridor space. The large, open kitchen with an island cook-top is convenient to the breakfast and dining rooms. The master bedroom suite has plenty of walk-in closet space and a well-planned master bath. A near-by bedroom would make an excellent guest room or study, with an adjacent full bath. An expansive rear deck boasts a location for a spa tub and generous space for outdoor living. The second level offers two bedrooms, with sloped ceilings and walk-in closets, and a full bath. A bonus room is available over the garage.

Design by
**Donald A. Gardner,
Architects, Inc.**

41

Design 9430

First Floor: 1,150 square feet
Second Floor: 543 square feet
Total: 1,693 square feet

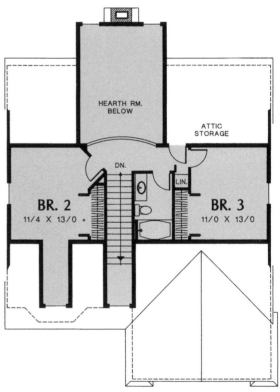

HEARTH RM. BELOW

ATTIC STORAGE

DN.

LIN.

BR. 2
11/4 X 13/0 +

BR. 3
11/0 X 13/0

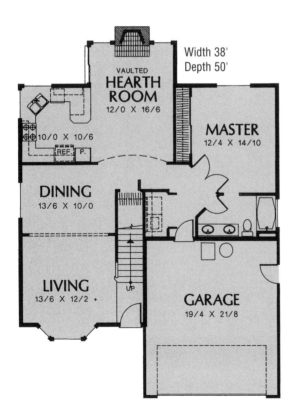

Width 38'
Depth 50'

VAULTED
HEARTH ROOM
12/0 X 16/6

10/0 X 10/6

REF. P.

MASTER
12/4 X 14/10

DINING
13/6 X 10/0

UP

LIVING
13/6 X 12/2 +

GARAGE
19/4 X 21/8

Design by
**Alan Mascord
Design Associates, Inc.**

Perfect for smaller lots, this functional cottage puts every inch of floor space to use with style. Enter into the formal living and dining room that's elegantly accented with a bay window. Casual living takes center stage in the fantastic hearth room with a dramatic two-story vaulted ceiling and windows flanking the fireplace. The adjoining kitchen has a sunny corner sink and a snack bar. The first floor master suite has double-door access, an extra-long closet, and a private master bath that also has a hall-access door. At the top of the stairs, a bowed balcony overlooks the hearth room while giving passage to the two secondary bedrooms and a full hall bath.

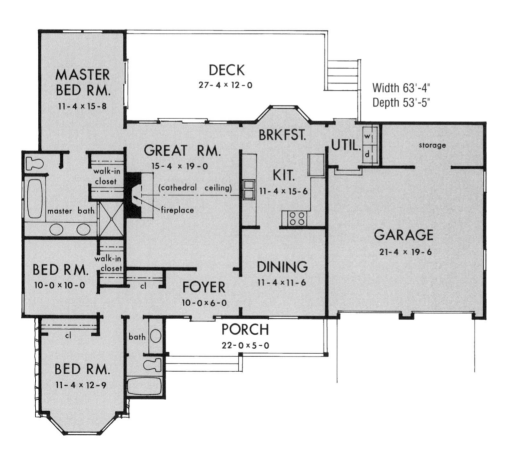

MASTER BED RM.
11-4 x 15-8

DECK
27-4 x 12-0

Width 63'-4"
Depth 53'-5"

BRKFST.

UTIL.

storage

GREAT RM.
15-4 x 19-0

walk-in closet

(cathedral ceiling)

fireplace

KIT.
11-4 x 15-6

master bath

GARAGE
21-4 x 19-6

BED RM.
10-0 x 10-0

walk-in closet

cl

DINING
11-4 x 11-6

FOYER
10-0 x 6-0

cl

bath

BED RM.
11-4 x 12-9

PORCH
22-0 x 5-0

Design 9679

Square Footage: 1,512

A multi-pane bay window, dormers, a cupola, a covered porch and a variety of building materials all combine to dress up this intriguing country cottage. The generous entry foyer leads to a formal dining room and an impressive great room with a cathedral ceiling and a fireplace. The kitchen includes a breakfast area with a bay window overlooking the deck. The great room and master bedroom also access the deck. An amenity-filled master suite is highlighted by a master bath that includes a double-bowl vanity, a shower and a garden tub. Two additional bedrooms are located at the front of the house for privacy and share a full bath.

Design by
**Donald A. Gardner,
Architects, Inc.**

Photo by Jon Riley

QUOTE ONE®

Cost to build? See page 214 to order complete cost estimate to build this house in your area!

BED RM.
10-4 × 11-9

walk-in closet

down

bath

cl

BED RM.
12-4 × 13-6

down

BONUS RM.
11-0 × 20-0

seat

DECK

spa

arched window above door

GREAT RM.
15-4 × 18-0
(cathedral ceiling)

fireplace

KIT./BRKFST.
16-8 × 16-0

master bath

walk-in closet

walk-in closet

pd. rm.

up

sto.

cl

MASTER BED RM.
13-0 × 13-6

FOYER
7-8 × 9-0

DINING
12-4 × 12-4

UTILITY
10-0 × 6-4

w

d

up

storage

PORCH

Width 58'-3"
Depth 68'-9"

GARAGE
20-0 × 20-0

Design 9661

First Floor: 1,416 square feet
Second Floor: 445 square feet
Total: 1,861 square feet

An arched entrance and windows provide a touch of class to the exterior of this plan. The foyer leads to all areas of the house, minimizing corridor space. The dining room displays round columns at the entrance while the great room boasts a cathedral ceiling, fireplace and arched window over exterior doors to the deck. The large kitchen is open to the breakfast nook, and sliding glass doors present a second access to the deck. In the master suite are two walk-in closets and a lavish bath. On the second level are two bedrooms and a full bath. Bonus space over the garage can be developed later. Please specify basement or crawlspace foundation when ordering.

Design by
Donald A. Gardner, Architects, Inc.

THIS IS THE FUTURE

Contemporary Plans With All the Comforts of Home

Some may ask what design elements and interior features are considered when describing a home as a contemporary style. After all, identifying a house as a Victorian or farmhouse style is relatively easy. What then makes a house *contemporary* when exterior styles and construction elements appear to differ greatly from house to house? Just as the modern family has a different definition today than it did twenty years ago, so does the contemporary home.

Looking at what features the couple of today desires in a home is the baseline of creating a livable design. Remember the adage "everything old is new again?" Well, that's true in home design as well. More so than a sleek modern design, a contemporary home is a mixing of architectural elements to fit a specific lifestyle. Take a closer look at Design 3314 (see page 46). Its strong Craftsman style is perfectly balanced with thoroughly modern amenities such as the spacious kitchen with a snack bar and the luxurious master suite with a spa-style bath.

You may be one of the thousands of Americans that is able to conduct business out of your home. Take a closer look at the den arrangements (which also double as cozy home offices) in Design 7221 (see page 66) or Design 9578 (see page 68). Many homeowners have told us that they don't need more than one spare bedroom. In response, we simply took those extra rooms out! Design 3453 (see page 63) offers an incredibly livable plan with a spacious feel—not to mention a fabulous master suite—with just one extra bedroom.

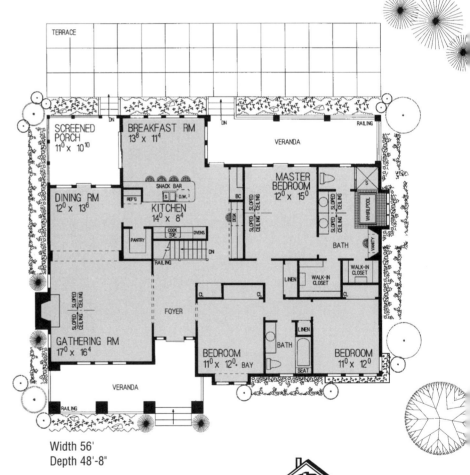

Design 3314

Square Footage: 1,951

L

This bountiful bungalow is an owner's paradise with a luxurious master suite that far exceeds its Craftsman-style roots. The large gathering room is joined to the dining room and is accented with a large brick fireplace. The galley kitchen has an abundance of cabinet space, a walk-in pantry and a full-size snack bar from the sunny breakfast room. A lovely screened porch that is accessed from both the dining room and the breakfast room adds an extra measure of charm to casual living. Two secondary bedrooms include one that can double as a den with a foyer entrance and another that is romanced with an expanse of corner windows and a wrap-around flower box.

California Engineered Plans and California Stock Plans are available for this home. Call 1-800-521-6797 for more information.

Design by
Home Planners

Width 56'
Depth 48'-8"

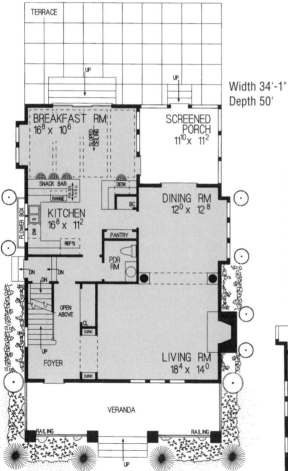

TERRACE

UP UP

BREAKFAST RM
16⁸ x 10⁶

SCREENED PORCH
11¹⁰ x 11²

SNACK BAR

DESK

RANGE

KITCHEN
16⁸ x 11²

FLOWER BOX

DW

REF'G

PANTRY

DINING RM
12⁰ x 12⁸

BC

PDR RM

DN DN

OPEN ABOVE

CL

CURIO

UP

FOYER

CURIO

LIVING RM
18⁴ x 14⁰

VERANDA

RAILING RAILING

UP

Width 34'-1"
Depth 50'

Design by
Home Planners

Design 3316

First Floor: 1,111 square feet
Second Floor: 886 square feet
Total: 1,997 square feet

L

Don't be fooled by a small-looking exterior. This plan offers three bedrooms and plenty of living space. Notice that the screened porch leads to a rear terrace with access to the breakfast room. A living room/dining room combination adds spaciousness to the floor plan. Other welcome amenities include: boxed windows in the breakfast room and dining room, fireplace in the living room, planning desk and pass-through snack bar in the kitchen, whirlpool tub in the master bath, an open two-story foyer. The thoughtfully placed flower box, beyond the kitchen window above the sink, adds a homespun touch to this already comfortable design.

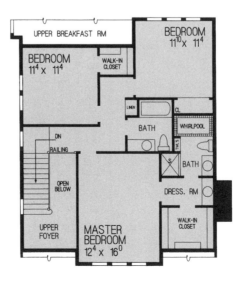

UPPER BREAKFAST RM

BEDROOM
11¹⁰ x 11⁴

BEDROOM
11⁴ x 11⁴

WALK-IN CLOSET

LINEN

BATH

WHIRLPOOL

DN

RAILING

OPEN BELOW

BATH

DRESS. RM

UPPER FOYER

MASTER BEDROOM
12⁴ x 16⁰

WALK-IN CLOSET

QUOTE ONE®

Cost to build? See page 214 to order complete cost estimate to build this house in your area!

Design 3321

First Floor: 1,636 square feet
Second Floor: 572 square feet
Total: 2,208 square feet

L **D**

Cozy and completely functional, this 1½-story bungalow has many amenities not often found in homes its size. The covered porch at the front opens at the entry to a foyer with an angled staircase. To the left is a media room, to the rear the gathering room with fireplace. Attached to the gathering room is a formal dining room with rear terrace access. The kitchen features a curved casual eating area and island work station. The right side of the first floor is dominated by the master suite. It has access to the rear terrace and a luxurious bath. Upstairs are two secondary bedrooms connected by a loft area overlooking the gathering room and foyer.

Design by
Home Planners

QUOTE ONE®

Cost to build? See page 214
to order complete cost estimate
to build this house in your area!

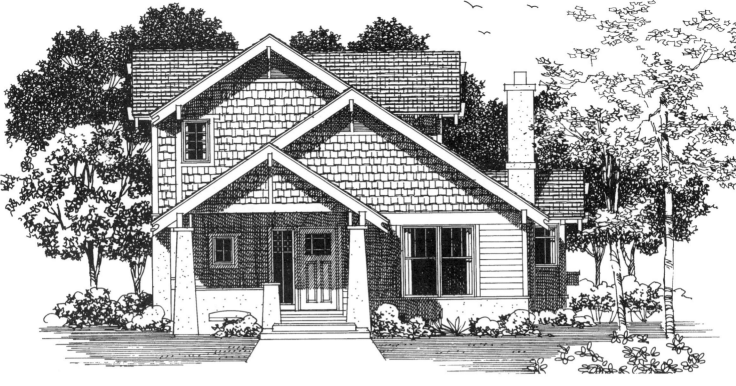

COVERED PORCH

MASTER
BEDRM
13⁴ x 18⁰

FAMILY
ROOM
15⁴ x 11⁶

LINEN

MASTER
BATH

BREAKFAST ROOM
15⁴ x 11⁸

DESK

KIT
13⁰ x 11⁴

WET
BAR

DINING
RM
13⁴ x 11⁰

5' HIGH SHELVES

UP   DW

OPEN ABOVE

LIVING
RM
13⁴ x 11⁴

PDR

FOYER

Width 35'-4"
Depth 66'

COVERED PORCH

Design by
Home Planners

Design **3497**

First Floor: 1,581 square feet
Second Floor: 592 square feet
Total: 2,173 square feet

This handsome bungalow is designed for easy-living with a floor plan that puts the owner's comfort first. A quaint living and dining room is separated with a half wall of built-in shelves. The large kitchen has an open wet bar to the dining room and a snack bar to the combination breakfast and family room. The extra-large family room has sliding glass doors off the breakfast area and a door opening onto the covered rear porch. The master suite offers privacy and convenience thanks to thoughtful first floor planning. The two spacious bedrooms upstairs share a twin-basin bath.

BEDRM
15⁴ x 11⁸

BATH

BEDRM
11⁸ x 11⁰

LINEN

DN

Quote One®

Cost to build? See page 214
to order complete cost estimate
to build this house in your area!

49

Design 9185

Square Footage: 1,567

Square columns supported by brick pedestals and a low-pitched roof are reminiscent of the Craftsman style brought to popularity in the early 1900s. Livability is the foremost consideration in this well-designed plan. To the left of the foyer is the cozy living room, warmed by an inviting fireplace. Straight ahead, the dining room shares space with an efficient, step-saving kitchen. A French door provides access to a covered porch for outdoor meals and entertaining. To the rear of the plan rests the master suite. The master bath is highlighted by a tub and a separate shower, a double-bowl vanity, a compartmented toilet and a large walk-in closet. Two family bedrooms, a full bath and a utility room with a linen closet complete this marvelous plan.

Design by
**Larry W. Garnett
& Associates, Inc.**

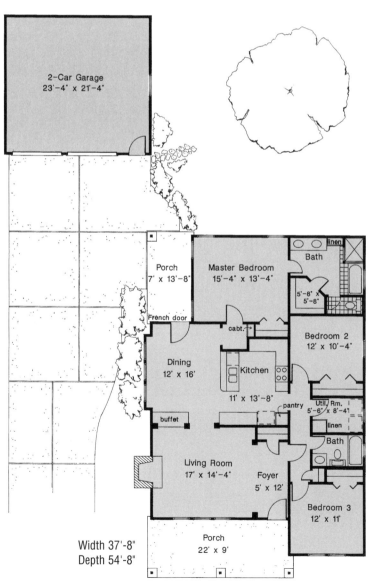

Width 37'-8"
Depth 54'-8"

Design 9529

This efficient floor plan carries three different exterior elevations to suite your taste. Inside, a living room or den opens to the right of the entry. It offers an optional built-in or closet. In the kitchen, an abundance of counter space and an accommodating layout make meal preparations simple. A great room and dining room connect to this area and will conform to everyday living. The master suite has a private bath, ample closet space and rear yard access. A secondary bedroom and a full hall bath complete this plan.

Design 9529
9530/9531
Square Footage: 1,420

Design 9530

Design 9531

MASTER
13/8 X 12/4 +/-

BR. 2
11/0 X 11/0

LINEN

DINING
10/0 X 11/0

GREAT RM.
14/4 X 15/0 +/-

13/0 X 13/0

PAN. REF.

LR./DEN
13/0 X 11/8 +/-

GARAGE
19/4 X 21/8

OPTIONAL
BUILT-IN
OR CLOSET

PORCH

Width 40'
Depth 58'

Design by
**Alan Mascord
Design Associates, Inc.**

Design 2918

Square footage: 1,693

D

Alternating use of stone and wood gives a textured look to this striking contemporary home with wide overhanging roof lines and a built-in planter box. The design is just as exciting on the inside, with two bedrooms, including a master suite, a study (or optional third bedroom), a rear gathering room with a fireplace and a sloped ceiling, a rear dining room and an efficient U-shaped kitchen with a pass-through to an adjoining breakfast room. A mud room and washroom are located between the kitchen and the spacious two-car garage.

California Engineered Plans and California Stock Plans are available for this home. Call 1-800-521-6797 for more information.

Design by
Home Planners

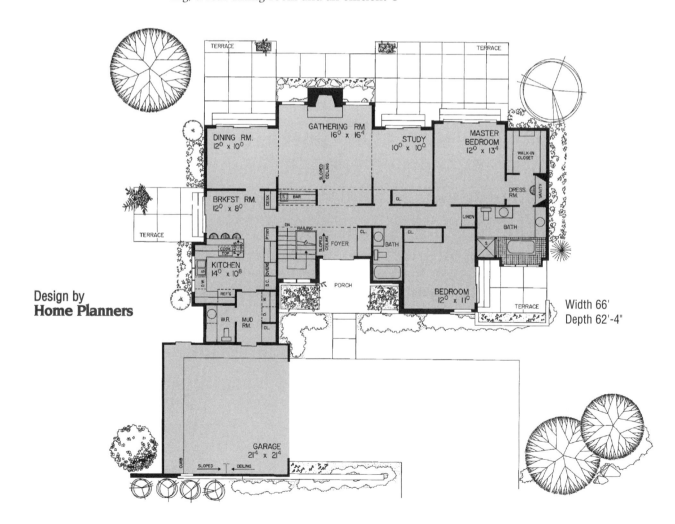

Width 66'
Depth 62'-4"

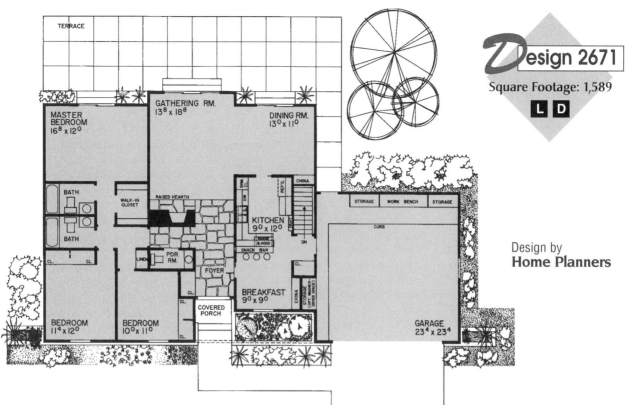

TERRACE

MASTER BEDROOM
16⁸ x 12⁰

GATHERING RM.
13⁸ x 18⁸

DINING RM.
13⁰ x 11⁰

BATH

WALK-IN CLOSET

RAISED HEARTH

CHINA

KITCHEN
9⁰ x 12⁰

STORAGE WORK BENCH STORAGE

CURB

BATH

CL.   CL.

LINEN

PDR. RM.

FOYER

SNACK BAR

BEDROOM
11⁴ x 12⁰

BEDROOM
10⁰ x 11⁰

CL.

CL.

COVERED PORCH

BREAKFAST
9⁰ x 9⁰

CHINA

STORAGE

GARAGE
23⁴ x 23⁴

Design 2671

Square Footage: 1,589

L D

Design by
Home Planners

Width 68'
Depth 40'-5"

The rustic exterior of this one-story home features vertical wood siding. The entry foyer is floored with flagstone and leads to the three areas of the plan: the sleeping, living and work center. The sleeping area features three bedrooms. The master bedroom utilizes sliding glass doors to the rear terrace. The living area, consisting of gathering and dining rooms, also enjoys access to the terrace. The work center is efficiently planned. It houses the kitchen with a snack bar, the breakfast room with a built-in china cabinet and stairs to the basement. This is a very livable plan. Special amenities include a raised-hearth fireplace and a walk-in closet in the master bedroom.

QUOTE ONE®

Cost to build? See page 214
to order complete cost estimate
to build this house in your area!

Design 3652

Square Footage: 2,076

L D

A contemporary, open floor plan updates this charming country home, perfect for starters, or empty-nesters. The cozy covered porch opens to a tiled foyer and then into the huge kitchen on the right. The kitchen connects to the living room/dining room area via a snack bar. The living room is accented with a lovely fireplace and a patio just off the dining area. Bedrooms are split with two secondary bedrooms and a full bath situated in a hall just off the dining room. The master suite has a large walk-in closet, double-basin vanity and a compartmented bath. A handy laundry room connects the two-car garage.

PATIO

MASTER BEDRM 17⁴ x 14⁰

LIVING RM 17⁰ x 15⁴

DINING RM 10⁰ x 12⁶

BEDRM 14⁴ x 12⁰

WALK-IN CLOSET

LINEN

BC

SNACK BAR

LINEN

BATH

MASTER BATH

SHOWER

GARDEN TUB

D

W

LT

LAUNDRY

FOYER

RANGE

DW

SINK

PANTRY

KIT 19⁰ x 11²

REFG

BEDRM 14⁴ x 14⁴

GARAGE 21⁴ x 20⁴

COVERED PORCH

RAILING

Width 64'-8"
Depth 54'-7"

Design by
Home Planners

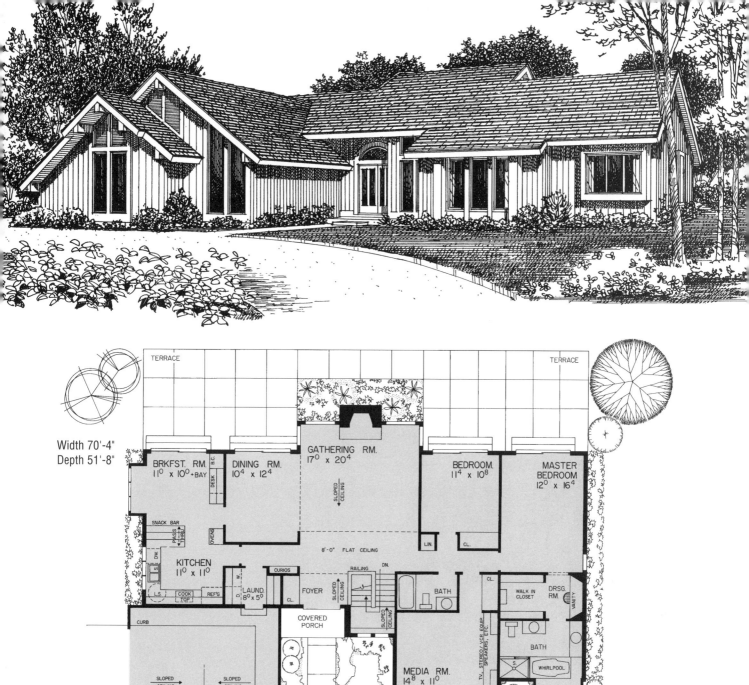

Width 70'-4"
Depth 51'-8"

TERRACE   TERRACE

BRKFST. RM.   DINING RM.   GATHERING RM.   BEDROOM.   MASTER
11⁰ x 10⁰+BAY   10⁴ x 12⁴   17⁰ x 20⁴   11⁴ x 10⁸   BEDROOM
                                                                                  12⁰ x 16⁴

SNACK BAR

KITCHEN
11⁰ x 11⁰   LAUND.   FOYER   RAILING   BATH   WALK IN   DRSG.
                   8⁰ x 5⁰   CLOSET   RM.
                          CURIOS

                                    8'-0" FLAT CEILING   BATH

                                                                                  WHIRLPOOL

COVERED
PORCH

GARAGE   SLOPED   SLOPED
21⁴ x 21⁸ + STORAGE CEILING   CEILING   MEDIA RM.
                                                 14⁸ x 11⁰

SLOPED   CEILING
STORAGE

Design by
Home Planners

This smart design features a multi-gabled roof, and vertical windows. It also offers efficient zoning by room functions and plenty of modern comforts for contemporary family living. A covered porch leads through a foyer to a large, central gathering room with a fireplace, a sloped ceiling, and its own special view of the rear terrace. A modern kitchen with a snack bar features a pass-through to the breakfast room with a view of the terrace. There's also an adjacent dining room. A media room is privately situated along with the bedrooms from the rest of the house to offer a quiet, private area for enjoying music or surfing-the-net. A master bedroom suite includes its own dressing area with a whirlpool tub in the bath. A large garage includes an extra storage room.

Design 2913

Square footage: 1,835

D

Design 8894

First Floor: 846 square feet
Second Floor: 400 square feet
Total: 1,246 square feet

Design by
**LifeStyle
HomeDesigns**

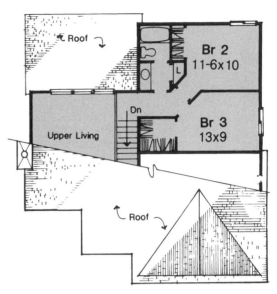

Br 2
11-6x10

Upper Living

Dn

Br 3
13x9

Roof

Roof

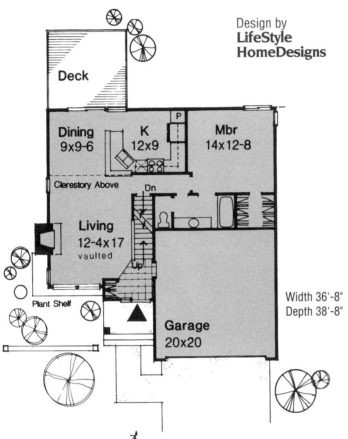

Deck

Dining
9x9-6

K
12x9

P

Mbr
14x12-8

Clerestory Above

Dn

Living
12-4x17
vaulted

Up

Plant Shelf

Garage
20x20

Width 36'-8"
Depth 38'-8"

A sloping roofline and wood siding lend a fresh look to this stunning Northwest contemporary plan. Inside, options include a second floor that can be built unfinished and completed as budgets allow. On the first floor, a tiled entryway reveals a vaulted living room with a fireplace. A space-saving kitchen serves a dining room that accesses a rear deck for outside enjoyments. Master-suite enhancements include corner windows, a walk-in closet and private passage to a full bath. Two bedrooms on the second floor include one with a walk-in closet. They share a full hall bath.

Photo by Laszlo Regos

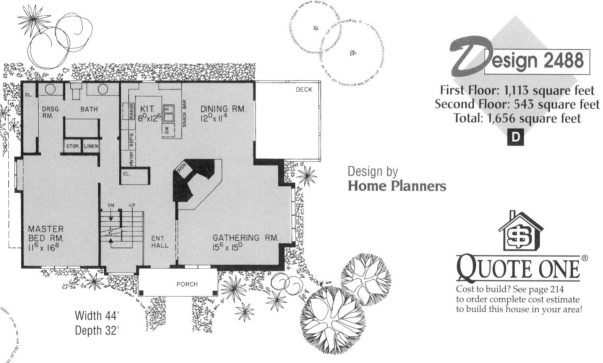

CL.

DRSG.
RM.   BATH

STOR. LINEN

RANGE   KIT.
        8⁰ x 12⁶   DINING RM.
DW REF'G   12⁰ x 11⁴
PANTRY
OVEN   SNACK BAR

CL.

DECK

MASTER
BED RM.
11⁶ x 16⁸

DN UP

ENT.
HALL   GATHERING RM.
            15⁶ x 15⁰

PORCH

Width 44'
Depth 32'

Design **2488**

First Floor: 1,113 square feet
Second Floor: 543 square feet
Total: 1,656 square feet

D

Design by
Home Planners

QUOTE ONE®

Cost to build? See page 214
to order complete cost estimate
to build this house in your area!

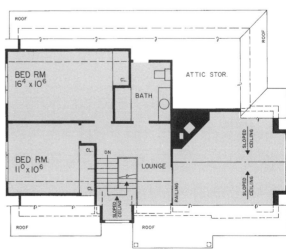

ROOF

BED RM.
16⁴ x 10⁶
            CL.
                    ATTIC STOR.
            BATH

BED RM.   SLOPED
11⁰ x 10⁶   CEILING
        CL.
            DN
        CL.   LOUNGE

                RAILING   SLOPED
                              CEILING
        SLOPED
        CEILING

ROOF   ROOF

For a lakeside retreat or as a retirement haven, this
charming design offers the best in livability. The gathering room has an oversized corner fireplace and a dramatic,
full length wall of windows. The space-saving, U-shaped
kitchen has a snack bar for meals on the go and an
attached dining room with doors to the lovely deck. The
first-floor master suite is completed with a compartmented
bath. Two bedrooms with a full bath and a balcony lounge
upstairs complement the design and provide sleeping
accommodations for family and guests.

**California Engineered Plans and California Stock
Plans are available for this home. Call 1-800-521-6797
for more information.**

greenhouse area off the dining room and living room
provides a cheerful focal point
for this comfortable three-bedroom home. The spacious living
room features a cozy fireplace
and a sloped ceiling. In addition
to the dining room, there's a less
formal breakfast room just off
the modern kitchen. Both
kitchen and breakfast areas look
out onto a front terrace. Stairs
just off the foyer lead down to a
basement recreation room. The
master bedroom suite opens to a
terrace. A mud room and a wash
room off the garage allow rear
entry to the house during
inclement weather.

Design by
Home Planners

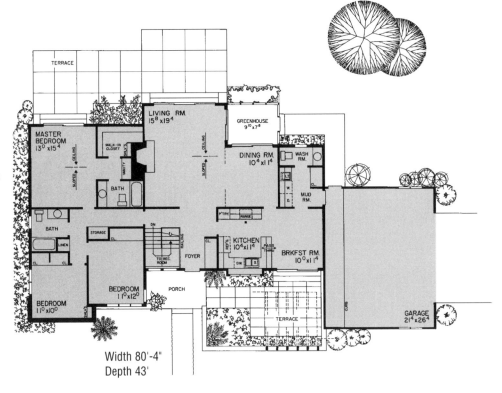

Width 80'-4"
Depth 43'

Design 2871

Living Area: 1,824 square feet
Greenhouse Area: 81 square feet
Total: 1,905 square feet

QUOTE ONE®

Cost to build? See page 214
to order complete cost estimate
to build this house in your area!

Photo by Bob Greenspan

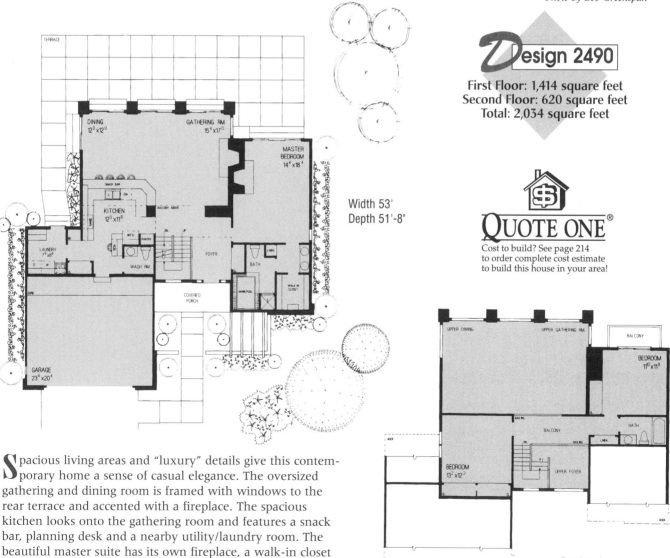

Width 53'
Depth 51'-8"

Design 2490

First Floor: 1,414 square feet
Second Floor: 620 square feet
Total: 2,034 square feet

QUOTE ONE®

Cost to build? See page 214
to order complete cost estimate
to build this house in your area!

Spacious living areas and "luxury" details give this contemporary home a sense of casual elegance. The oversized gathering and dining room is framed with windows to the rear terrace and accented with a fireplace. The spacious kitchen looks onto the gathering room and features a snack bar, planning desk and a nearby utility/laundry room. The beautiful master suite has its own fireplace, a walk-in closet and a whirlpool tub. Upstairs, a balcony overlooking the foyer and gathering room leads to the two secondary bedrooms and a full hall bath.

Design by
Home Planners

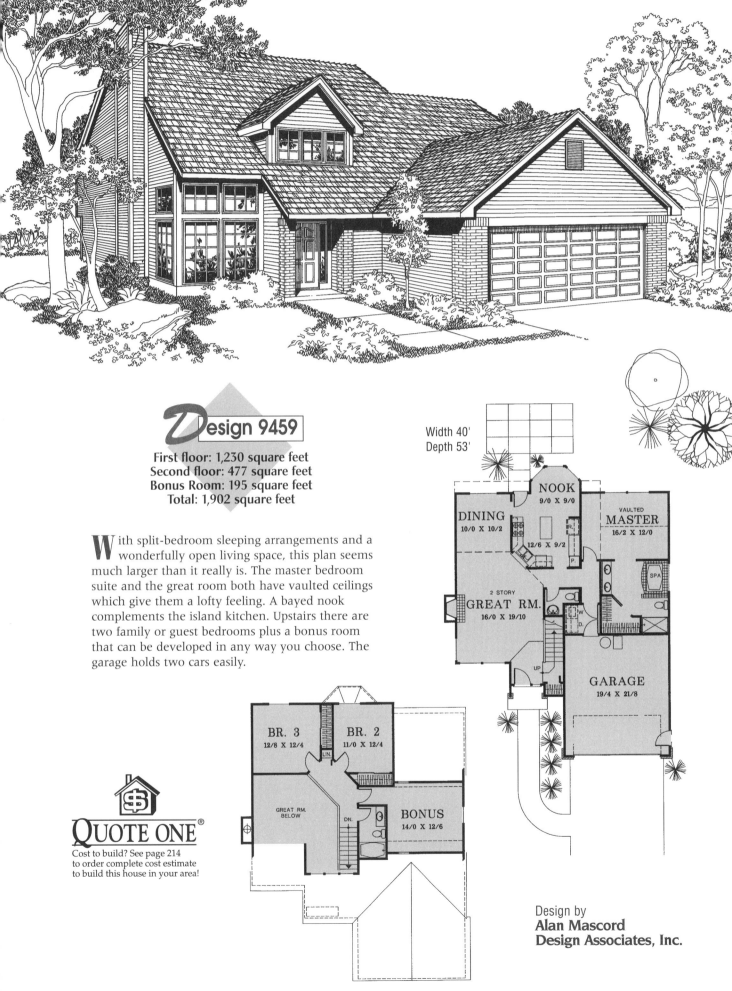

Design 9459

First floor: 1,230 square feet
Second floor: 477 square feet
Bonus Room: 195 square feet
Total: 1,902 square feet

With split-bedroom sleeping arrangements and a wonderfully open living space, this plan seems much larger than it really is. The master bedroom suite and the great room both have vaulted ceilings which give them a lofty feeling. A bayed nook complements the island kitchen. Upstairs there are two family or guest bedrooms plus a bonus room that can be developed in any way you choose. The garage holds two cars easily.

QUOTE ONE®

Cost to build? See page 214 to order complete cost estimate to build this house in your area!

Width 40'
Depth 53'

NOOK
9/0 X 9/0

DINING
10/0 X 10/2

VAULTED
MASTER
16/2 X 12/0

12/6 X 9/2

SPA

2 STORY

GREAT RM.
16/0 X 19/10

UP

GARAGE
19/4 X 21/8

BR. 3
12/8 X 12/4

BR. 2
11/0 X 12/4

LIN.

GREAT RM.
BELOW

DN.

BONUS
14/0 X 12/6

Design by
Alan Mascord
Design Associates, Inc.

60

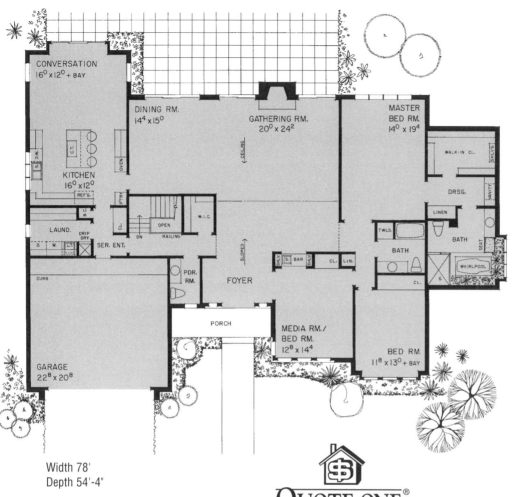

CONVERSATION
16⁰ x 12⁰ + BAY

DINING RM.
14⁴ x 15⁰

GATHERING RM.
20⁰ x 24²

MASTER
BED RM.
14⁰ x 19⁴

WALK-IN CL.

DRSG.

KITCHEN
16⁰ x 12⁰

REF'G.

P'TRY.

OPEN

W.I.C.

LINEN

VANITY

TWLS.

BATH

SEAT

LAUND.

DRIP
DRY

DN   RAILING

BATH

WHIRLPOOL

SER. ENT.

SHLV'S   BAR   SHLV'S   CL.   LIN.

PDR.
RM.

FOYER

CURB

PORCH

MEDIA RM./
BED RM.
12⁸ x 14⁴

BED RM.
11⁸ x 13⁰ + BAY

GARAGE
22⁸ x 20⁸

Width 78'
Depth 54'-4"

Design 3368

Square Footage: 2,720

L D

Roof lines are the key to the interesting exterior of this design. Their configuration allows for sloped ceilings in the gathering room and large foyer. The master bedroom suite has a huge walk-in closet, garden whirlpool and separate shower. Two family bedrooms share a full bath. One of these bedrooms could be used as a media room with pass-through wet bar. Note the large gourmet-style kitchen with both a snack bar and a conversation bay and the wide terrace to the rear.

Design by
Home Planners

Design 9422

Square footage: 1,417

This compact home leaves nothing out in the way of great features. Most rooms of the home have ten-and-a-half-foot ceilings, allowing transom windows to be used extensively. The kitchen and nook look out on a lovely front terrace. Note the unique shape of the great room with fireplace and vaulted ceiling. The master suite has rear-yard access and is complemented by a second smaller bedroom. Because of the narrow width of the home, it can sit comfortably on many small-sized lots.

Design by
**Alan Mascord
Design Associates, Inc.**

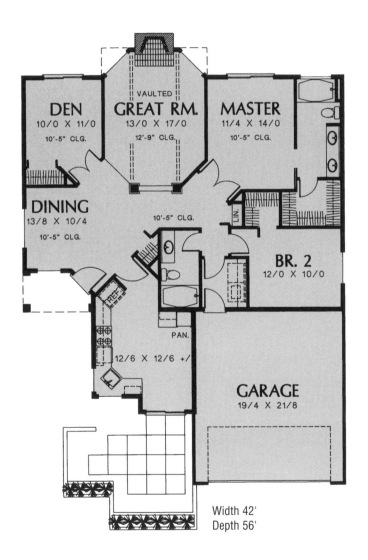

DEN
10/0 X 11/0
10'-5" CLG.

VAULTED
GREAT RM.
13/0 X 17/0
12'-9" CLG.

MASTER
11/4 X 14/0
10'-5" CLG.

DINING
13/8 X 10/4
10'-5" CLG.

10'-5" CLG.

LIN.

BR. 2
12/0 X 10/0

PAN.

12/6 X 12/6 +/

GARAGE
19/4 X 21/8

Width 42'
Depth 56'

Design by
Home Planners

Terrace

TRAY CLG.

MASTER
BEDRM
13⁰ X14⁰

LIVING RM.
14⁰ X15⁰

DINING
RM.
11⁴ X13⁰

SHLVS

W.I.C.

KITCHEN
9⁴ X14⁴

PTRY

REFG

SHWR

MASTER BATH

LIN

W. D.

FOYER

BATH

LIN

DN

CL.

CL.

BEDRM
11⁶ X11²

GARAGE
18⁴ X18⁸

Width 40'
Depth 57'-4"

Design **3453**

Square Footage: 1,442

L

This volume home impresses with its stately rooflines and stucco exterior. The front porch opens to an eleven-foot ceiling in the foyer. Straight ahead, an elegant living room serves as a prelude to the dramatic circular dining bay. Here, family and guests alike will revel in the fine views out the back of the house. The kitchen with a built-in snack bar offers an abundance of counter and cabinet space. The front bedroom, with its closet space and access to a full hall bath, could easily convert to a media room. In the master bedroom you'll find a lengthy closet in addition to a stunning bath. Glass block provides privacy to the toilet and shower while the spa tub delights in its well-illuminated nook. Dual lavatories complete the amenities in this room.

$

QUOTE ONE ®

Cost to build? See page 214
to order complete cost estimate
to build this house in your area!

63

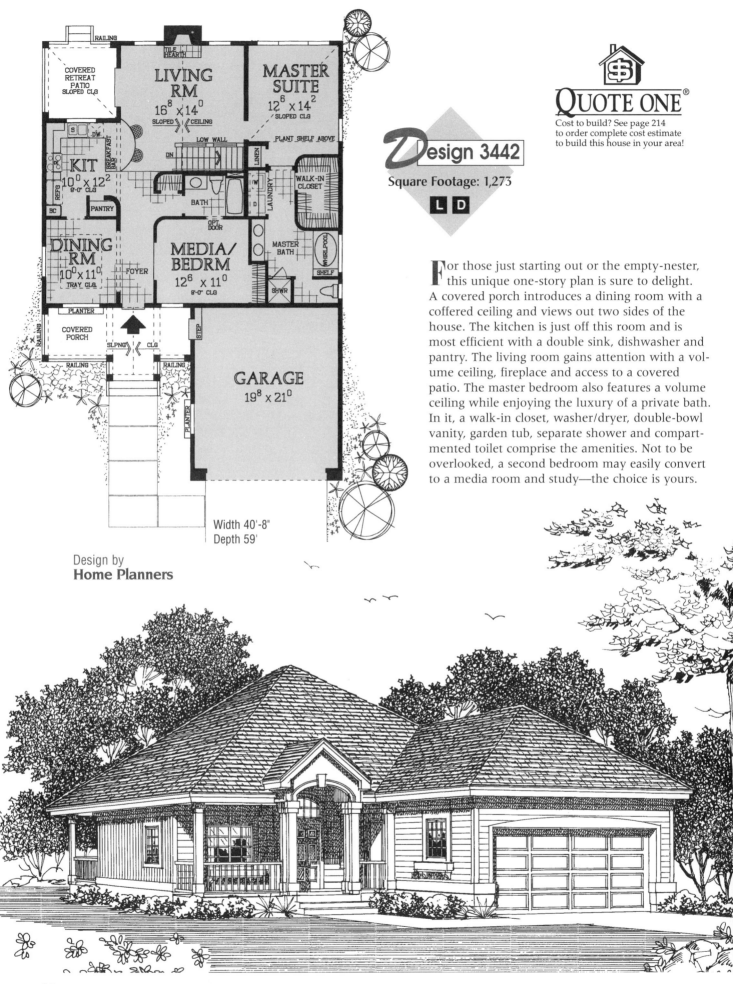

COVERED
RETREAT
PATIO
SLOPED CLG

LIVING
RM
16⁸ x 14⁰
SLOPED CEILING

TILE HEARTH

MASTER
SUITE
12⁶ x 14²
SLOPED CLG

KIT
10⁰ x 12²
9'-0" CLG

BREAKFAST
BAR

LOW WALL

DN

PLANT SHELF ABOVE

LINEN

WALK-IN
CLOSET

LAUNDRY

BATH

OPT
DOOR

MASTER
BATH

WHIRLPOOL

SHELF

PANTRY

BC

DINING
RM
10⁰ x 11⁰
TRAY CLG

FOYER

MEDIA/
BEDRM
12⁶ x 11⁰
8'-0" CLG

SHWR

PLANTER

COVERED
PORCH

STEP

SLPNG CLG

RAILING

GARAGE
19⁸ x 21⁰

PLANTER

Width 40'-8"
Depth 59'

Design by
Home Planners

QUOTE ONE®
Cost to build? See page 214
to order complete cost estimate
to build this house in your area!

Design 3442

Square Footage: 1,273

L **D**

For those just starting out or the empty-nester, this unique one-story plan is sure to delight. A covered porch introduces a dining room with a coffered ceiling and views out two sides of the house. The kitchen is just off this room and is most efficient with a double sink, dishwasher and pantry. The living room gains attention with a volume ceiling, fireplace and access to a covered patio. The master bedroom also features a volume ceiling while enjoying the luxury of a private bath. In it, a walk-in closet, washer/dryer, double-bowl vanity, garden tub, separate shower and compartmented toilet comprise the amenities. Not to be overlooked, a second bedroom may easily convert to a media room and study—the choice is yours.

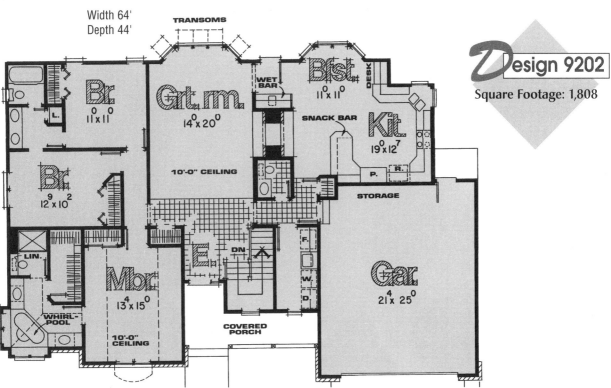

Width 64'
Depth 44'

TRANSOMS

Br.
11 x 11

Grt. rm.
14⁰ x 20⁰

WET
BAR

Bfst.
11⁰ x 11⁰

DESK

Design 9202

Square Footage: 1,808

SNACK BAR

Kit.
19⁰ x 12⁷

10'-0" CEILING

Br.
12 x 10²

P.

R.

STORAGE

LIN.

Mbr
13⁴ x 15⁰

DN

F.

W.

D.

Gar
21⁴ x 25⁰

WHIRL-
POOL

10'-0"
CEILING

COVERED
PORCH

Discriminating buyers will love the refined yet inviting look of this three-bedroom ranch plan. A tiled entry with ten-foot ceilings leads into the spacious great room with large bay window. An open-hearth fireplace warms both the great room and kitchen. The sleeping area features a large master suite with a dramatic arched window and a bath with whirlpool, His and Hers vanities and a walk-in closet. Don't miss the storage space in the oversized garage.

Design by
Design Basics, Inc.

Design 7221

Square Footage: 1,580

Brick wing walls give a visually expansive front elevation to this charming home. From the entry, traffic flows into the bright great room that has an impressive two-sided fireplace. The dining room opens to the great room, offering a view of the fireplace. French doors off the entry lead to the kitchen. Here, a large pantry, a planning desk and a snack bar are appreciated amenities. The breakfast nook accesses a large, comfortable screened porch. The laundry room is strategically located off the kitchen and provides direct access to the garage. The master suite features a formal ceiling, French doors and a pampering bath. Two secondary bedrooms and a full hall bath complete the sleeping wing.

Design by
Design Basics, Inc.

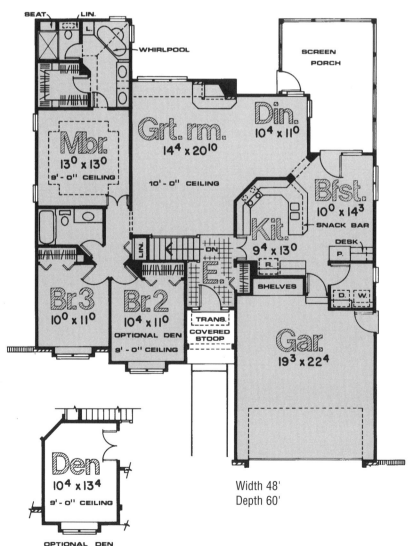

Width 48'
Depth 60'

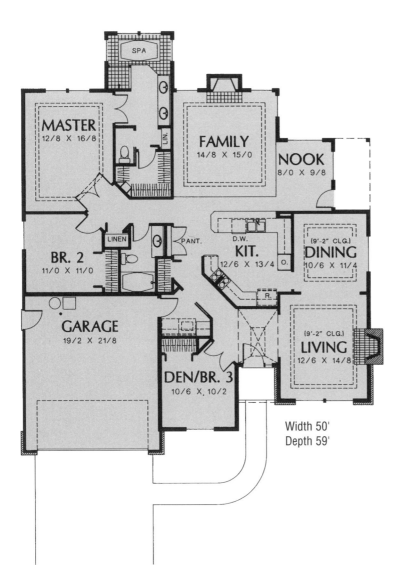

MASTER
12/8 X 16/8

FAMILY
14/8 X 15/0

SPA

NOOK
8/0 X 9/8

LIN.

BR. 2
11/0 X 11/0

LINEN

PANT.

D.W.

KIT.
12/6 X 13/4

O.

(9'-2" CLG.)

DINING
10/6 X 11/4

R.

GARAGE
19/2 X 21/8

(9'-2" CLG.)

LIVING
12/6 X 14/8

DEN/BR. 3
10/6 X 10/2

Width 50'
Depth 59'

Design 9502

Square Footage: 1,865

Don't let the small size of this home fool you. It adequately serves both formal and informal occasions. A living room and dining room are found to the right of the plan and are open to one another. The well-planned kitchen is nearby and also serves a nook eating area and the casual family room. The master suite is filled with amenities not usually found in a smaller home such as French doors, a walk-in closet and a luxurious spa bathroom. One secondary bedroom has a full bath nearby.

Design by
**Alan Mascord
Design Associates, Inc.**

Design 9578

Square Footage: 2,225

This home exemplifies clever floor patterning. Casual living takes off in the kitchen, nook and family room. A stylish corner fireplace will warm gatherings. The formal dining room is nicely set off the kitchen to lend an elegant tone to entertaining. A see-through fireplace joins the living room and den. In the master bedroom suite, a garden tub and dual lavatories top the list of accommodations. Two secondary bedrooms share a hall bath, also with dual lavatories. The two-car garage joins the house through the laundry room.

QUOTE ONE®

Cost to build? See page 214 to order complete cost estimate to build this house in your area!

Design by
**Alan Mascord
Design Associates, Inc.**

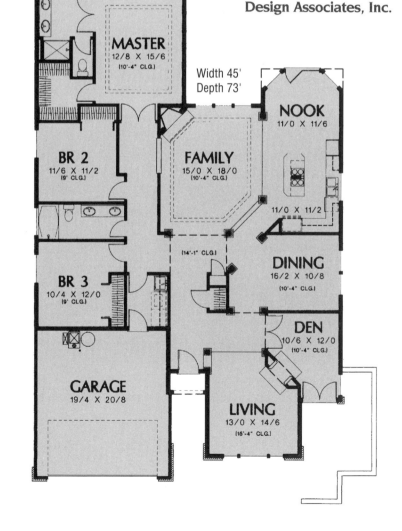

MASTER
12/8 X 15/6
(10'-4" CLG.)

Width 45'
Depth 73'

NOOK
11/0 X 11/6

BR 2
11/6 X 11/2
(9' CLG.)

FAMILY
15/0 X 18/0
(10'-4" CLG.)

11/0 X 11/2

(14'-1" CLG.)

DINING
16/2 X 10/8
(10'-4" CLG.)

BR 3
10/4 X 12/0
(9' CLG.)

DEN
10/6 X 12/0
(10'-4" CLG.)

GARAGE
19/4 X 20/8

LIVING
13/0 X 14/6
(15'-4" CLG.)

Design 9483

First floor: 1,697 square feet
Second floor: 433 square feet
Total: 2,130 square feet

Design by
**Alan Mascord
Design Associates, Inc.**

A high, hipped roof allows for a volume look with expansive windows in this two-story plan. The main living areas of the plan are clustered on the first floor with the second floor reserved for two secondary bedrooms and a full hall bath. From the spacious entry, the joined living and dining rooms create a nice place for entertaining. The large family room welcomes casual living with its fireplace. The gourmet kitchen has a great cooktop island that will keep the cook in the loop of family room activities. The master suite has a nearby den, walk-in closet and a large, compartmented bath.

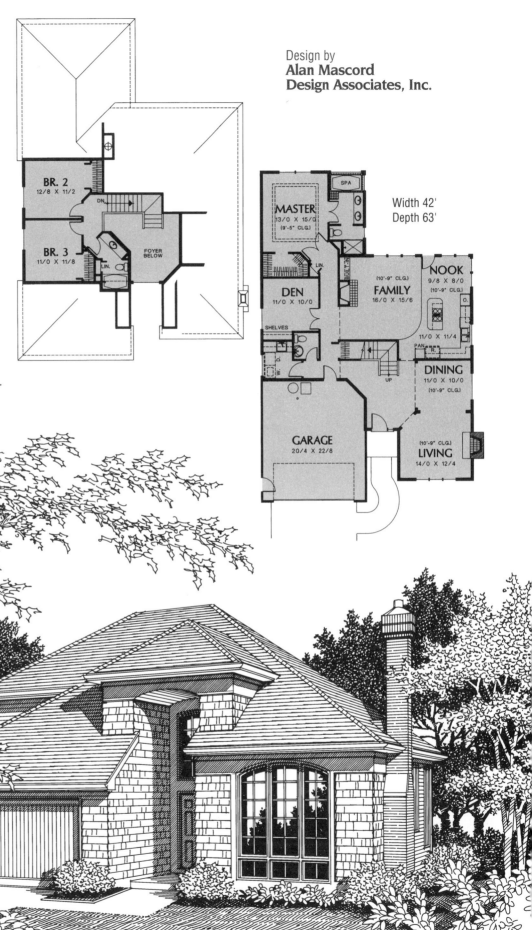

Width 42'
Depth 63'

Design 9237

Square Footage: 1,697

This volume-look home gives the impression of size and scope in just under 1,700 square feet. The large great room with fireplace is perfect for entertaining. The spacious kitchen has a snack bar and a breakfast room with a dramatic valley cathedral ceiling. Besides a large walk-in closet, other features in the master bedroom include a whirlpool tub, double vanity, sky-lit dressing area and convenient linen storage. Two family bedrooms share a full bath with a skylight and offer ample closet space.

Design by
Design Basics, Inc.

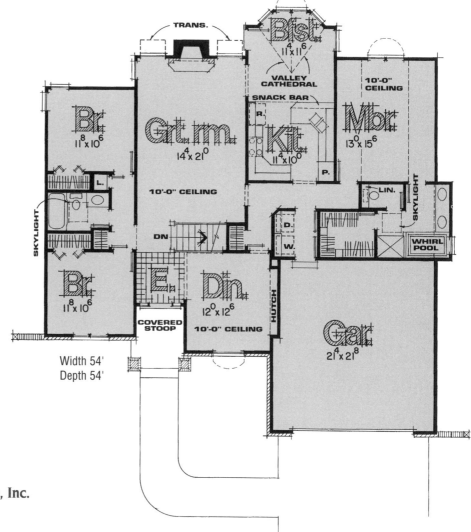

Width 54'
Depth 54'

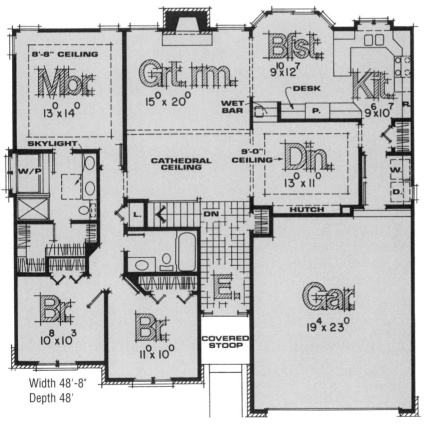

8'-8" CEILING

Mbr
13⁰ x 14⁰

SKYLIGHT

W/P

Grt. rm.
15⁰ x 20⁰

WET BAR

CATHEDRAL CEILING

L.

DN

Br
10⁸ x 10³

Br
11⁰ x 10⁰

COVERED STOOP

Bfst
9¹⁰ x 12⁷

DESK

P.

Kit.
9⁶ x 10⁷

R.

9'-0" CEILING

Dn.
13⁰ x 11

HUTCH

W.

D.

Gar.
19⁴ x 23⁰

Width 48'-8"
Depth 48'

QUOTE ONE®
Cost to build? See page 214
to order complete cost estimate
to build this house in your area!

Design by
Design Basics, Inc.

Design 9200
Square Footage: 1,604

Thoughtful arrangement makes this uncomplicated three-bedroom plan comfortable. The living and working areas are grouped together for convenience—a great room with cathedral ceiling, dining room with wet bar pass-through and kitchen with breakfast room. The sleeping area features a spacious master suite with a skylight and whirlpool in the bath, and a walk-in closet. Two smaller bedrooms accommodate guests graciously. A convenient service entrance leads from the garage, through the laundry room and into the kitchen. An alternate elevation is available at no extra cost.

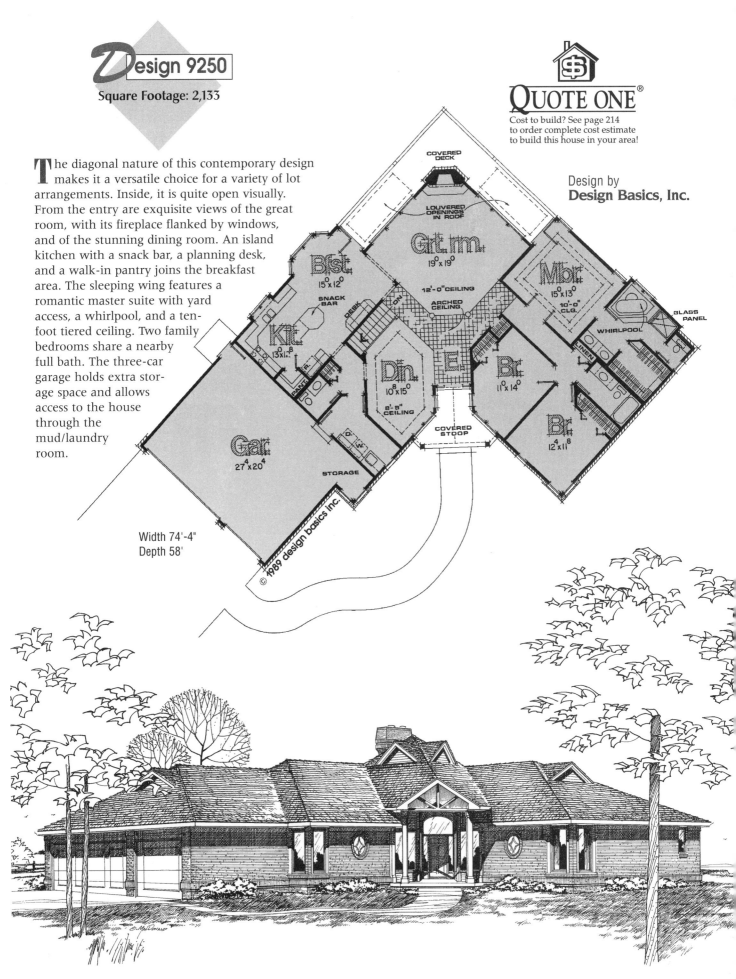

Design 9250

Square Footage: 2,133

Quote One®
Cost to build? See page 214
to order complete cost estimate
to build this house in your area!

Design by
Design Basics, Inc.

The diagonal nature of this contemporary design makes it a versatile choice for a variety of lot arrangements. Inside, it is quite open visually. From the entry are exquisite views of the great room, with its fireplace flanked by windows, and of the stunning dining room. An island kitchen with a snack bar, a planning desk, and a walk-in pantry joins the breakfast area. The sleeping wing features a romantic master suite with yard access, a whirlpool, and a ten-foot tiered ceiling. Two family bedrooms share a nearby full bath. The three-car garage holds extra storage space and allows access to the house through the mud/laundry room.

Width 74'-4"
Depth 58'

© 1989 design basics inc.

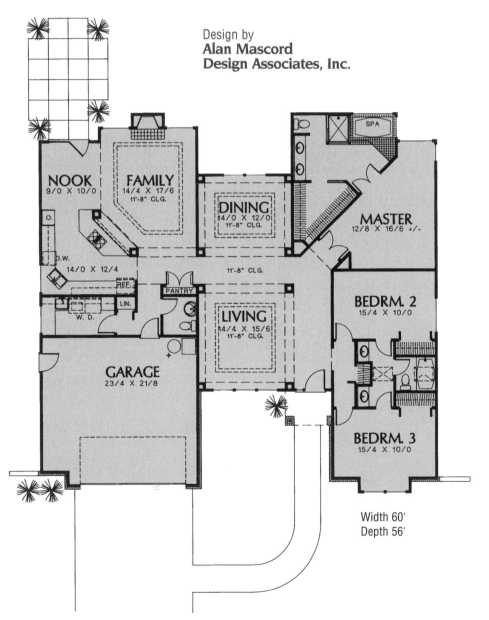

Design by
**Alan Mascord
Design Associates, Inc.**

NOOK
9/0 X 10/0

FAMILY
14/4 X 17/6
11'-8" CLG.

DINING
14/0 X 12/0
11'-8" CLG.

MASTER
12/8 X 16/6 +/-

11'-8" CLG.

14/0 X 12/4

D.W.

O.

REF.

PANTRY

LIN.

W. D.

LIVING
14/4 X 15/6
11'-8" CLG.

BEDRM. 2
15/4 X 10/0

GARAGE
23/4 X 21/8

BEDRM. 3
15/4 X 10/0

SPA

Width 60'
Depth 56'

Design 9432

Square Footage: 2,276

This elegant single-level plan puts its best foot forward with a brick facade, deeply hipped roof and multi-paned windows. The interior is something to brag about as well. All main living areas have tall ceilings with stepped-tray vaults and transom windows. The large kitchen features an island with a built-in cabinet on the opposite side that is perfect for the home entertainment system in the family room. Formal living and dining rooms face one another in the central hallway, giving an open feeling to both rooms. Three bedrooms include the master suite with angled wall and double doors. A convenient full bath with double vanity is shared by the two family bedrooms. The two-car garage allows space for a workshop along one side.

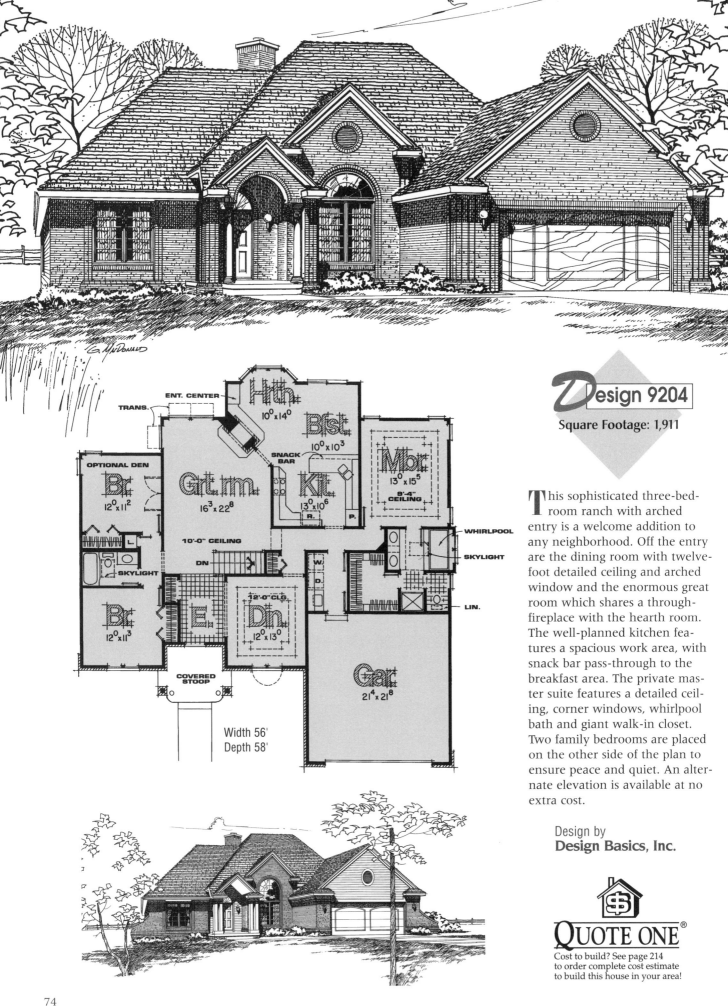

Design 9204

Square Footage: 1,911

This sophisticated three-bedroom ranch with arched entry is a welcome addition to any neighborhood. Off the entry are the dining room with twelve-foot detailed ceiling and arched window and the enormous great room which shares a through-fireplace with the hearth room. The well-planned kitchen features a spacious work area, with snack bar pass-through to the breakfast area. The private master suite features a detailed ceiling, corner windows, whirlpool bath and giant walk-in closet. Two family bedrooms are placed on the other side of the plan to ensure peace and quiet. An alternate elevation is available at no extra cost.

Design by
Design Basics, Inc.

QUOTE ONE®

Cost to build? See page 214
to order complete cost estimate
to build this house in your area!

Hrth.
10⁰ x 14⁰

ENT. CENTER

TRANS.

Brst.
10⁰ x 10³

SNACK BAR

Mbr.
13⁰ x 15⁵

9'-4" CEILING

WHIRLPOOL

SKYLIGHT

OPTIONAL DEN

Br.
12⁰ x 11²

Grt. rm.
16³ x 22⁸

Kit.
13⁰ x 10⁶

R.

P.

10'-0" CEILING

DN

SKYLIGHT

LIN.

Br.
12⁰ x 11³

E.

Dn.
12⁰ x 13⁰

12'-0" CLG.

W. D.

Gar.
21⁴ x 21⁸

COVERED STOOP

Width 56'
Depth 58'

Old-World Accents
Revisit a European Heritage

With a large slice of America's melting-pot pie made with a mix of European backgrounds, it is easy to see these influences occurring and reoccurring in contemporary times. No place is this more evident than in the creation of a residential home.

More than just an architectural style that is both beautiful to look at and extremely easy to live in, the European-style home gives much more to the homeowner. Through the use of time-honored materials such as stone and stucco, brick and shingles, the European-style home provides the owner with an unparalleled sense of stability and roots. While the home may be brand new, the feeling evoked is of a cherished home passed down from generation to generation.

Spend some time looking through this section for the homes that speak to your ancestral foundation. For example, the charming country house on page 81 (Design 7818) welcomes casual living. The eclectic Tudor (Design 8164, page 91) shows your flair for the unique—in a square footage that's more manageable that all the queen's men. All the homes here offer superior livability and elegant design—sure to win the family's heart over for generations to come.

Width 64'
Depth 64'-4"

Design 9831

Square Footage: 2,150
Expandable Lower Level: 2,150

Design by
**Stephen Fuller/
Design Traditions**

QUOTE ONE®
Cost to build? See page 214
to order complete cost estimate
to build this house in your area!

This home draws its inspiration from both French and English country homes. From the foyer and across the spacious great room, French doors give a generous view of the covered rear porch. The adjoining dining room is subtly defined by the use of columns and a large triple window. The kitchen, with its generous work island, adjoins the breakfast area and keeping room with fireplace, a vaulted ceiling and an abundant use of windows. The study to the front of the first floor could be a guest room. It shares a bath with the bedroom beside it. The home is completed by a quiet master suite located at the rear. It contains a bay window, a garden tub and His and Hers vanities. This home is designed with a basement foundation that can be developed later.

Width 62'
Depth 61'-6"

BEDROOM NO. 3
11'-6" X 11'-0"

BATH

BEDROOM NO. 2
11'-4" X 11'-0"

SUN ROOM
12'-0" X 13'-8"

PORCH

MASTER BATH

W.I.C.

PORCH

BREAKFAST
10'-0" X 9'-0"

FAMILY ROOM
18'-0" X 14'-0"

MASTER BEDROOM
13'-4" X 15'-6"

LAUNDRY

KITCHEN
12'-0" X 13'-2"

BATH

STORAGE

DN

TWO CAR GARAGE
20'-4" X 19'-8"

DINING ROOM
11'-4" X 11'-4"

FOYER
6'-8" X 11'-10"

DEN/GUEST BEDROOM
11'-4" X 14'-0"

PORCH

QUOTE ONE®

Cost to build? See page 214
to order complete cost estimate
to build this house in your area!

Design by
**Stephen Fuller/
Design Traditions**

Design 9862

Square Footage: 2,170

This classic cottage features a stone-and-wood exterior with an arch-detailed porch and a box-bay window. From the foyer, double doors open to the den with built-in bookcases and a fireplace. A full bath is situated next to the den, allowing for an optional guest room. The family room is centrally located, just beyond the foyer. Its hearth is framed by windows overlooking the porch at the rear of the home. The master bedroom opens onto the rear porch. The master bath, with a large walk-in closet, double vanities, a corner tub and a separate shower, completes this relaxing retreat. Left of the family room awaits a sun room with access to the covered porch. A breakfast area complements the attractive and efficiently designed kitchen. Two secondary bedrooms with large closets share a full bath featuring double vanities. This home is designed with a basement foundation.

Design 7800

First Floor: 1,831 square feet
Second Floor: 651 square feet
Total: 2,482 square feet
Bonus Room: 394 square feet

Master Bedroom 15⁰x16⁰

Breakfast 14⁹x12⁹

Porch

Kitchen 14⁹x10⁰

Great Room 21⁰x15⁰

Dining Room 11⁹x14³

Porch

Two Car Garage 22⁰x26⁹

Width 55'
Depth 77'

Design by
**Stephen Fuller/
Design Traditions**

Bedroom No. 2 14⁹x13⁹

Open To Below

Bedroom No. 3 13⁰x11⁹

Unfin Bonus 9⁹x32⁹

This purely country home characterizes all the charm of a rural lifestyle. From the covered porch entrance, the front door opens to a formal dining room and great room with a fireplace. A rear porch offers outdoor livability to the great room. The U-shaped kitchen and adjoining breakfast room are nearby and offer space for casual eating. Located on the first floor for privacy, the master bedroom features two large walk-in closets and a master bath designed for relaxation. A laundry room and a powder room complete this floor. Upstairs are two family bedrooms—each with a walk-in closet—and a shared bath with separate dressing areas. A large bonus space that might make another bedroom or handy study is also on the second floor. This plan is designed with a basement foundation.

Design 9853

Square Footage: 2,090

Design by
**Stephen Fuller/
Design Traditions**

This traditional home features board-and-batten siding and cedar shingles in an attractively proportioned exterior. Finishing touches include a covered entrance and porch with column detailing and an arched transom, flower boxes and shuttered windows. The foyer opens to both the dining room and great room beyond with French doors opening onto the porch. Through the double doors to the right of the foyer is the combination bedroom/study. A short hallway leads to a full bath and a secondary bedroom with ample closet space. The master bedroom is spacious, with walk-in closets on both sides of the entrance to the master bath. With separate vanities, a shower and a toilet, the master bath forms a private retreat at the rear of the home. Convenient to both the great room and dining room, the kitchen opens to an attractive breakfast area featuring a bay window. An additional room is remotely located off the kitchen, providing a retreat for today's at-home office or guests. This home is designed with a basement foundation.

QUOTE ONE®
Cost to build? See page 214 to order complete cost estimate to build this house in your area!

PORCH

MASTER BATH

MASTER BEDROOM
16'-4" X 13'-6"

BREAKFAST
13'-4" X 9'-0"

BEDROOM/
OFFICE
10'-4" X 11'-0"

GREAT ROOM
17'-0" X 17'-8"

BEDROOM NO. 2
10'-4" X 12'-0"

KITCHEN
13'-4" X 10'-6"

DN

BATH

BATH

LAUNDRY

TWO CAR GARAGE
20'-6" X 19'-6"

DINING ROOM
11'-4" X 12'-10"

FOYER
5'-4" X
12'-10"

BEDROOM/
STUDY
11'-2" X 12'-0"

PORCH

Width 61'
Depth 70'-6"

79

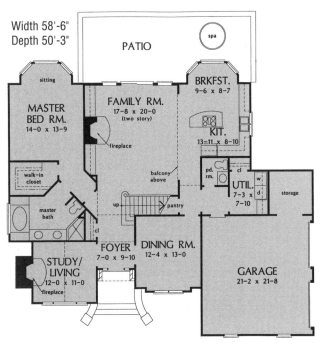

Width 58'-6"
Depth 50'-3"

PATIO

spa

MASTER BED RM.
14-0 x 13-9

sitting

FAMILY RM.
17-8 x 20-0
(two story)

fireplace

walk-in closet

balcony above

BRKFST.
9-6 x 8-7

KIT.
13-11 x 8-10

pd. rm.

cl

UTIL.
7-3 x 7-10

w d

storage

master bath

up

pantry

cl

STUDY/ LIVING
12-0 x 11-0

fireplace

FOYER
7-0 x 9-10

DINING RM.
12-4 x 13-0

GARAGE
21-2 x 21-8

Design 9757

First Floor: 1,715 square feet
Second Floor: 620 square feet
Total: 2,335 square feet

With a decided European flavor, this two-story home features country living at its best. The foyer opens to a study or living room on the left. The dining room on the right offers large proportions and full windows. The family room remains open to the kitchen and breakfast room. Here, sunny meals are guaranteed with a bay window overlooking the rear yard. In the master suite, a bayed sitting area, a walk-in closet and a pampering bath are sure to please. Upstairs, two bedrooms flank a loft or study area and a full hall bath.

Design by
Donald A. Gardner, Architects, Inc.

clerestory window with arched top

BED RM.
13-7 x 11-0

great room below

walk-in closet

LOFT/ STUDY
8-4 x 12-5

railing

bath

attic storage

down

attic storage

walk-in closet

foyer below

BED RM.
12-4 x 13-0

lin.

skylights

BONUS RM.
11-4 x 21-8

B. NATHAN.

Design 7818

First Floor: 1,805 square feet
Second Floor: 765 square feet
Total: 2,570 square feet

Stone and stucco—with the delicate addition of a latticed front porch—present this French country home with a gracious welcome. Open living spaces invite casual times in the expansive great room with a full measure of windows and a fireplace rising the full two-stories. An adjoining breakfast room with patio doors provides a casual place for meals with easy access from the kitchen. From the gourmet kitchen, the formal dining room is served through a rear passage. Entertaining is a joy here with the added beauty of a bay window in the dining room and a box-bay in the formal living room. The secluded master suite is fashioned with a formal ceiling and a spacious bath highlighted with a spa tub and a walk-in closet. Upstairs, the balcony hall that overlooks the great room leads to a loft and two secondary bedrooms that share a private bath. This home is designed with a basement foundation.

Design by
Stephen Fuller/
Design Traditions

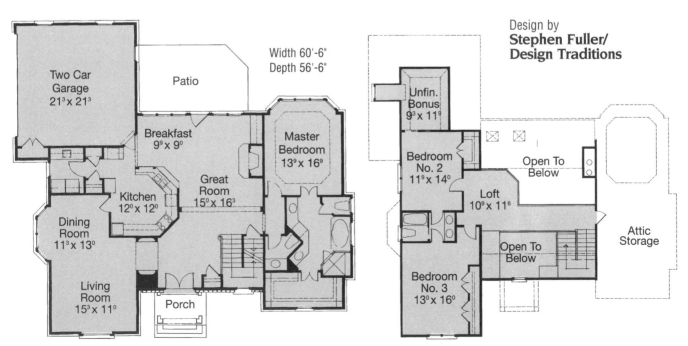

81

Design 7806

Square Footage: 2,598

A formal entry and gallery hall combine with open living spaces to create a casually elegant plan that is designed for easy living. The large great room has a massive fireplace serving as a focal point and three sets of French doors opening onto the rear deck. The kitchen is nicely tucked away from living spaces and is open to a traditional keeping room with a warming fireplace and breakfast nook. The sleeping wing is highlighted with a lovely master suite with a spa-style bath and large walk-in closet. Two additional bedrooms share a private bath. Extra storage space is available in the two-car garage. This house is designed with a basement foundation.

Design by
Stephen Fuller/
Design Traditions

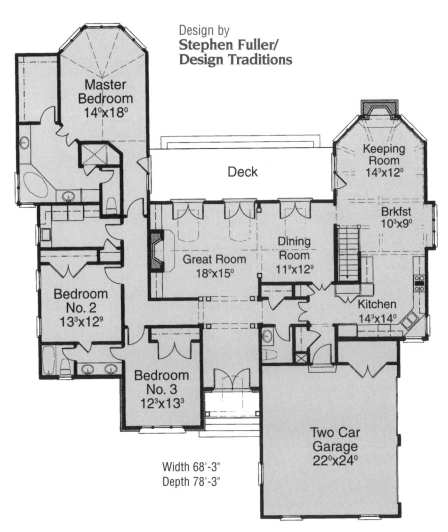

Master Bedroom 14⁰x18⁰

Deck

Keeping Room 14³x12⁰

Brkfst 10³x9⁰

Great Room 18⁰x15⁰

Dining Room 11⁹x12⁹

Bedroom No. 2 13³x12⁹

Kitchen 14³x14⁰

Bedroom No. 3 12³x13³

Two Car Garage 22⁰x24⁰

Width 68'-3"
Depth 78'-3"

Design by
**Stephen Fuller/
Design Traditions**

Porch

Master
Bedroom
16³ x 13⁶

Bedroom
Office
10³ x 11⁰

Breakfast
13³ x 9⁰

Kitchen
13³ x 10⁶
Dn

Great
Room
17⁰ x 17⁹

Bedroom
No. 2
10³ x 12⁰

Dining
Room
11³ x 12⁹

Bedroom
No. 3
11³ x 12⁰

Two Car
Garage
20⁶ x 19⁶

Width 61'
Depth 73'-8"

Design 7820

Square Footage: 2,127

A quaint stucco and stone facade with detailed windows sets a cozy mood in this delightful French cottage. The foyer is set apart from the formal dining room with stately columns. The great room will accommodate easy living with a grand fireplace and doors to the rear porch. A gourmet-style kitchen has a cooktop island and a bayed breakfast nook. The sleeping wing is set off with its own hall for privacy. The master suite features twin walk-in closets and a luxury bath. Two secondary bedrooms share a hall bath. An additional bedroom and bath off the kitchen would make a nice guest suite or a home office. This house is designed with a basement foundation.

Copyright 1992 Stephen S. Fuller, Inc.

Design 9885

Square Footage: 2,295

One-story living takes a lovely traditional turn in this stately brick home. The entry foyer opens directly to the dining room and great room, with columned accents to separate the areas. A large island kitchen adjoins the breakfast nook and the keeping room that's highlighted with a fireplace. The bedrooms are found to the left of the plan. A master suite is cloistered to the rear and has a large master bath and bayed sitting area. Two additional bedrooms share a full bath. This home is designed with a basement foundation.

Width 69'
Depth 49'-6"

DECK

SITTING AREA
12'-0" X 12'-0"

MASTER SUITE
13'-0" X 17'-6"

M.BATH

M.CLOSET

BREAKFAST
11'-4" X 10'-0"

KITCHEN
10'-0" X 18'-0"

KEEPING ROOM
11'-4" X 11'-0"

GREAT ROOM
20'-6" X 19'-0"

CLO. CLO.

BATH

LIN.

PNTRY

DN. LAUNDRY

BEDROOM NO. 3
12'-0" X 11'-8"

COAT

FOYER
8'-0" X 14'-4"

DINING ROOM
12'-0" X 14'-4"

BEDROOM NO. 2
13'-10" X 12'-6"

TWO CAR GARAGE
21'-4" X 21'-5"

STOOP

QUOTE ONE®

Cost to build? See page 214 to order complete cost estimate to build this house in your area!

Design by
**Stephen Fuller/
Design Traditions**

Design 9949

Square Footage: 1,770

Wood frame, weatherboard siding and stacked stone give this home its country cottage appeal. The concept is reinforced by the double elliptical arched front porch, a Colonial balustrade and a roof-vent dormer. Inside, the foyer leads to the great room and the dining room. The well-planned kitchen easily services the breakfast room. A rear deck makes outdoor living extra enjoyable. Three bedrooms include a master suite with a tray ceiling and a luxurious bath. The two secondary bedrooms share a compartmented bath. This home is designed with a basement foundation.

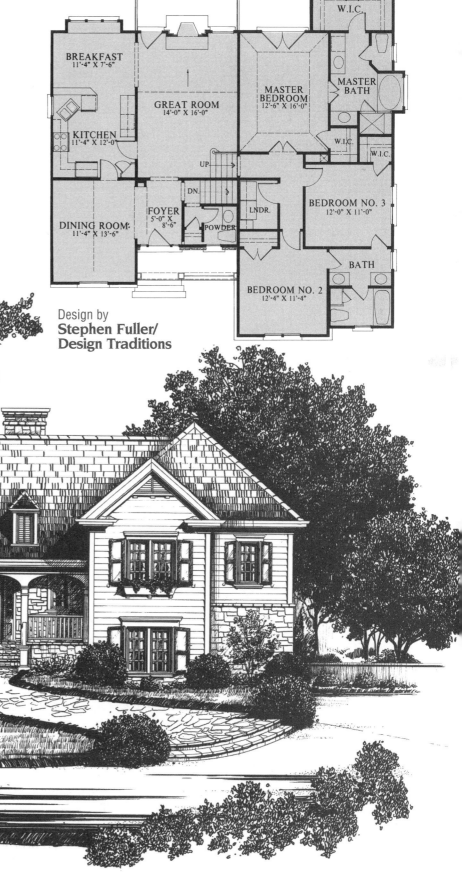

Width 48'
Depth 47'-5"

DECK

BREAKFAST
11'-4" X 7'-6"

GREAT ROOM
14'-0" X 16'-0"

MASTER
BEDROOM
12'-6" X 16'-0"

W.I.C.

MASTER
BATH

KITCHEN
11'-4" X 12'-0"

W.I.C.

W.I.C.

UP

DN.

LNDR.

BEDROOM NO. 3
12'-0" X 11'-0"

FOYER
5'-0" X
8'-6"

POWDER

DINING ROOM
11'-4" X 13'-6"

BATH

BEDROOM NO. 2
12'-4" X 11'-4"

Design by
**Stephen Fuller/
Design Traditions**

Copyright 1992 Stephen S. Fuller, Inc.

 **Design 9884**

Square Footage: 2,120

Design by
Stephen Fuller/
Design Traditions

Arch-top windows act as graceful accents for this wonderful design. Inside, the floor plan is compact but commodious. A central family room serves as the center of activity. It has a fireplace and connects to a lovely sun room with rear porch access. The formal dining room is to the front of the plan and is open to the entry foyer. A private den complete with a cozy fireplace also opens off the foyer with double doors. The kitchen area opens to the sun room and it contains an island work counter. Bedrooms are split, with the master suite to the right side of the design. Two secondary bedrooms that share a private bath are just off the sun room. This home is designed with a basement foundation.

BEDROOM NO. 3 11'-6" X 11'-0"

BATH

BEDROOM NO. 2 11'-4" X 11'-0"

SUN ROOM 12'-0" X 13'-9"

MASTER BATH

W.I.C.

PORCH

BREAKFAST 10'-0" X 9'-0"

FAMILY ROOM 18'-0" X 14'-0"

MASTER BEDROOM 13'-4" X 15'-8"

LAUNDRY

KITCHEN 12'-0" X 13'-9"

BATH

DN.

TWO CAR GARAGE 20'-4" X 20'-8"

DINING ROOM 10'-6" X 13'-6"

FOYER

DEN 11'-4" X 12'-6"

STOOP

Width 62'
Depth 62'-6"

Quote One®

Cost to build? See page 214 to order complete cost estimate to build this house in your area!

Design 9904

Square Footage: 2,090

People will surely stop to admire this exquisite house. Its European styling will work well in a variety of environments. As for livability, this plan has it all. Begin with the front door which opens into the dining and great rooms—the latter complete with fireplace and doors that open onto the back porch. The kitchen combines with the breakfast nook to create ample space for meals and quiet socializing—whatever your fancy. This plan incorporates four bedrooms; you may want to use one bedroom as an office and another as a study. The master bedroom houses a fabulous bath; be sure to check out the walk-in closets and spa tub. This home is designed with a basement foundation.

Design by
**Stephen Fuller/
Design Traditions**

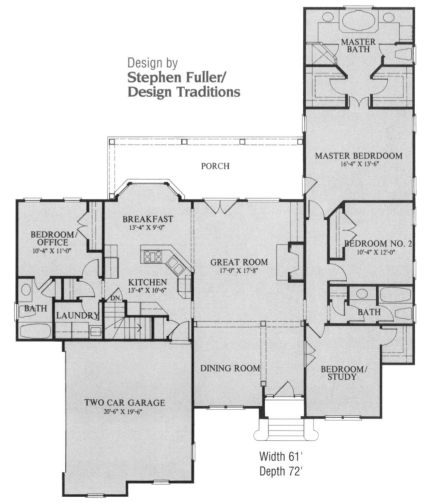

PORCH

BREAKFAST
13'-4" X 9'-0"

BEDROOM/
OFFICE
10'-4" X 11'-0"

GREAT ROOM
17'-0" X 17'-8"

MASTER BEDRDOOM
16'-4" X 13'-6"

MASTER
BATH

BEDRROOM NO. 2
10'-4" X 12'-0"

KITCHEN
13'-4" X 10'-6"

DN.

BATH

LAUNDRY

BATH

TWO CAR GARAGE
20'-6" X 19'-6"

DINING ROOM

BEDROOM/
STUDY

Width 61'
Depth 72'

Design 9361

Square Footage: 1,666

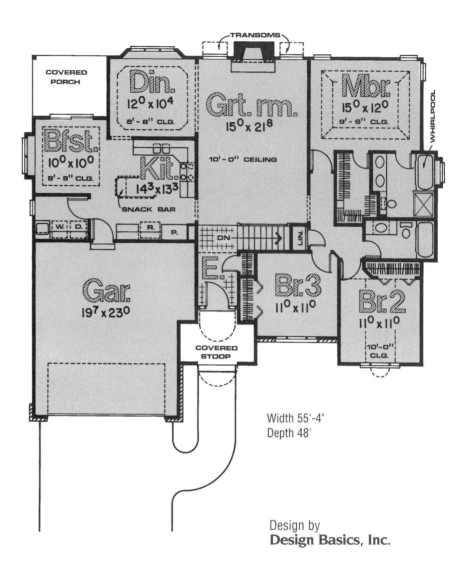

COVERED PORCH

Din.
12⁰ x 10⁴
8' - 8" CLG.

Bfst.
10⁰ x 10⁰
8' - 8" CLG.

Kit.
14³ x 13³

SNACK BAR

Grt. rm.
15⁰ x 21⁸
10' - 0" CEILING

TRANSOMS

Mbr.
15⁰ x 12⁰
9' - 6" CLG.

WHIRLPOOL

W. D.   R.   P.

DN

LIN.

Gar.
19⁷ x 23⁰

Br.3
11⁰ x 11⁰

Br.2
11⁰ x 11⁰
10' - 0" CLG.

COVERED STOOP

Width 55'-4"
Depth 48'

Design by
Design Basics, Inc.

The delightfully updated European plan has brick and stucco on the dramatic front elevation, showcased by sleek lines and decorative windows. An inviting entry has a view into the great room and is enhanced by an arched window and plant shelves above. The great room's fireplace is framed by sunny windows with transoms above. The bay-windowed dining room is nestled between the great room and the superb eat-in kitchen. The secluded master suite has a roomy walk-in closet and a luxurious bath with dual lavatories and whirlpool tub. Two additional bedrooms share a hall bath.

Design by
**Donald A. Gardner,
Architects, Inc.**

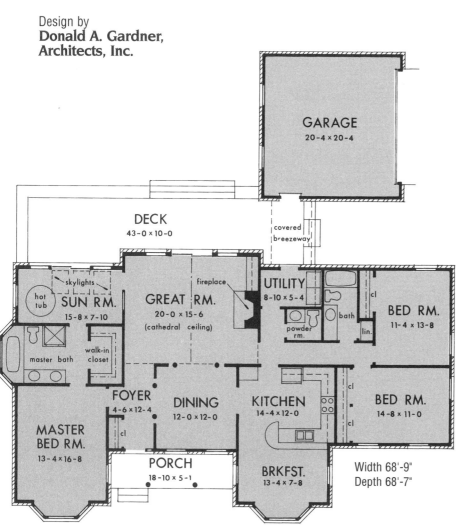

GARAGE
20-4 x 20-4

DECK
43-0 x 10-0

covered
breezeway

skylights

hot
tub

SUN RM.
15-8 x 7-10

fireplace

GREAT RM.
20-0 x 15-6
(cathedral ceiling)

UTILITY
8-10 x 5-4

bath

cl

BED RM.
11-4 x 13-8

master bath

walk-in
closet

powder
rm.

lin.

FOYER
4-6 x 12-4

DINING
12-0 x 12-0

KITCHEN
14-4 x 12-0

cl

BED RM.
14-8 x 11-0

MASTER
BED RM.
13-4 x 16-8

cl

cl

PORCH
18-10 x 5-1

BRKFST.
13-4 x 7-8

Width 68'-9"
Depth 68'-7"

esign 9660
Square Footage: 2,108

Multi-pane windows, dormers, copper-covered bay windows, a covered porch with round columns and brick siding help to emphasize the sophisticated appearance of this three-bedroom home. An added special feature to this plan is the sun room with hot tub that's accessible to both the master bath and great room. The great room has a fireplace, cathedral ceiling and sliding glass door with arched window above to allow plenty of natural light. The spacious master bedroom contains a walk-in closet and a bath with double-bowl vanity, shower and garden tub. Two family bedrooms are located at the opposite end of the house for privacy.

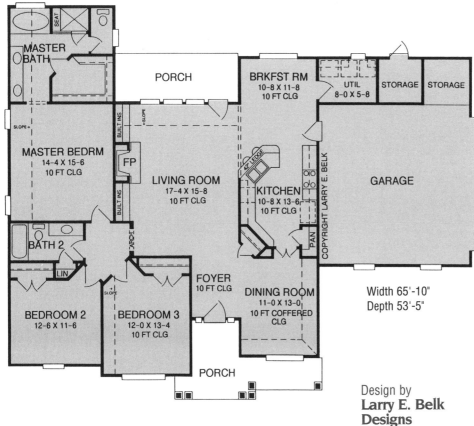

MASTER BATH

SEAT

PORCH

BRKFST RM
10-8 X 11-8
10 FT CLG

UTIL
8-0 X 5-8

STORAGE

STORAGE

MASTER BEDRM
14-4 X 15-6
10 FT CLG

SLOPE

BUILT INS

SLOPE

FP

BUILT INS

LIVING ROOM
17-4 X 15-8
10 FT CLG

ART LEDGE

KITCHEN
10-8 X 13-6
10 FT CLG

PAN

COPYRIGHT LARRY E. BELK

GARAGE

ARCH

BATH 2

LIN

SLOPE

FOYER
10 FT CLG

BEDROOM 2
12-6 X 11-6

BEDROOM 3
12-0 X 13-4
10 FT CLG

DINING ROOM
11-0 X 13-0
10 FT COFFERED CLG

PORCH

Width 65'-10"
Depth 53'-5"

Design by
**Larry E. Belk
Designs**

Design 8183

Square Footage: 1,890

Small, elegant and classi-cally styled, this home appears larger from the curb. Inside, ten-foot ceilings give the home a spacious feel. The roomy living room features a centerpiece fireplace flanked by built-in bookcases. An angled bar opens the nearby kitchen and breakfast room to the living room. The master suite has a huge walk-in closet and a lush compartmented bath. Two secondary bedrooms share a full hall bath. Two separate storage rooms are part of the garage. Please specify slab or crawlspace foundation when ordering.

Design 8164

First Floor: 1,276 square feet
Second Floor: 378 square feet
Total: 1,654 square feet

Designed for utmost livability, this English mini-estate is full of cottage charm. A turret entrance leads to the vaulted foyer and the great room beyond. An adjacent kitchen features a breakfast bar, a walk-in pantry and a planning desk. The spacious, multi-windowed breakfast room allows access to the octagonal porch, perfect for outdoor dining. Located on the first floor, the master suite is filled with amenities that include a relaxing bath and an enormous walk-in closet. On the second floor, an additional bedroom has a private bath. A large expandable area is available off the balcony and can be used for storage or finished for additional living space. Please specify crawlspace or slab foundation when ordering.

Design by
Larry E. Belk
Designs

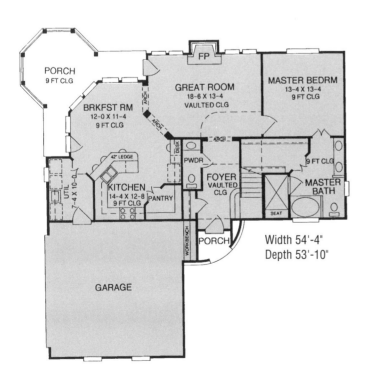

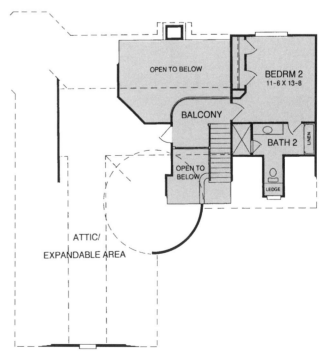

SCREENED
PORCH
12-6 X 11-0
10 FT CLG

GREAT ROOM
17-4 X 17-6
12 FT CLG

FP

BUILT IN

SITTING
11-2 X 13-6
10 FT CLG

MASTER BEDROOM
15-2 X 15-2
10 FT CLG

MASTER
BATH
10 FT CLG

K.S.

LEDGE

LIN

CHEST

BRKFST RM
12-6 X 11-0
10 FT CLG

PWDR

BUILT IN

ARCH

ARCH

FOYER
10 FT CLG

ARCH

BATH 2

42" LEDGE

KITCHEN
15-4 X 13-6

10 FT CLG

DINING ROOM
15-4 X 13-4
10 FT CLG

ARCH

LIN

BEDROOM 3
12-4 X 12-0
10 FT CLG

BEDROOM 2
12-6 X 12-6
10 FT CLG

PAN

UTIL

RAISED PLANTER

Width 81'-2"
Depth 67'-10"

GARAGE

Design by
**Larry E. Belk
Designs**

*D*esign 8224

Square Footage: 2,439

G raceful arches and columns are a delicate complement to the easy-care
brick facade of this English farmhouse.
An extended foyer introduces an exciting
interior plan—ten-foot ceilings throughout offer a spacious look. Guests and
family alike will appreciate a cozy fireplace in the great room, and the nearby
screen porch. An efficient kitchen with a
cooktop island counter and an angled
dual sink serves both a breakfast room
with screen porch access and the formal
dining room. The master suite offers privacy at the rear of the plan. It features a
large walk-in closet with built-in chest,
knee-space vanity, dual sinks, garden tub
and compartment toilet. Two family bedrooms are clustered nearby and share a
full bath. Please specify crawlspace or
slab foundation when ordering.

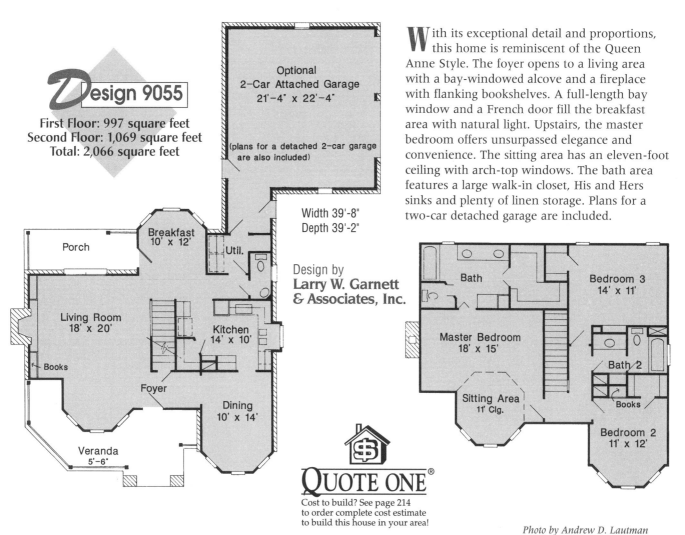

Design 9055

First Floor: **997 square feet**
Second Floor: **1,069 square feet**
Total: **2,066 square feet**

Optional
2-Car Attached Garage
21'-4" x 22'-4"

(plans for a detached 2-car garage
are also included)

Width 39'-8"
Depth 39'-2"

Porch

Breakfast
10' x 12'

Util.

Living Room
18' x 20'

Books

Kitchen
14' x 10'

Foyer

Dining
10' x 14'

Veranda
5'-6"

Design by
**Larry W. Garnett
& Associates, Inc.**

Bath

Bedroom 3
14' x 11'

Master Bedroom
18' x 15'

Bath 2

Books

Sitting Area
11' Clg.

Bedroom 2
11' x 12'

QUOTE ONE®

Cost to build? See page 214
to order complete cost estimate
to build this house in your area!

With its exceptional detail and proportions, this home is reminiscent of the Queen Anne Style. The foyer opens to a living area with a bay-windowed alcove and a fireplace with flanking bookshelves. A full-length bay window and a French door fill the breakfast area with natural light. Upstairs, the master bedroom offers unsurpassed elegance and convenience. The sitting area has an eleven-foot ceiling with arch-top windows. The bath area features a large walk-in closet, His and Hers sinks and plenty of linen storage. Plans for a two-car detached garage are included.

Photo by Andrew D. Lautman

Photo by Jon Riley

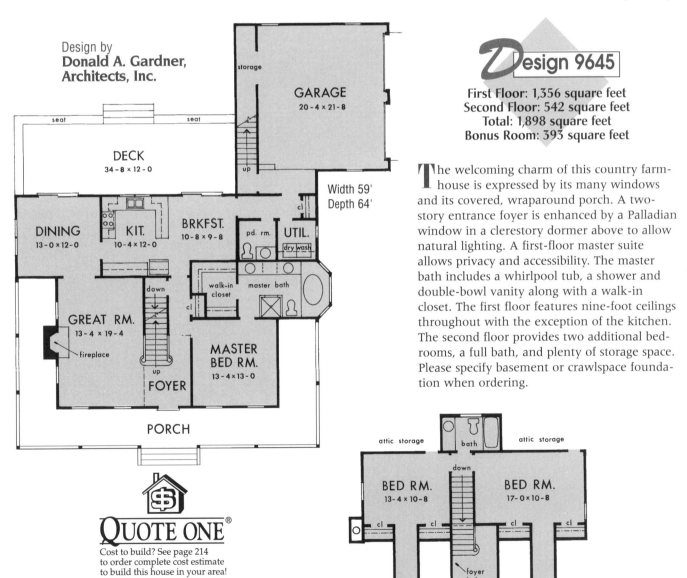

Design by
**Donald A. Gardner,
Architects, Inc.**

GARAGE
20-4 × 21-8

storage

seat   seat

DECK
34-8 × 12-0

Width 59'
Depth 64'

DINING
13-0 × 12-0

KIT.
10-4 × 12-0

BRKFST.
10-8 × 9-8

pd. rm.

UTIL.
dry wash

down

walk-in
closet

cl

master bath

GREAT RM.
13-4 × 19-4

fireplace

up   FOYER

MASTER
BED RM.
13-4 × 13-0

PORCH

Design 9645

First Floor: 1,356 square feet
Second Floor: 542 square feet
Total: 1,898 square feet
Bonus Room: 393 square feet

The welcoming charm of this country farm-house is expressed by its many windows and its covered, wraparound porch. A two-story entrance foyer is enhanced by a Palladian window in a clerestory dormer above to allow natural lighting. A first-floor master suite allows privacy and accessibility. The master bath includes a whirlpool tub, a shower and double-bowl vanity along with a walk-in closet. The first floor features nine-foot ceilings throughout with the exception of the kitchen. The second floor provides two additional bed-rooms, a full bath, and plenty of storage space. Please specify basement or crawlspace founda-tion when ordering.

QUOTE ONE®

Cost to build? See page 214
to order complete cost estimate
to build this house in your area!

attic storage   bath   attic storage

down

BED RM.
13-4 × 10-8

BED RM.
17-0 × 10-8

cl   cl   cl   cl

foyer
below

clerestory with palladian window

94

Design by
Larry W. Garnett & Associates, Inc.

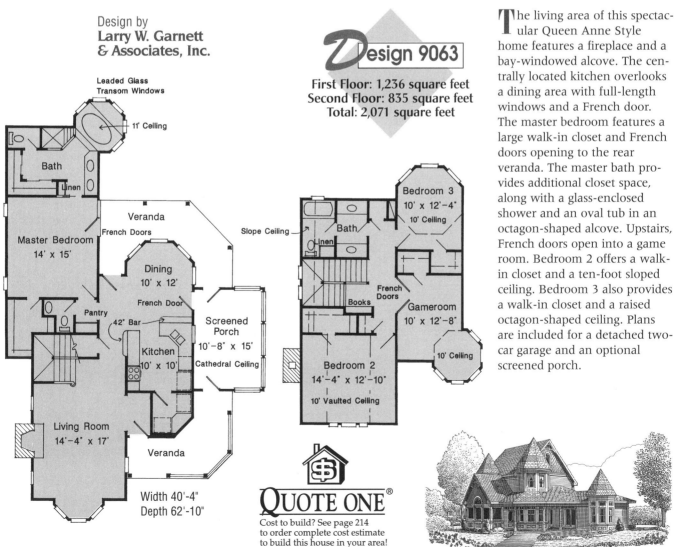

Leaded Glass
Transom Windows

11' Ceiling

Bath

Linen

Veranda
French Doors

Master Bedroom
14' x 15'

Pantry

42" Bar

Dining
10' x 12'

French Door

Kitchen
10' x 10'

Screened
Porch
10'-8" x 15'

Cathedral Ceiling

Living Room
14'-4" x 17'

Veranda

Width 40'-4"
Depth 62'-10"

Slope Ceiling

Bath

Linen

Books

French
Doors

Bedroom 3
10' x 12'-4"
10' Ceiling

Gameroom
10' x 12'-8"

10' Ceiling

Bedroom 2
14'-4" x 12'-10"

10' Vaulted Ceiling

Design 9063

First Floor: 1,236 square feet
Second Floor: 835 square feet
Total: 2,071 square feet

The living area of this spectacular Queen Anne Style home features a fireplace and a bay-windowed alcove. The centrally located kitchen overlooks a dining area with full-length windows and a French door. The master bedroom features a large walk-in closet and French doors opening to the rear veranda. The master bath provides additional closet space, along with a glass-enclosed shower and an oval tub in an octagon-shaped alcove. Upstairs, French doors open into a game room. Bedroom 2 offers a walk-in closet and a ten-foot sloped ceiling. Bedroom 3 also provides a walk-in closet and a raised octagon-shaped ceiling. Plans are included for a detached two-car garage and an optional screened porch.

QUOTE ONE®

Cost to build? See page 214
to order complete cost estimate
to build this house in your area!

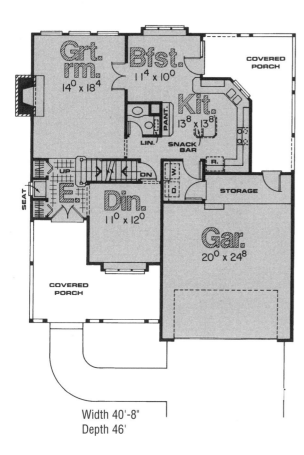

Design 7220

First Floor: 905 square feet
Second Floor: 863 square feet
Total: 1,768 square feet

A covered porch and Victorian accents create a classical elevation. Double doors to the entry open to a spacious great room and an elegant dining room. In the gourmet kitchen, features include an island snack bar and a large pantry. French doors lead to the breakfast area which also enjoys access to a covered porch. Cathedral ceilings in the master bedroom and dressing area add an exquisite touch. His and Hers walk-in closets, a large dressing area with dual sinks and a whirlpool complement the master bedroom. A vaulted ceiling in Bedroom 2 accents a window seat and an arched transom window.

Width 40'-8"
Depth 46'

Design by
Design Basics, Inc.

Design 3331

First Floor: 1,115 square feet
Second Floor: 690 square feet
Total: 1,805 square feet

L

This quaint tudor cottage has an open floor plan that is designed for easy living. The gathering room is accented with a cathedral ceiling and a full Palladian window. The dining room is joined to the efficient kitchen with extra entertaining space available on the deck. The first-floor master suite has a large compartmented bath and bumped-out windows. Upstairs, a lounge overlooks the gathering room. Two additional bedrooms and a full hall bath complete the second floor.

California Engineered Plans and California Stock Plans are available for this home. Call 1-800-521-6797 for more information.

Design by
Home Planners

QUOTE ONE®

Cost to build? See page 214 to order complete cost estimate to build this house in your area!

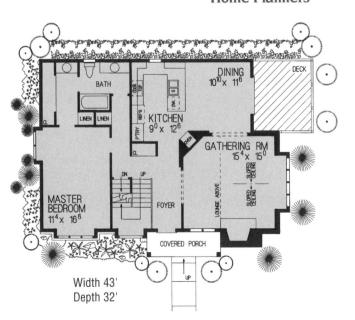

Width 43'
Depth 32'

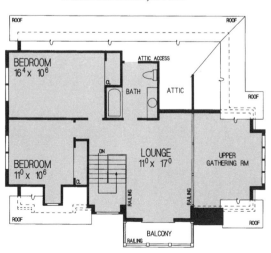

B. NATHAN

Floor Plan

DECK
25-2 × 10-0

seat

MASTER
BED RM.
13-4 × 17-8

master
bath

walk-in
closet

storage

skylights

SUN RM.
16-0 × 7-6

wet bar

BRKFST.
8-6 × 10-10

pantry

BED RM.
11-4 × 11-8

cl

fireplace

GREAT RM.
18-0 × 16-2
(cathedral ceiling)

KIT.
12-0 × 10-0

cl

UTIL.

GARAGE
21-0 × 19-6

bath

lin.

cl

storage

cl

FOYER
12-4 × 5-6

vaulted
clerestory

DINING
12-0 × 12-0

BED RM.
12-0 × 12-0

PORCH
15-2 × 4-9

Width 72'-6"
Depth 53'-10"

Alternate Basement Plan

pantry

cl

down

kitchen

garage

storage

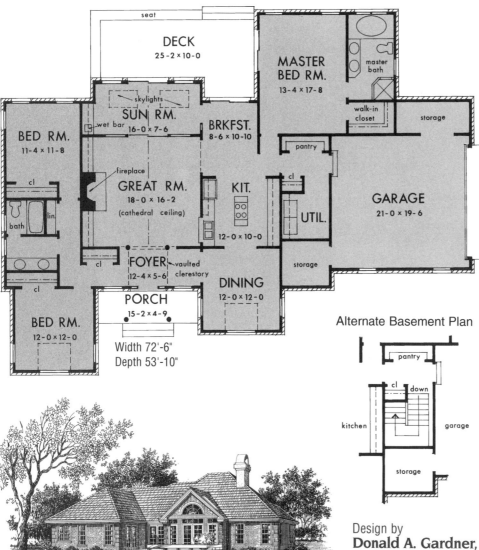

Design by
**Donald A. Gardner,
Architects, Inc.**

Design 9634

Square Footage: 2,099

This enchanting design incorporates the best in floor planning all on one level. The central great room is the hub of the plan from which all other rooms radiate. It is highlighted with a fireplace and cathedral ceiling. Nearby is a skylit sun room with sliding glass doors to the rear deck and a built-in wet bar. The galley-style kitchen adjoins an attached breakfast room that also connects to the sun room. The master suite is split from the family bedrooms and contains access to the rear deck. Its bathroom contains such special amenities as a large walk-in closet and double vanity. Family bedrooms share a full bath also with double vanity. Extra storage space is contained in the garage. Please specify basement or crawlspace foundation when ordering.

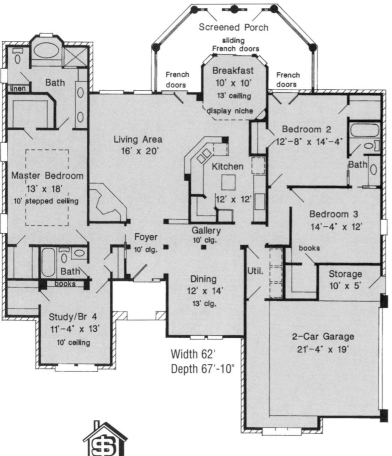

Screened Porch

sliding
French doors

French
doors

Breakfast
10' x 10'
13' ceiling

French
doors

display niche

Bath

linen

Living Area
16' x 20'

Kitchen
12' x 12'

Bedroom 2
12'-8" x 14'-4"

Bath

Master Bedroom
13' x 18'
10' stepped ceiling

Gallery
10' clg.

Bedroom 3
14'-4" x 12'

books

Foyer
10' clg.

Bath
books

Dining
12' x 14'
13' clg.

Util.

Storage
10' x 5'

Study/Br 4
11'-4" x 13'
10' ceiling

2-Car Garage
21'-4" x 19'

Width 62'
Depth 67'-10"

Design 8923

Square Footage: 2,361

The combination of finely detailed brick and shingle siding recalls some of the distinctive architecture of the East Coast during the early part of this century. The foyer and gallery provide for a functional traffic pattern. The formal dining room to the front of the home is outlined by columns and features a thirteen-foot ceiling. The extensive living area offers a corner fireplace. A screened porch surrounding the breakfast room is an ideal entertainment area. The master suite features two spacious closets and a bath with a garden tub and an oversized shower. Bedroom 4 can serve as a study, nursery, guest room or home office.

Design by
Larry W. Garnett & Associates, Inc.

Design 9089

Square Footage: 1,849

Design by
**Larry W. Garnett
& Associates, Inc.**

QUOTE ONE®

Cost to build? See page 214
to order complete cost estimate
to build this house in your area!

A wonderful floor plan is found on the interior of this cozy one-story plan. The large living room and conveniently placed dining room both open from the raised foyer. In between is the galley kitchen with a snack bar, a huge pantry and attached breakfast area. French doors flanking the fireplace in the living room open to the rear yard. To the right of the plan is the master bedroom with walk-in closet, compartmented bath and double sinks. To the left of the plan are two family bedrooms sharing a full, compartmented bath in between.

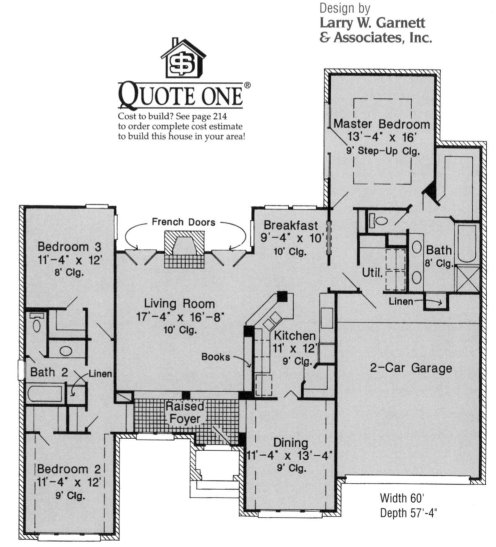

Design 3622

First Floor: 1,566 square feet
Second Floor: 837 square feet
Total: 2,403 square feet
Apartment Option: 506 square feet

L

This elegant English mini-estate offers a traditional country lifestyle in a home that is still manageable enough for a couple. True to country manor style, the foyer opens to the great hall. In this grand central room space is provided for a living room area around the fireplace, a dining room area with pass-through service to the kitchen and lovely, bumped-out window seats. The large country kitchen has gourmet effects, a snack bar and bayed breakfast nook. Also on the first floor, the master suite is fashioned with a window seat, romantic fireplace and a luxurious bath with a walk-in closet. Upstairs, a balcony hall joins three additional bedrooms and two full baths. Offered as a special option, a self-containing apartment can be built over the garage. Complete with a kitchen, living room and bedroom suite this apartment will make the perfect accommodations for extended-stay guests or as a rental.

Design by
Home Planners

Width 116'-3"
Depth 55'-1"

QUOTE ONE®

Cost to build? See page 214
to order complete cost estimate
to build this house in your area!

Design 2964

First Floor: 1,441 square feet
Second Floor: 621 square feet
Total: 2,062 square feet

Tudor houses have their own unique exterior features, most notably simulated beam work on a stucco and brick exterior and diamond-lite windows. The living room is dramatically spacious. It has a two-story sloping ceiling and large glass windows across the back. A large kitchen has a snack bar opening into the breakfast room. The first floor master suite has sliding doors to the terrace, a dressing area with walk-in closet and a bath with whirlpool tub. Two secondary bedrooms and a full hall bath lie just beyond the upstairs lounge that overlooks the living room.

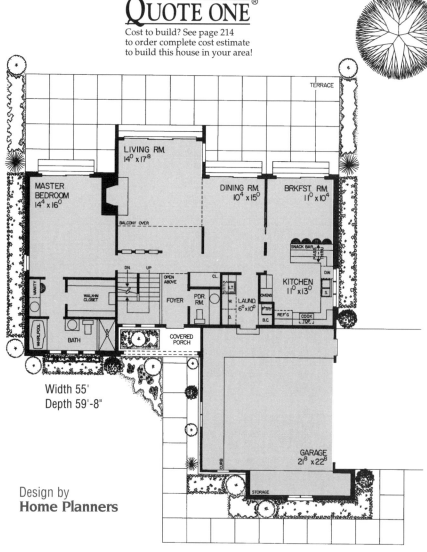

Quote One®

Cost to build? See page 214 to order complete cost estimate to build this house in your area!

Width 55'
Depth 59'-8"

Design by
Home Planners

Design 2802

Square Footage: 1,729

L D

Design by
Home Planners

QUOTE ONE®

Cost to build? See page 214
to order complete cost estimate
to build this house in your area!

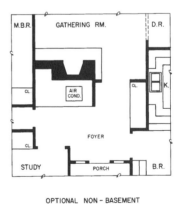

OPTIONAL NON-BASEMENT

This attractive plan displays an effective use of half-timbered stucco and brick as well as an authentic bay window to create an elegant Tudor elevation. The covered porch serves as a fitting introduction to all the inside amenities. The gathering room will be a favorite place for friends and family with its rustic appeal and rear terrace doors. A full sized kitchen with snack bar and breakfast room is well suited for the gourmet. The master bedroom has a large walk-in closet, private bath and doors to the terrace. Two additional bedrooms share a hall bath. A large storage area or shop space is available in the two-car garage.

LIVING RM.
18²x21²

DINING RM.
9⁴x13¹⁰

KITCHEN
10⁰x13¹⁰

BRKFST. RM.
10⁰x15¹⁰

RANGE

SLOPED

CEILING

RAILING

LAUNDRY

CHINA   BRM CL

PDR.
RM.

DESK   PANTRY

BATH

WHIRLPOOL

BATH

WALK-IN
CLOSET

LINEN

FOYER

STUDY
10⁰x11⁰

COVERED
PORCH

GARAGE
19⁶x19⁶

MASTER BEDROOM
13²x16²

BEDROOM
13⁶x11⁰

Width 63'-4"
Depth 54'-10"

Design by
Home Planners

This home's English Tudor exterior houses a contemporary, well-planned interior. Each of the three main living areas—sleeping, living and working—are but a couple of steps from the foyer. Open planning, a sloped ceiling and plenty of glass create a nice environment for the living-dining area. Its appeal is further enhanced by the open staircase to the lower level recreation/hobby area. The L-shaped kitchen with its island range and work surface opens onto the large, sunny breakfast room. Nearby is the step-saving laundry room. The sleeping area has the flexibility of functioning as a two- or three-bedroom plan.

Cost to build? See page 214
to order complete cost estimate
to build this house in your area!

Width 67'-4"
Depth 49'-8"

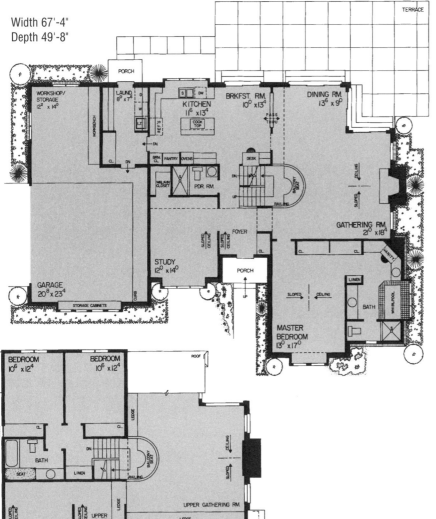

Design by
Home Planners

Design 2967

**First Floor: 1,877 square feet
Second Floor: 467 square feet
Total: 2,344 square feet**

L

Special interior amenities abound in this unique 1½-story Tudor. Living areas include an open gathering room/dining room area with fireplace and pass-through to the breakfast room. Quiet time can be spent in a sloped-ceiling study. Look for plenty of workspace in the island kitchen. Sleeping areas are separated for utmost privacy: an elegant master suite on the first floor, two bedrooms and a full bath on the second. Note the unusual curved balcony seat in the stairwell and the second floor ledge—a perfect spot for displaying plants or collectibles.

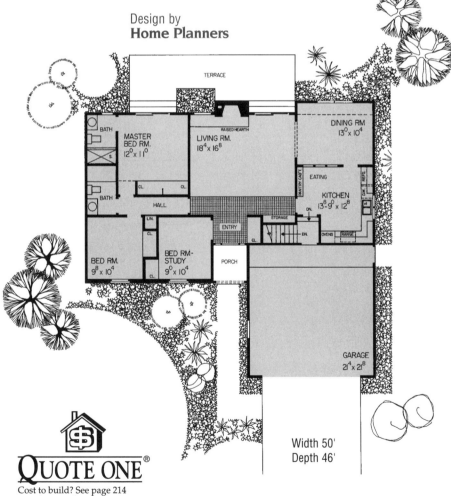

TERRACE

RAISED HEARTH

BATH

MASTER
BED RM.
12⁰ x 11⁰

LIVING RM.
18⁴ x 16⁸

DINING RM
13⁰ x 10⁴

BATH

CL.

CL.

PANTRY CAB'T

EATING

REFR.

DW.

HALL

KITCHEN
13-9⁰ x 12⁸

LIN.

CL.

ENTRY

STORAGE

DN.

CL.

DN.

OVENS

RANGE

BED RM.
9⁸ x 10⁴

BED RM-
STUDY
9⁰ x 10⁴

CL.

PORCH

GARAGE
21⁴ x 21⁸

Width 50'
Depth 46'

esign 2707

Square Footage: 1,267

L **D**

Here is a charming Early American adaptation that will serve as a picturesque and practical home. The living area, highlighted by the raised hearth fireplace, is spacious and comfortable. The efficient kitchen features an eating nook, convenient passage to the formal dining room and an easy service entrance. The bedroom wing offers three bedrooms and two full baths. The front facing secondary bedroom would make an ideal study or media room.

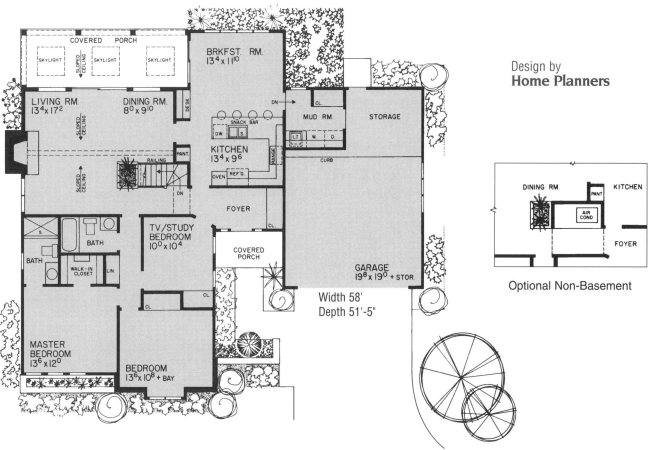

COVERED PORCH

SKYLIGHT | SLOPED CEILING | SKYLIGHT | SKYLIGHT

BRKFST. RM.
13⁴ x 11¹⁰

LIVING RM.
13⁴ x 17²

DINING RM.
8⁰ x 9¹⁰

SLOPED CEILING

DESK

SNACK BAR

DW. | S.

KITCHEN
13⁴ x 9⁶

RANGE

OVEN | REF'G.

PANT.

RAILING

DN

SLOPED CEILING

DN

CL.

MUD RM.

STORAGE

L.T. | W. | D.

CURB

FOYER

BATH

BATH

WALK-IN CLOSET

LIN.

TV/STUDY BEDROOM
10⁰ x 10⁴

COVERED PORCH

CL.

GARAGE
19⁸ x 19⁰ + STOR.

MASTER BEDROOM
13⁶ x 12⁰

CL.

BEDROOM
13⁶ x 10⁸ + BAY

Width 58'
Depth 51'-5"

Design by
Home Planners

DINING RM. | PANT. | KITCHEN

AIR COND

FOYER

Optional Non-Basement

Design 2805

Square Footage: 1,547

L **D**

This appealing Tudor home offers a practical and economical floor plan. The living/dining room at the rear of the plan has direct access to the covered porch. Notice the built-in planter adjacent to the open staircase leading to the basement. A breakfast room overlooks the covered porch. A desk, snack bar and mud room with laundry facilities are near the U-shaped kitchen. The master bedroom features a private bath and a walk-in closet. The large front bedroom has a bay window, while a third bedroom may serve as a study.

QUOTE ONE®

Cost to build? See page 214 to order complete cost estimate to build this house in your area!

Design by
Home Planners

Quote One®

Cost to build? See page 214
to order complete cost estimate
to build this house in your area!

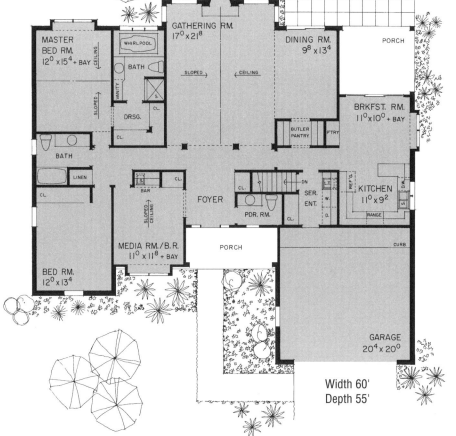

MASTER BED RM. 12⁰ x 15⁴ + BAY

WHIRLPOOL

BATH

GATHERING RM. 17⁰ x 21⁸

DINING RM. 9⁸ x 13⁴

PORCH

VANITY

DRSG.

SLOPED

CEILING

CL.

S.

BUTLER PANTRY

P'TRY

BRKFST. RM. 11⁰ x 10⁰ + BAY

BATH

LINEN

CL.

BAR

CL.

S.

SLOPED CEILING

FOYER

CL.

PDR. RM.

SER. ENT.

REF'G.

W.

D.

RANGE

KITCHEN 11⁰ x 9²

S.

BED RM. 12⁰ x 13⁴

MEDIA RM./B.R. 11⁰ x 11⁸ + BAY

PORCH

DN

CL.

PORCH

CURB

GARAGE 20⁴ x 20⁰

Width 60'
Depth 55'

Design 3376

Square Footage: 1,999

L D

Small families or empty-nesters will appreciate the layout of this traditional stone country home. The foyer opens to the gathering room with a dramatic centered fireplace and sloped ceiling. The dining room is open to the gathering room for entertaining ease and offers sliding doors to the rear terrace. The breakfast room also provides access to a covered porch for dining outdoors. The media room to the left of the foyer offers a box-bay window and a wet bar, and can double as a third bedroom. The master bedroom is accented with a sloping ceiling, a dressing area and a bath with both a shower and separate whirlpool tub. An additional bedroom and a full hall bath complete this comfortable plan.

Time to Relax

Porches That Welcome Easy Times

Down home comfort and style has never been as thoughtfully conceived as in the modern farmhouse—presented here with decidedly up-town amenities. Take a break from the hustle and bustle of your everyday life, or perhaps set your sights on an easy retirement in a delightful country home that caters to a more relaxed lifestyle.

No single amenity says "welcome home" like a covered porch. Either located in the front or rear, wrapping around one corner or all four, your porch is sure to be a favorite destination. The porch is the perfect place for lively gatherings with friends and family or quiet relaxing with a good book and a glass of lemonade. And this easy living pattern is transferred throughout the home with open living areas that speak of casual elegance.

The beautiful farmhouse styles we've selected for this section are sure to please the choosy home builder thanks to superior design and, of course, that always popular porch. The porch design in Design 7601 (page 118) offers front, side and rear exposure with an area large enough for a small dining table plus, a screened-in section around back. A full measure of country charm is added to the mix in Design 3679 (page 132) with a full wraparound porch and a quaint balcony off the upstairs master suite. Now all you need to do is sit back and get ready to relax.

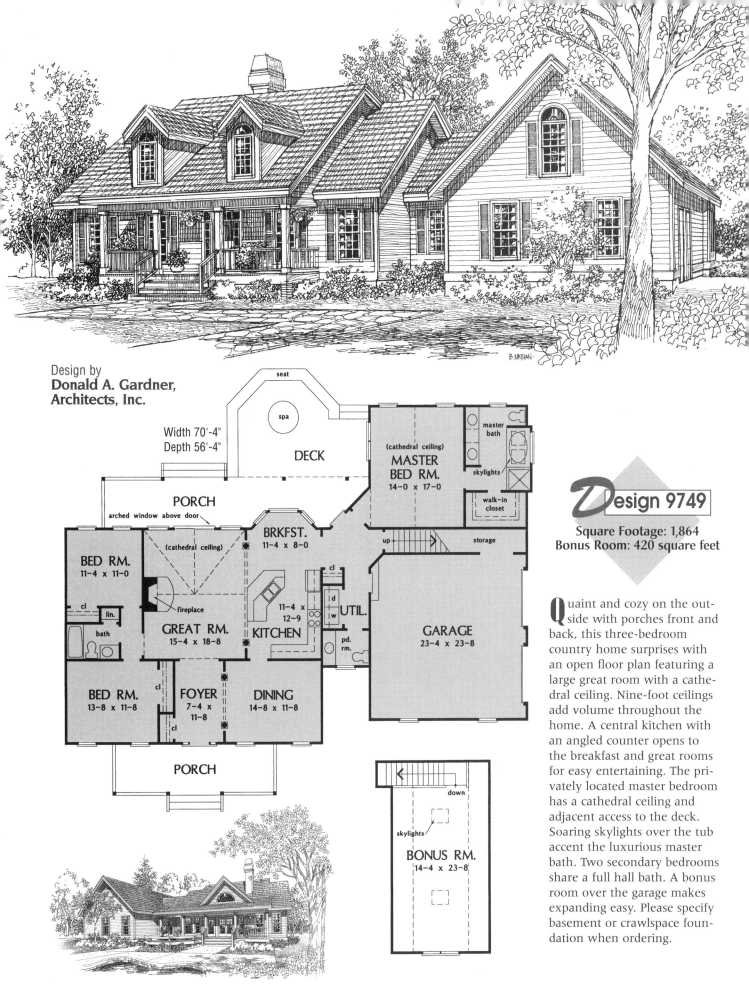

Design by
**Donald A. Gardner,
Architects, Inc.**

Width 70'-4"
Depth 56'-4"

DECK

seat

spa

PORCH

arched window above door

BRKFST.
11-4 x 8-0

(cathedral ceiling)

MASTER
BED RM.
14-0 x 17-0

master bath

skylights

walk-in closet

up

storage

Design 9749

**Square Footage: 1,864
Bonus Room: 420 square feet**

BED RM.
11-4 x 11-0

cl

lin.

(cathedral ceiling)

fireplace

GREAT RM.
15-4 x 18-8

KITCHEN

11-4 x 12-9

cl

d w

UTIL.

pd. rm.

GARAGE
23-4 x 23-8

bath

BED RM.
13-8 x 11-8

cl

FOYER
7-4 x 11-8

cl

DINING
14-8 x 11-8

PORCH

BONUS RM.
14-4 x 23-8

down

skylights

Quaint and cozy on the outside with porches front and back, this three-bedroom country home surprises with an open floor plan featuring a large great room with a cathedral ceiling. Nine-foot ceilings add volume throughout the home. A central kitchen with an angled counter opens to the breakfast and great rooms for easy entertaining. The privately located master bedroom has a cathedral ceiling and adjacent access to the deck. Soaring skylights over the tub accent the luxurious master bath. Two secondary bedrooms share a full hall bath. A bonus room over the garage makes expanding easy. Please specify basement or crawlspace foundation when ordering.

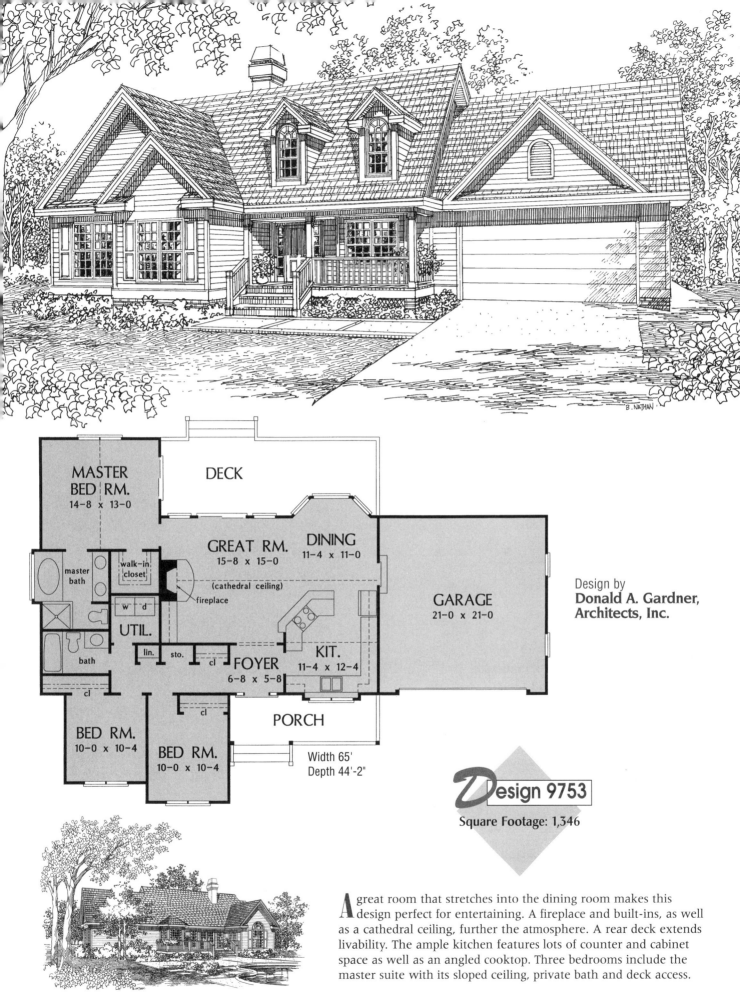

MASTER BED RM.
14-8 x 13-0

DECK

master bath

walk-in closet

w | d

UTIL.

bath

cl

GREAT RM.
15-8 x 15-0

(cathedral ceiling)

fireplace

DINING
11-4 x 11-0

GARAGE
21-0 x 21-0

lin. sto. cl

FOYER
6-8 x 5-8

KIT.
11-4 x 12-4

cl

BED RM.
10-0 x 10-4

BED RM.
10-0 x 10-4

PORCH

Width 65'
Depth 44'-2"

B. NATHAN

Design by
**Donald A. Gardner,
Architects, Inc.**

Design 9753

Square Footage: 1,346

A great room that stretches into the dining room makes this design perfect for entertaining. A fireplace and built-ins, as well as a cathedral ceiling, further the atmosphere. A rear deck extends livability. The ample kitchen features lots of counter and cabinet space as well as an angled cooktop. Three bedrooms include the master suite with its sloped ceiling, private bath and deck access.

111

Design 2947

Square Footage: 1,830

L D

This lovely one-story home greets visitors with a covered porch and plenty of traditional charm. A galley-style kitchen shares a snack bar with the spacious gathering room. An ample master suite includes a luxury bath with a whirlpool tub and a separate dressing area. Two family bedrooms, one that could double as a study, are located at the front of the home.

California Engineered Plans and California Stock Plans are available for this home. Call 1-800-521-6797 for more information.

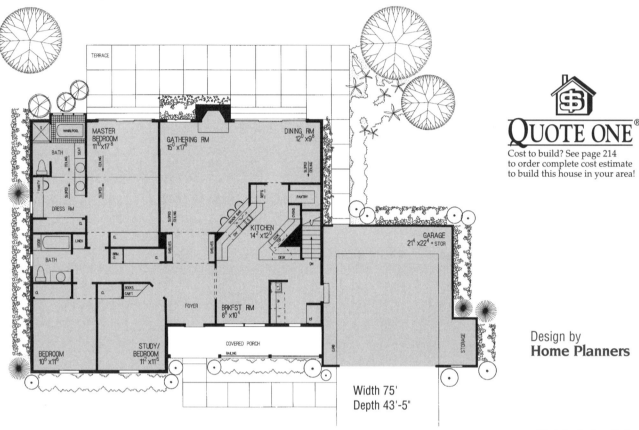

QUOTE ONE®

Cost to build? See page 214
to order complete cost estimate
to build this house in your area!

Design by
Home Planners

Width 75'
Depth 43'-5"

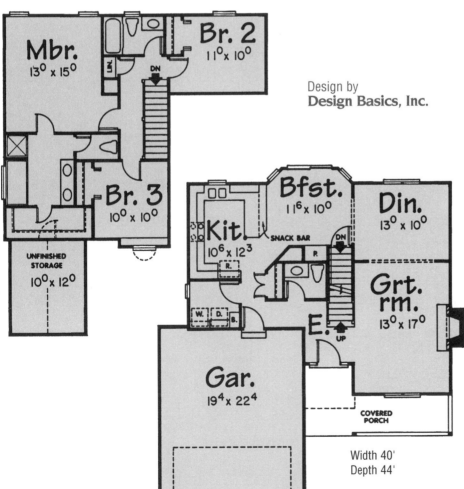

Mbr.
13⁰ x 15⁰

Br. 2
11⁰ x 10⁰

Br. 3
10⁰ x 10⁰

LIN.

DN

UNFINISHED STORAGE
10⁰ x 12⁰

Bfst.
11⁶ x 10⁰

Din.
13⁰ x 10⁰

Kit.
10⁶ x 12³

SNACK BAR

DN

P.

Grt. rm.
13⁰ x 17⁰

W. D. B.

E.

UP

Gar.
19⁴ x 22⁴

COVERED PORCH

Width 40'
Depth 44'

Design by
Design Basics, Inc.

*D*esign 7291

First Floor: 862 square feet
Second Floor: 780 square feet
Total: 1,642 square feet

A wide, gabled porch provides this home with its country identity and comfortable welcome. Inside, the foyer opens on the right to a great room and formal dining room that flow together to create a wonderful space for entertaining. The step-saving kitchen connects to a sunny, bay-windowed breakfast nook that provides direct access to the backyard. A convenient laundry room and a powder room complete the first floor. Upstairs, two family bedrooms share a hall bath and a linen closet. Designed for ultimate relaxation, the master suite features a private bath with a compartmented toilet, a double-bowl vanity and a large walk-in closet with access to plenty of unfinished storage space.

Design 9726

Square Footage: 1,498

This charming country home utilizes multi-pane windows, columns, dormers, and a covered porch to offer a welcoming front exterior. Inside, the great room with a dramatic cathedral ceiling commands attention; the kitchen and breakfast room are just beyond a set of columns. The tiered-ceilinged dining room presents a delightfully formal atmosphere for dinner parties or family gatherings. A tray ceiling in the master bedroom contributes to its pleasant atmosphere, as do the large walk-in closet and the gracious master bath with a garden tub and a separate shower. The secondary bedrooms are located at the opposite end of the house for privacy. Please specify basement or crawlspace foundation when ordering.

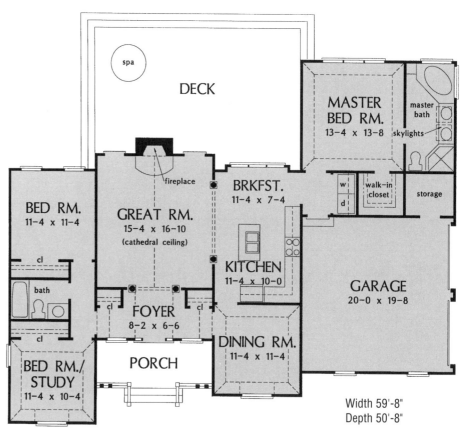

Width 59'-8"
Depth 50'-8"

Design by
Donald A. Gardner, Architects, Inc.

114

Design 8175

Square Footage: 1,302

Design by
Larry E. Belk Designs

Width 58'-10"
Depth 46'

A roomy wraparound porch accents this farmhouse-style elevation. Inside, ten-foot ceilings in the living room, kitchen and dining room give this home a spacious look. The efficiently designed kitchen includes a large pantry and plenty of cabinet and counter space. The dining room is nearby and perfect for either family gatherings or more formal entertaining. The master bedroom is located at the rear of the home and features a functional master bath with double vanities. Two additional bedrooms and a full hall bath complete this quaint farmhouse. Please specify crawlspace or slab foundation when ordering.

MASTER BEDRM 13-8 X 12-6

BEDRM 2 11-8 X 12-6

LIN

MASTER BATH

BATH 2

BEDRM 3 11-8 X 10-4

ARCH

GARAGE

DINING RM 12-8 X 9-8 10 FT CLG

SLOPE→

42" LEDGE

KITCHEN 12-8 X 9-8 10 FT CLG

PAN

ENTRY

ARCH

LIVING RM 16-6 X 13-8 10 FT CLG

STOR

FP

PORCH

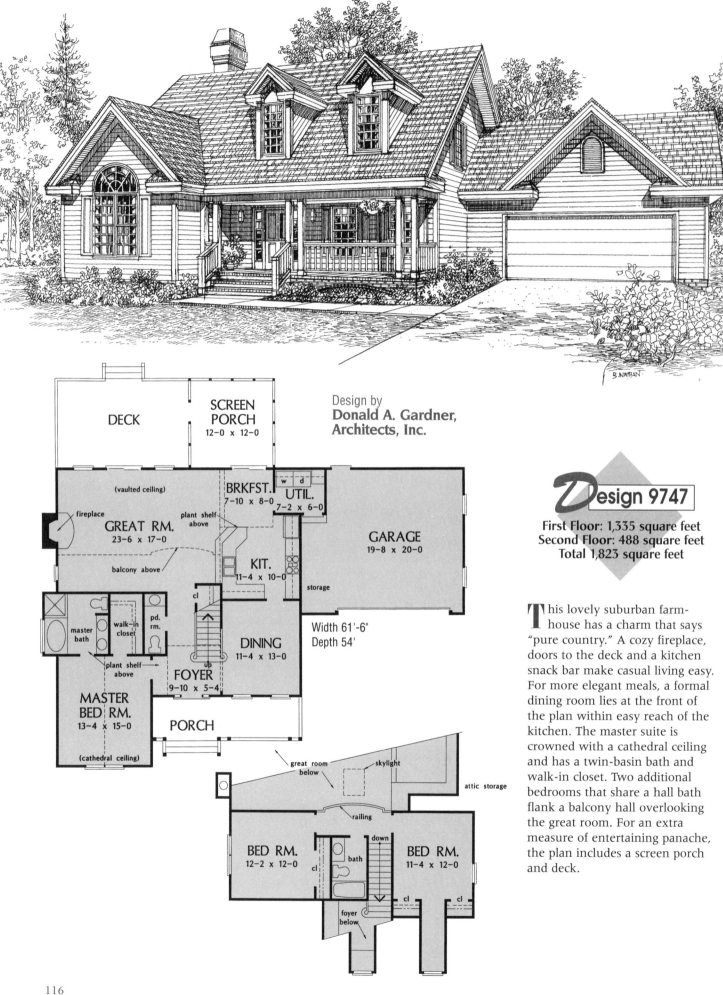

DECK

SCREEN
PORCH
12-0 x 12-0

Design by
**Donald A. Gardner,
Architects, Inc.**

(vaulted ceiling)

fireplace

GREAT RM.
23-6 x 17-0

plant shelf
above

balcony above

BRKFST.
7-10 x 8-0

UTIL.
7-2 x 6-0

w d

KIT.
11-4 x 10-0

storage

GARAGE
19-8 x 20-0

cl

master
bath

walk-in
closet

pd.
rm.

plant shelf
above

DINING
11-4 x 13-0

up

FOYER
9-10 x 5-4

Width 61'-6"
Depth 54'

**MASTER
BED RM.**
13-4 x 15-0

(cathedral ceiling)

PORCH

Design 9747

First Floor: 1,335 square feet
Second Floor: 488 square feet
Total 1,823 square feet

great room
below

skylight

attic storage

railing

BED RM.
12-2 x 12-0

cl

down

bath

BED RM.
11-4 x 12-0

cl

cl

foyer
below

This lovely suburban farmhouse has a charm that says
"pure country." A cozy fireplace,
doors to the deck and a kitchen
snack bar make casual living easy.
For more elegant meals, a formal
dining room lies at the front of
the plan within easy reach of the
kitchen. The master suite is
crowned with a cathedral ceiling
and has a twin-basin bath and
walk-in closet. Two additional
bedrooms that share a hall bath
flank a balcony hall overlooking
the great room. For an extra
measure of entertaining panache,
the plan includes a screen porch
and deck.

Design 9764

Square Footage: 1,815

Design by
**Donald A. Gardner,
Architects, Inc.**

Dormers, arched windows and covered porches lend this home its country appeal. Inside, the foyer opens to the dining room on the right and leads through a columned entrance to the great room warmed by a fireplace. Access is provided to the covered, skylit rear porch for outdoor livability. The open kitchen easily serves the great room, the bayed breakfast area and the dining room. A cathedral ceiling graces the master bedroom with its walk-in closet and private bath with a dual vanity and a whirlpool tub. Two additional bedrooms share a full bath. A detached garage with a skylit bonus room is connected to the covered rear porch.

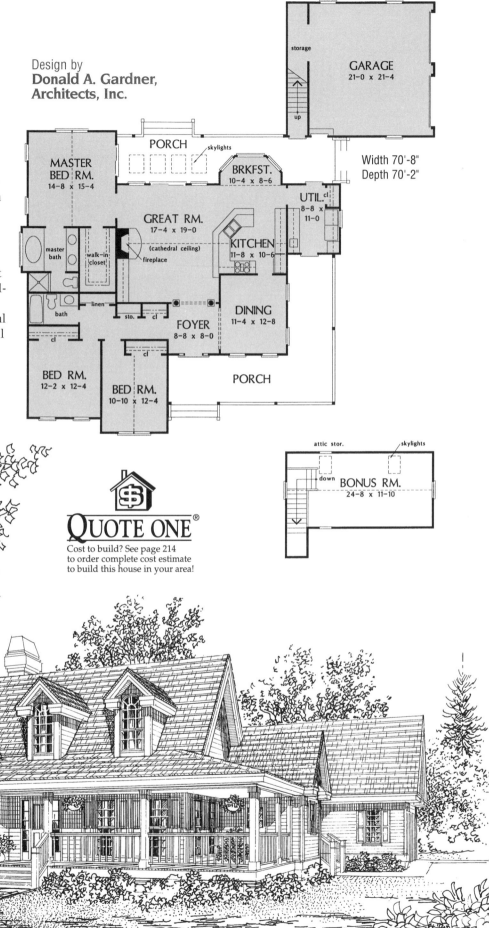

Width 70'-8"
Depth 70'-2"

QUOTE ONE®

Cost to build? See page 214
to order complete cost estimate
to build this house in your area!

117

B. NATHAN

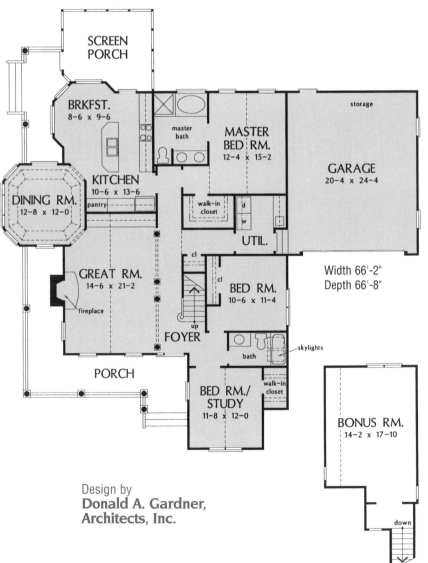

SCREEN PORCH

BRKFST.
8-6 x 9-6

master bath

MASTER BED RM.
12-4 x 15-2

storage

GARAGE
20-4 x 24-4

KITCHEN
10-6 x 13-6

DINING RM.
12-8 x 12-0

pantry

walk-in closet

d w

UTIL.

cl

Width 66'-2"
Depth 66'-8"

GREAT RM.
14-6 x 21-2

fireplace

cl

BED RM.
10-6 x 11-4

up

FOYER

bath

skylights

PORCH

BED RM./ STUDY
11-8 x 12-0

walk-in closet

BONUS RM.
14-2 x 17-10

Design by
Donald A. Gardner,
Architects, Inc.

down

Design 7601

Square Footage: 1,787
Bonus Room: 326 square feet

A neighborly porch as friendly as a handshake wraps around this charming country home, warmly greeting family and friends alike. Inside, cathedral ceilings promote a feeling of spaciousness. To the left of the foyer, the great room is enhanced with a fireplace and built-in book-shelves. A uniquely shaped formal dining room separates the kitchen and breakfast area. Outdoor pur-suits—rain or shine—will be enjoyed from the screen porch. The master suite is located at the rear of the plan for privacy and features a walk-in closet and a luxurious bath. Two additional bedrooms, one with a walk-in closet, share a skylit bath. A second-floor bonus room is available to develop later as a study, home office or play area. Please specify basement or crawlspace foundation when ordering.

Design 9664

Square footage: 1,287

This economical plan offers an impressive visual statement with its comfortable and well-proportioned appearance. The entrance foyer leads to all areas of the house. The great room, dining area and kitchen are all open to one another allowing visual interaction. The great room and dining area both have a cathedral ceiling. The fireplace is flanked by bookshelves and cabinets. The master suite has a cathedral ceiling, walk-in closet and master bath with double-bowl vanity, whirlpool tub and shower. Two secondary bedrooms share a full hall bath. Please specify basement or crawl-space foundation when ordering.

Design by
**Donald A. Gardner,
Architects, Inc.**

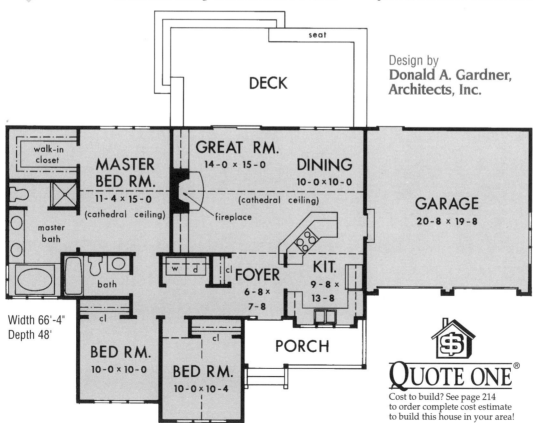

Width 66'-4"
Depth 48'

Quote One®
Cost to build? See page 214
to order complete cost estimate
to build this house in your area!

Design 9763

Square Footage: 1,807

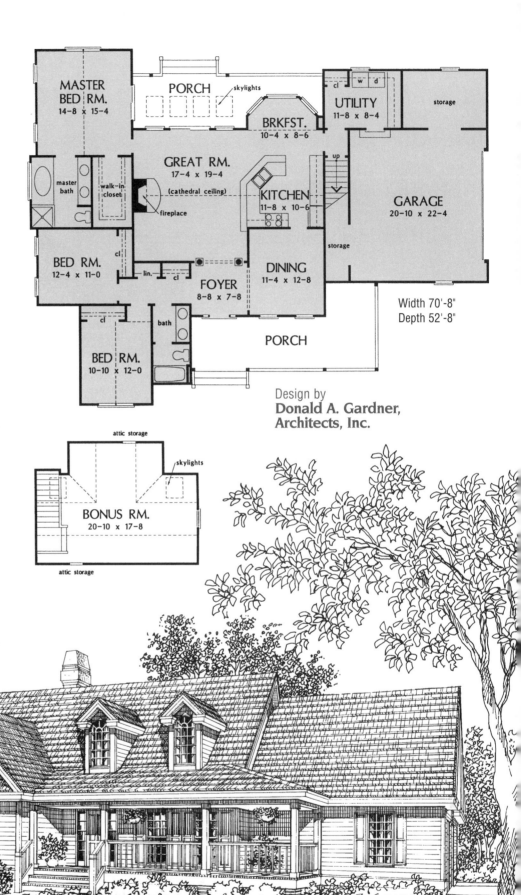

Dormers and arched windows provide this country home with lots of charm. The foyer opens through stately columns into the great room crowned with a cathedral ceiling and accented with a fireplace. An open kitchen easily serves the great room, the bayed breakfast area and the dining room. The master bedroom contains a huge walk-in closet and a private bath featuring a whirlpool tub, a separate shower and a double-bowl vanity. Two family bedrooms share a full bath. A handy utility room gives a place for laundry and hobbies while providing a service entrance through the garage. Extra storage space is available in the garage.

MASTER BED RM.
14-8 x 15-4

PORCH

skylights

UTILITY
11-8 x 8-4

storage

cl w d

master bath

walk-in closet

BRKFST.
10-4 x 8-6

GREAT RM.
17-4 x 19-4

(cathedral ceiling)

fireplace

KITCHEN
11-8 x 10-6

up

GARAGE
20-10 x 22-4

BED RM.
12-4 x 11-0

cl

lin.   cl

FOYER
8-8 x 7-8

DINING
11-4 x 12-8

storage

cl

bath

BED RM.
10-10 x 12-0

PORCH

Width 70'-8"
Depth 52'-8"

Design by
**Donald A. Gardner,
Architects, Inc.**

attic storage

skylights

BONUS RM.
20-10 x 17-8

attic storage

B. NATHAN

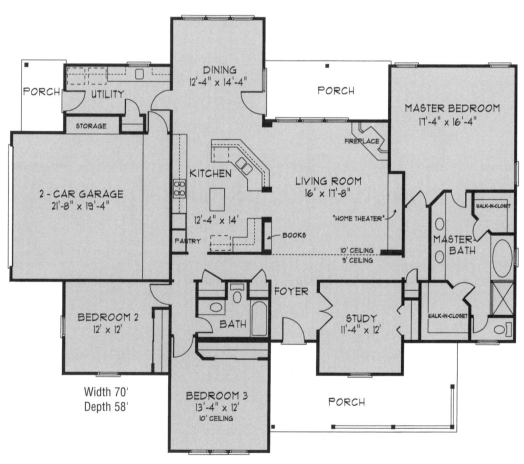

PORCH

UTILITY

STORAGE

DINING
12'-4" x 14'-4"

PORCH

MASTER BEDROOM
17'-4" x 16'-4"

2 - CAR GARAGE
21'-8" x 19'-4"

KITCHEN

12'-4" x 14'

PANTRY

FIREPLACE

LIVING ROOM
16' x 17'-8"

"HOME THEATER"

BOOKS

10' CEILING
9' CEILING

WALK-IN-CLOSET

MASTER
BATH

Design by
**Larry W. Garnett
& Associates, Inc.**

BEDROOM 2
12' x 12'

BATH

FOYER

STUDY
11'-4" x 12'

WALK-IN-CLOSET

Width 70'
Depth 58'

BEDROOM 3
13'-4" x 12'
10' CEILING

PORCH

Design 8992

Square Footage: 2,313

This favorite country design takes a turn for today with great floor planning in a split-bedroom plan. The covered front porch leads to a private study on the right and an open living room and dining area to the rear. A covered porch provides a splendid setting for casual, outdoor dining. The master suite is on the right side of the plan—located for privacy—away from family bedrooms to the left. It contains a well-appointed bath and two walk-in closets. The two-car garage, with its large storage area, connects to the main house by way of a handy utility room.

Design 7292

First Floor: 1,210 square feet
Second Floor: 405 square feet
Total: 1,615 square feet

An interesting front porch furnishes the exterior of this delightful home with a country mile of charm. Inside, an expansive great room, enhanced by a warming fireplace, is sure to be the focus of this efficient three-bedroom plan. The kitchen will please even the fussiest of gourmets with its large pantry, abundance of counter space and corner snack bar. Connecting the kitchen and great room is a sun-filled breakfast room with a bumped-out bay and access to the rear yard. Located on the first floor for privacy, the master suite supplies the perfect retreat to relax and pamper yourself. On the second floor, two comfortable family bedrooms share a full hall bath with twin lavatories.

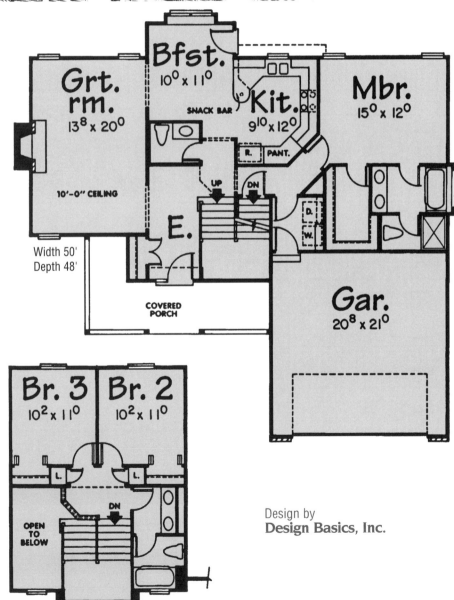

Grt. rm.
13⁸ x 20⁰
10'-0" CEILING

Bfst.
10⁰ x 11⁰
SNACK BAR

Kit.
9¹⁰ x 12⁰
R.   PANT.

Mbr.
15⁰ x 12⁰

UP   DN

E.

Gar.
20⁸ x 21⁰

Width 50'
Depth 48'

COVERED PORCH

Br. 3
10² x 11⁰

Br. 2
10² x 11⁰

DN

OPEN TO BELOW

Design by
Design Basics, Inc.

122

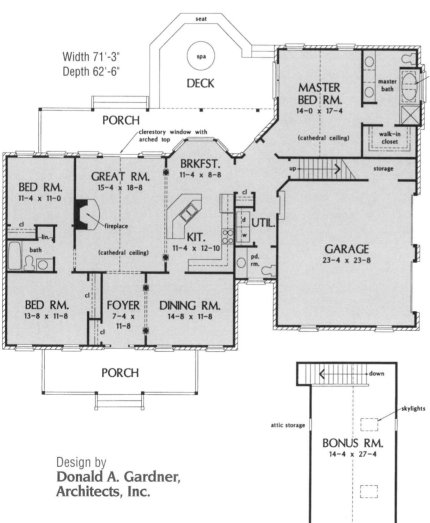

Width 71'-3"
Depth 62'-6"

seat

spa

DECK

PORCH

cleristory window with arched top

GREAT RM.
15-4 x 18-8

BRKFST.
11-4 x 8-8

MASTER BED RM.
14-0 x 17-4

master bath

(cathedral ceiling)

up

walk-in closet

storage

BED RM.
11-4 x 11-0

cl

lin.

bath

fireplace

(cathedral ceiling)

cl

KIT.
11-4 x 12-10

d
w

UTIL.

cl

pd. rm.

GARAGE
23-4 x 23-8

BED RM.
13-8 x 11-8

cl

FOYER
7-4 x 11-8

cl

DINING RM.
14-8 x 11-8

PORCH

attic storage

down

skylights

BONUS RM.
14-4 x 27-4

Design by
Donald A. Gardner, Architects, Inc.

Square Footage: 1,954
Bonus Room: 436 square feet

This beautiful brick country home has all the amenities needed for today's active family. Covered front and back porches along with a rear deck provide plenty of room for outdoor enjoyment. Inside, the focus is on the large great room with its cathedral ceiling and welcoming fireplace. To the right, columns separate the kitchen and breakfast room while keeping this area open. Resident gourmets will certainly appreciate the convenience of the kitchen with its center island and additional eating space. The master bedroom provides a splendid private retreat, featuring a cathedral ceiling and a large walk-in closet. A double-bowl vanity, a separate shower and a relaxing skylit whirlpool tub enhance the luxurious master bath. At the opposite end of the plan, two additional bedrooms share a full bath. A skylit bonus room above the garage allows for additional living space.

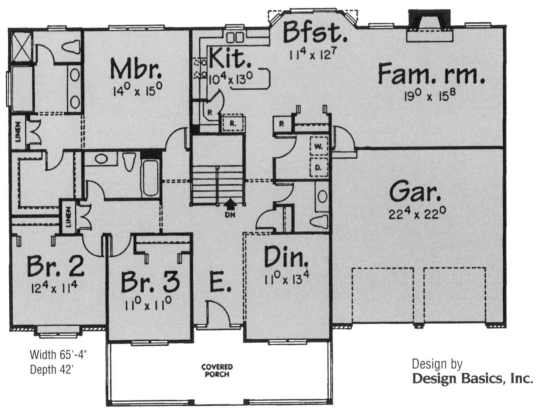

Width 65'-4"
Depth 42'

Mbr.
14⁰ x 15⁰

Kit.
10⁴ x 13⁰

Bfst.
11⁴ x 12⁷

Fam. rm.
19⁰ x 15⁸

Br. 2
12⁴ x 11⁴

Br. 3
11⁰ x 11⁰

E.

Din.
11⁰ x 13⁴

Gar.
22⁴ x 22⁰

DN

LINEN

LINEN

COVERED PORCH

Design by
Design Basics, Inc.

Design 7299

Square Footage: 2,042

This traditional farmhouse style gives a smart first impression with its classic front porch and open view of the formal dining room from the foyer. A generous living space in the rear of the home connects the large family room, breakfast nook and island kitchen. Special amenities here include a grand fireplace, bayed windows and an abundance of cabinet space. The master bedroom features an oversized walk-in closet and a compartmented bath. Two additional family bedrooms share a full hall bath.

124

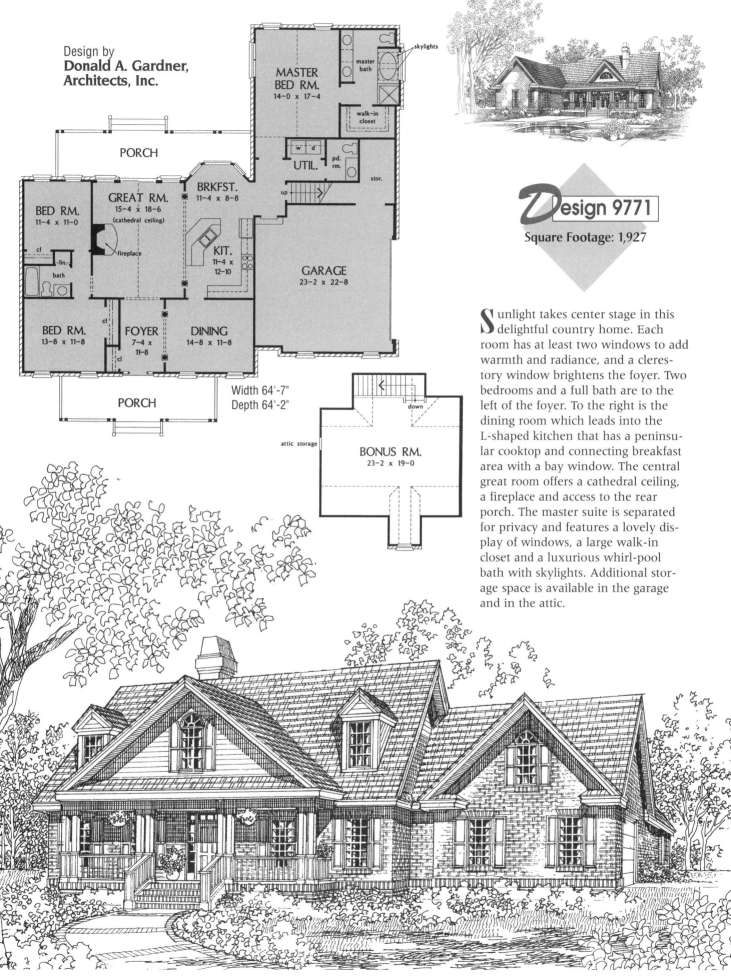

Design by
**Donald A. Gardner,
Architects, Inc.**

PORCH

BED RM.
11-4 x 11-0

cl

lin.

bath

BED RM.
13-8 x 11-8

cl

FOYER
7-4 x
11-8

cl

GREAT RM.
15-4 x 18-6
(cathedral ceiling)

fireplace

DINING
14-8 x 11-8

PORCH

BRKFST.
11-4 x 8-8

KIT.
11-4 x
12-10

MASTER
BED RM.
14-0 x 17-4

skylights

master
bath

walk-in
closet

UTIL.

w   d

pd.
rm.

stor.

up

GARAGE
23-2 x 22-8

Width 64'-7"
Depth 64'-2"

attic storage

down

BONUS RM.
23-2 x 19-0

Design 9771

Square Footage: 1,927

Sunlight takes center stage in this delightful country home. Each room has at least two windows to add warmth and radiance, and a clerestory window brightens the foyer. Two bedrooms and a full bath are to the left of the foyer. To the right is the dining room which leads into the L-shaped kitchen that has a peninsular cooktop and connecting breakfast area with a bay window. The central great room offers a cathedral ceiling, a fireplace and access to the rear porch. The master suite is separated for privacy and features a lovely display of windows, a large walk-in closet and a luxurious whirl-pool bath with skylights. Additional storage space is available in the garage and in the attic.

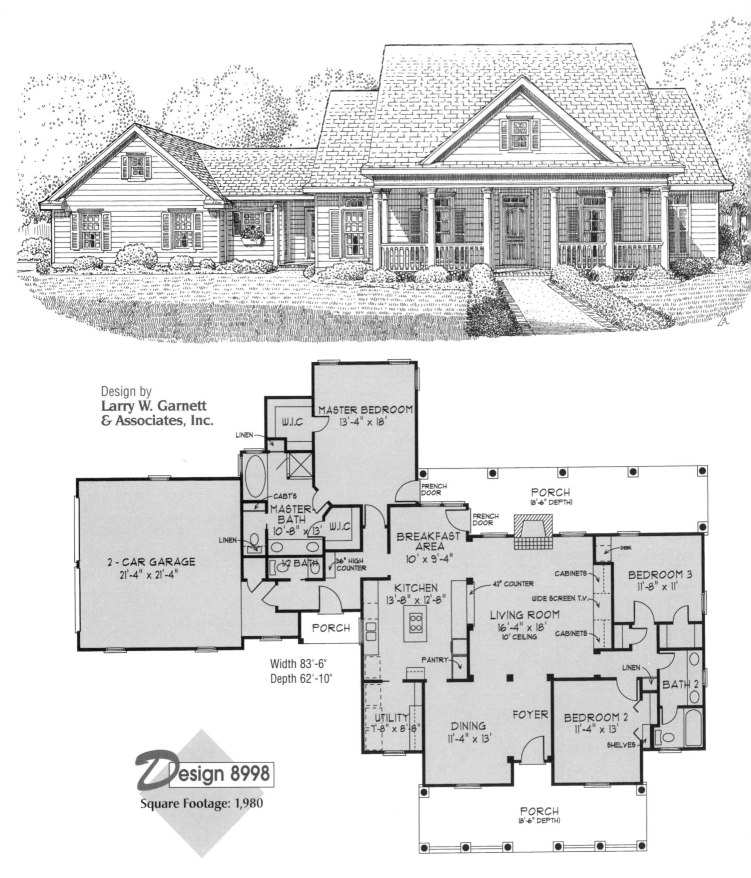

Design by
**Larry W. Garnett
& Associates, Inc.**

MASTER BEDROOM
13'-4" x 18'

W.I.C

LINEN

2 - CAR GARAGE
21'-4" x 21'-4"

CABT'S

MASTER
BATH
10'-8" x 13'

LINEN

W.I.C

1/2 BATH

36" HIGH
COUNTER

PORCH

FRENCH
DOOR

PORCH
(8'-6" DEPTH)

FRENCH
DOOR

BREAKFAST
AREA
10' x 9'-4"

DESK

CABINETS

BEDROOM 3
11'-8" x 11'

WIDE SCREEN T.V.

KITCHEN
13'-8" x 12'-8"

42" COUNTER

LIVING ROOM
16'-4" x 18'
10' CEILING

CABINETS

LINEN

Width 83'-6"
Depth 62'-10"

PANTRY

BATH 2

Design 8998

Square Footage: 1,980

UTILITY
7'-8" x 8'-8"

DINING
11'-4" x 13'

FOYER

BEDROOM 2
11'-4" x 13'

SHELVES

PORCH
(8'-6" DEPTH)

Encompassing just one floor, this farmhouse plan provides excellent livability. From the large covered porch, the foyer opens to a dining room on the left and a center living room with space for a wide-screen TV flanked by cabinets and a fireplace with a scenic view on each side. The large kitchen sports an island cooktop and easy accessibility to the rear breakfast area, the utility room, and the dining room. While the family bedrooms reside on the right side of the plan and share a full bath with twin vanities, the master bedroom takes advantage of its secluded rear location. It features twin walk-in closets and vanities, a windowed corner tub, a separate shower and private access to the rear covered porch.

A breezy front porch welcomes easy times while giving an appropriate introduction to the casual plan of this home. The entry opens to the formal dining room with the large great room and its magnificent fireplace flanked with transom windows directly ahead. The great room is open to the eat-in country kitchen that is complete with a work island, extra counter space and access to the rear yard. The master bedroom has a private bath tucked behind double French doors. Two family bedrooms share a full hall bath. Plus, the plan includes a spacious home office that has a separate outside entrance.

Design 7293

Square Footage: 2,151

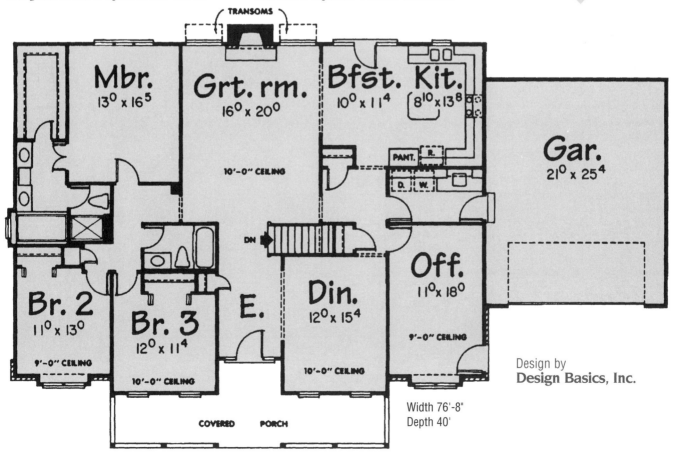

Design by
Design Basics, Inc.

Width 76'-8"
Depth 40'

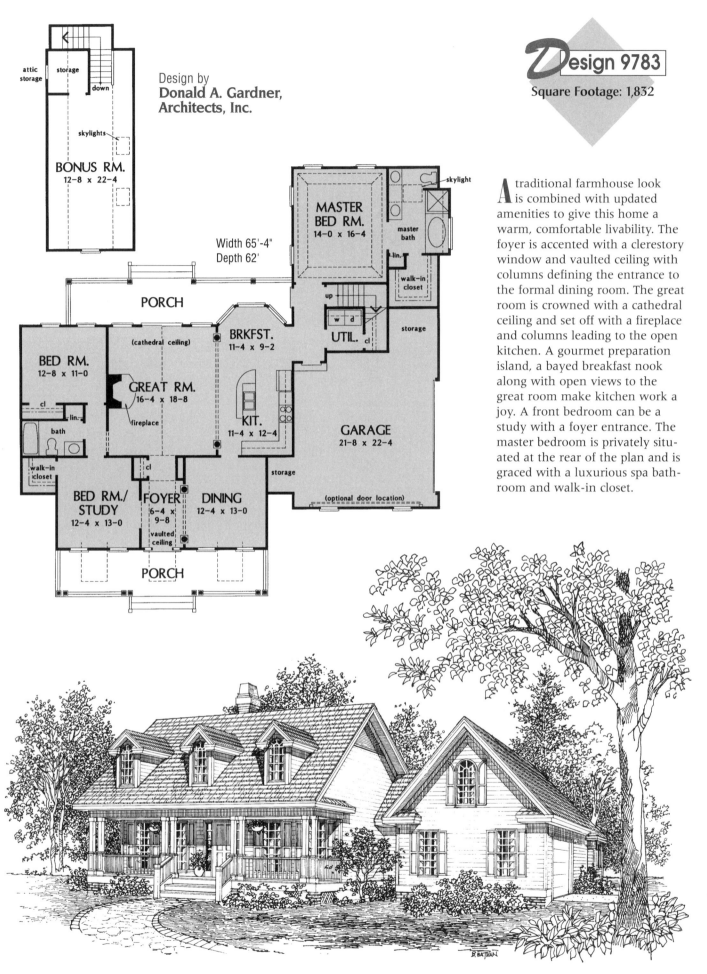

attic storage

storage

down

skylights

BONUS RM.
12-8 x 22-4

Design by
**Donald A. Gardner,
Architects, Inc.**

Width 65'-4"
Depth 62'

MASTER BED RM.
14-0 x 16-4

skylight

master bath

lin.

walk-in closet

up

UTIL.

cl

storage

PORCH

(cathedral ceiling)

BRKFST.
11-4 x 9-2

w   d

BED RM.
12-8 x 11-0

cl

lin.

GREAT RM.
16-4 x 18-8

fireplace

bath

KIT.
11-4 x 12-4

GARAGE
21-8 x 22-4

walk-in closet

cl

storage

BED RM./ STUDY
12-4 x 13-0

FOYER
6-4 x 9-8

DINING
12-4 x 13-0

(optional door location)

vaulted ceiling

PORCH

Design 9783

Square Footage: 1,832

A traditional farmhouse look is combined with updated amenities to give this home a warm, comfortable livability. The foyer is accented with a clerestory window and vaulted ceiling with columns defining the entrance to the formal dining room. The great room is crowned with a cathedral ceiling and set off with a fireplace and columns leading to the open kitchen. A gourmet preparation island, a bayed breakfast nook along with open views to the great room make kitchen work a joy. A front bedroom can be a study with a foyer entrance. The master bedroom is privately situated at the rear of the plan and is graced with a luxurious spa bathroom and walk-in closet.

B. BATMAN

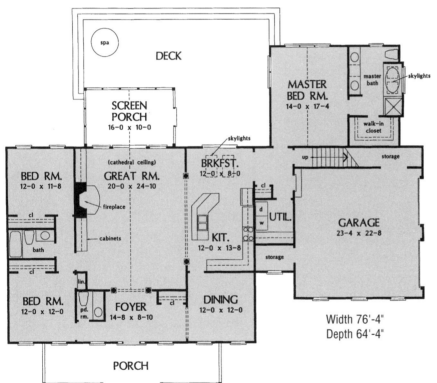

DECK

spa

SCREEN PORCH
16-0 x 10-0

(cathedral ceiling)
GREAT RM.
20-0 x 24-10

skylights

BRKFST.
12-0 x 8-0

MASTER BED RM.
14-0 x 17-4

master bath

skylights

walk-in closet

BED RM.
12-0 x 11-8

fireplace

cl

cabinets

cl

bath

KIT.
12-0 x 13-8

d
w

UTIL.

up

storage

GARAGE
23-4 x 22-8

storage

BED RM.
12-0 x 12-0

lin.

pd. rm.

FOYER
14-8 x 8-10

cl

DINING
12-0 x 12-0

PORCH

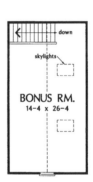

down

skylights

BONUS RM.
14-4 x 26-4

Width 76'-4"
Depth 64'-4"

Design by
Donald A. Gardner, Architects, Inc.

QUOTE ONE®

Cost to build? See page 214
to order complete cost estimate
to build this house in your area!

Design 9738

Square Footage: 2,136
Bonus Room: 405 square feet

This exciting three-bedroom country home overflows with amenities. Traditional details such as columns, cathedral ceilings and open living areas combine to create the ideal floor plan for today's active family lifestyle. The spacious great room features built-in cabinets and a fireplace and a cathedral ceiling which continues into the adjoining screened porch. An efficient kitchen with a food preparation island is conveniently grouped with the great room, the dining room and the skylit breakfast area for the cook who enjoys visiting while preparing meals. A private master bedroom features a cathedral ceiling, a large walk-in closet and a relaxing master bath with a skylit whirlpool tub and a separate shower. Two secondary bedrooms share a full bath at the opposite end of the home.

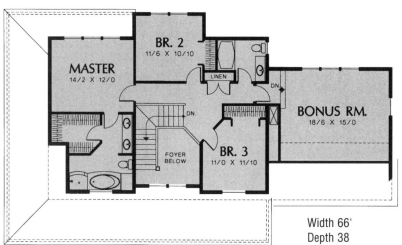

MASTER
14/2 X 12/0

BR. 2
11/6 X 10/10

LINEN

BONUS RM.
18/6 X 15/0

DN.

DN.

FOYER
BELOW

BR. 3
11/0 X 11/10

Width 66'
Depth 38

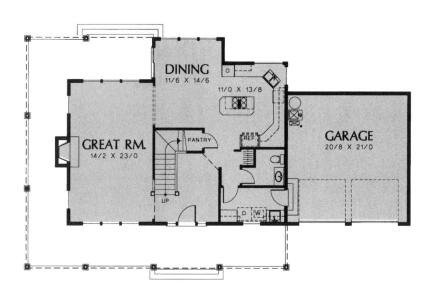

DINING
11/6 X 14/6

11/0 X 13/8

GREAT RM.
14/2 X 23/0

PANTRY

REF

GARAGE
20/8 X 21/0

UP

D W

Design 9588

First Floor: 1,032 square feet
Second Floor: 870 square feet
Total: 1,902 square feet
Bonus Room: 306 square feet

A wraparound covered porch and symmetrical dormers produce an inviting appearance to this farmhouse. Inside, the two-story foyer leads directly to the large great room graced by a fireplace and an abundance of windows. The U-shaped island kitchen is convenient to the sunny dining room and has a powder room nearby. The utility room offers access to the two-car garage. Upstairs, two family bedrooms share a full hall bath and have convenient access to a large bonus room. The master suite is full of amenities including a walk-in closet and a pampering bath.

Design by
**Alan Mascord
Design Associates, Inc.**

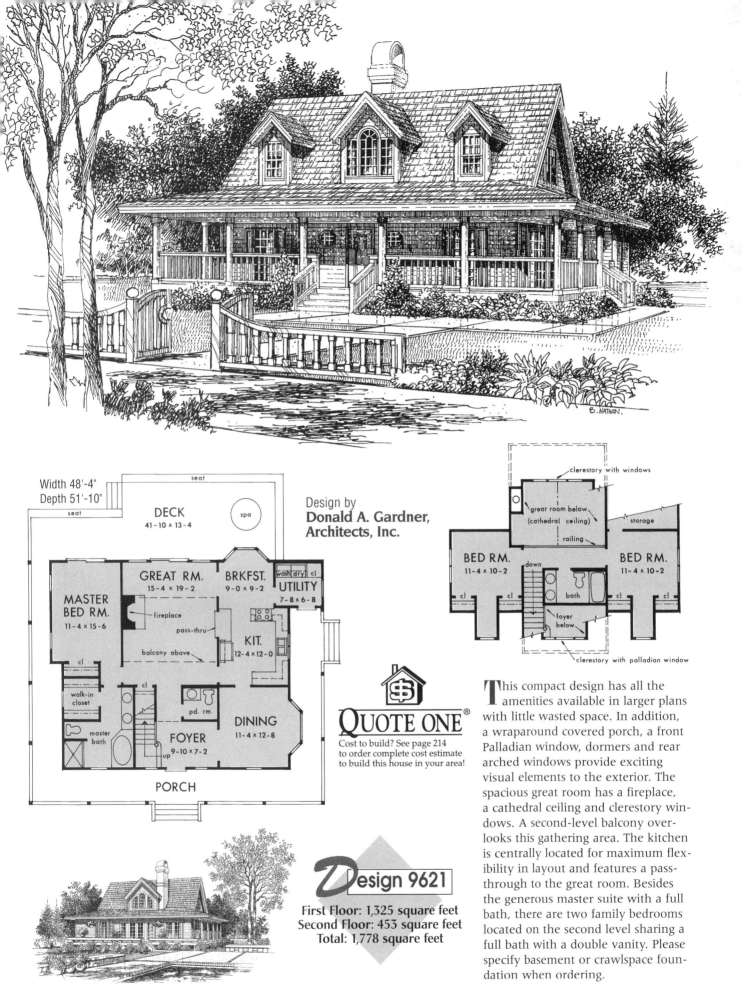

B. NATHAN.

Width 48'-4"
Depth 51'-10"

seat

seat

DECK
41-10 × 13-4

spa

Design by
**Donald A. Gardner,
Architects, Inc.**

GREAT RM.
15-4 × 19-2

BRKFST.
9-0 × 9-2

UTILITY
7-8 × 6-8

wash dry cl

MASTER
BED RM.
11-4 × 15-6

fireplace

pass-thru

balcony above

KIT.
12-4 × 12-0

cl

walk-in
closet

cl

pd. rm.

master
bath

up

FOYER
9-10 × 7-2

DINING
11-4 × 12-8

PORCH

clerestory with windows

great room below
(cathedral ceiling)

storage

railing

BED RM.
11-4 × 10-2

down

BED RM.
11-4 × 10-2

cl

cl

bath

cl

cl

foyer
below

clerestory with palladian window

QUOTE ONE®

Cost to build? See page 214
to order complete cost estimate
to build this house in your area!

Design 9621

First Floor: 1,325 square feet
Second Floor: 453 square feet
Total: 1,778 square feet

This compact design has all the amenities available in larger plans with little wasted space. In addition, a wraparound covered porch, a front Palladian window, dormers and rear arched windows provide exciting visual elements to the exterior. The spacious great room has a fireplace, a cathedral ceiling and clerestory windows. A second-level balcony overlooks this gathering area. The kitchen is centrally located for maximum flexibility in layout and features a pass-through to the great room. Besides the generous master suite with a full bath, there are two family bedrooms located on the second level sharing a full bath with a double vanity. Please specify basement or crawlspace foundation when ordering.

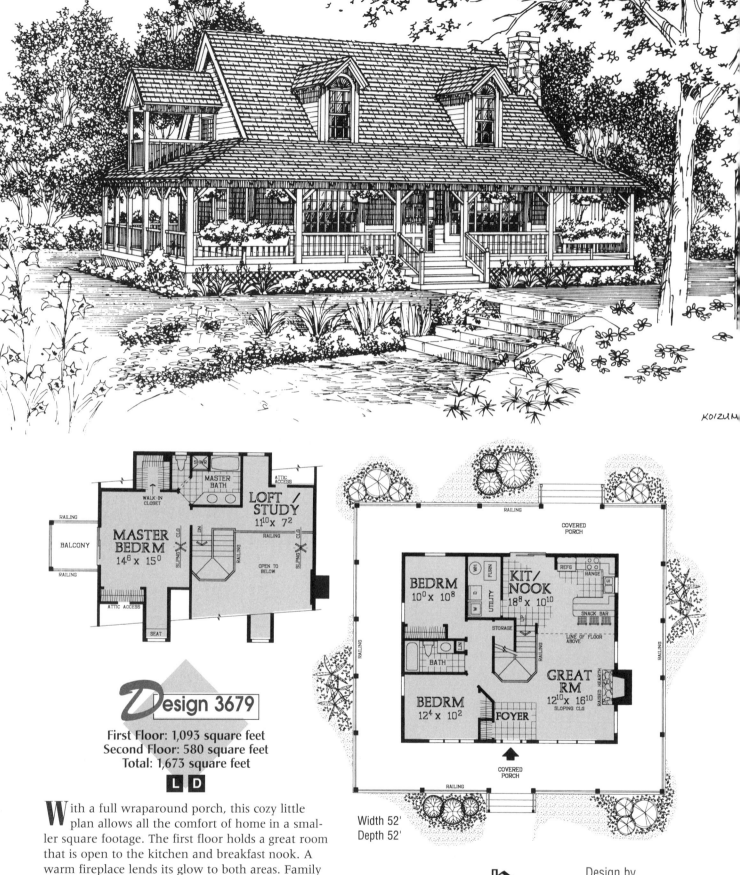

Design 3679

First Floor: 1,093 square feet
Second Floor: 580 square feet
Total: 1,673 square feet

L **D**

MASTER BATH

WALK-IN CLOSET

SHWR

ATTIC ACCESS

LOFT / STUDY
11¹⁰ x 7²

MASTER BEDRM
14⁶ x 15⁰

BALCONY

RAILING

OPEN TO BELOW

ATTIC ACCESS

SEAT

COVERED PORCH

RAILING

BEDRM
10⁰ x 10⁸

WH

FURN

UTILITY

W

D

KIT / NOOK
18⁸ x 10¹⁰

REFG

RANGE

SNACK BAR

STORAGE

LINE OF FLOOR ABOVE

BATH

LIN

BEDRM
12⁴ x 10²

FOYER

GREAT RM
12¹⁰ x 16¹⁰
SLOPING CLG

RAISED HEARTH

RAILING

COVERED PORCH

RAILING

Width 52'
Depth 52'

With a full wraparound porch, this cozy little plan allows all the comfort of home in a smaller square footage. The first floor holds a great room that is open to the kitchen and breakfast nook. A warm fireplace lends its glow to both areas. Family bedrooms on this floor share a full bath and are separated from the master suite on the second floor. With its own private balcony, the master bedroom has a fine bath with separate shower and tub, and a compartmented toilet. A loft or study area that overlooks the great room completes this owner's retreat.

Design by Home Planners

QUOTE ONE®

Cost to build? See page 214
to order complete cost estimate
to build this house in your area!

Design by
Larry W. Garnett & Associates, Inc.

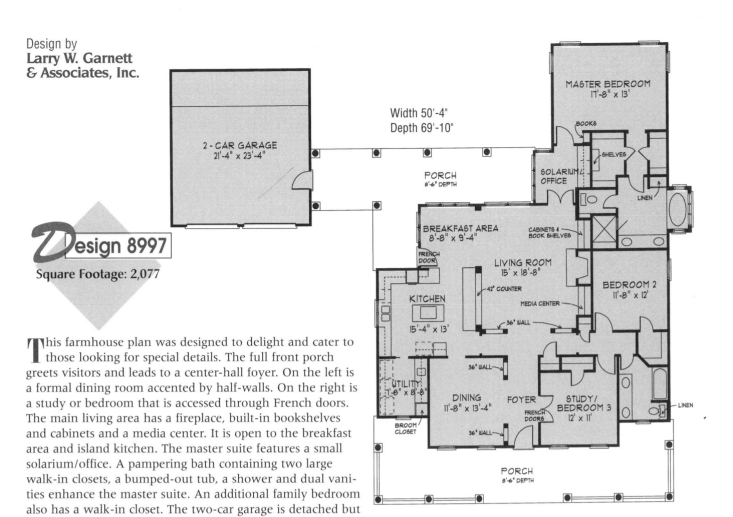

Width 50'-4"
Depth 69'-10"

2 - CAR GARAGE
21'-4" x 23'-4"

MASTER BEDROOM
17'-8" x 13'

BOOKS
SHELVES
SOLARIUM OFFICE
LINEN
PORCH
8'-6" DEPTH

BREAKFAST AREA
8'-8" x 9'-4"
CABINETS & BOOK SHELVES

FRENCH DOOR

LIVING ROOM
15' x 18'-8"
42" COUNTER
MEDIA CENTER
36" WALL

BEDROOM 2
11'-8" x 12'

KITCHEN
15'-4" x 13'

UTILITY
7'-8" x 8'-8"

36" WALL

DINING
11'-8" x 13'-4"

FOYER
FRENCH DOORS
36" WALL

STUDY/ BEDROOM 3
12' x 11'

LINEN

BROOM CLOSET

PORCH
8'-6" DEPTH

Design 8997
Square Footage: 2,077

This farmhouse plan was designed to delight and cater to those looking for special details. The full front porch greets visitors and leads to a center-hall foyer. On the left is a formal dining room accented by half-walls. On the right is a study or bedroom that is accessed through French doors. The main living area has a fireplace, built-in bookshelves and cabinets and a media center. It is open to the breakfast area and island kitchen. The master suite features a small solarium/office. A pampering bath containing two large walk-in closets, a bumped-out tub, a shower and dual vanities enhance the master suite. An additional family bedroom also has a walk-in closet. The two-car garage is detached but is reached by the rear covered porch.

Design 9605

First Floor: 1,562 square feet
Second Floor: 537 square feet
Total: 2,099 square feet

Outdoor living is enjoyed with the wraparound covered porch at the front and sides of this house, as well as on the open deck with storage to the rear. Also notice how the country feel is updated with arched rear windows and a sun room. Inside, you'll find the spacious great room with fireplace, cathedral ceiling and clerestory with arched windows. The kitchen occupies a central location between the dining room and the great room for equally convenient formal and informal occasions. A generous master suite has a fireplace and access to the sun room and covered porch. On the second level are two more bedrooms, a full bath and storage space.

Design by
**Donald A. Gardner,
Architects, Inc.**

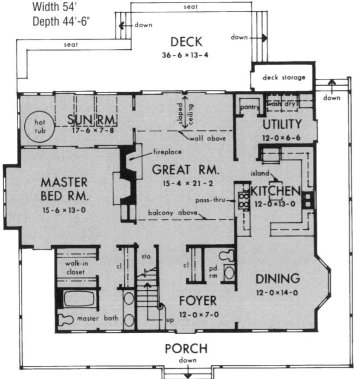

Width 54'
Depth 44'-6"

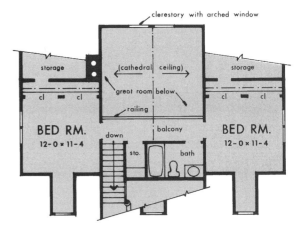

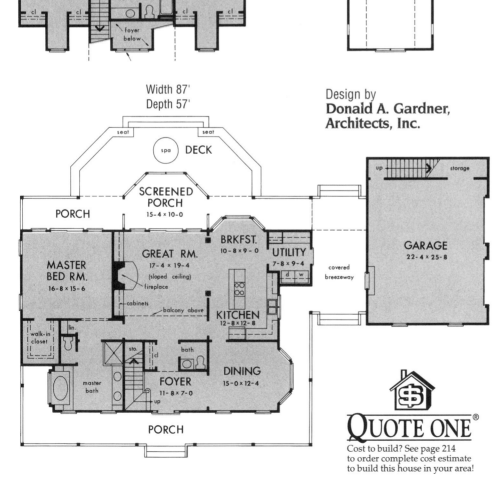

clerestory window with arched top

great room below
railing
balcony
down

BED RM.
12-8 x 12-0

BED RM.
12-8 x 12-0

cl | cl | cl | cl

bath

foyer below

down

BONUS RM.
15-4 x 29-4

down

Width 87'
Depth 57'

Design by
Donald A. Gardner, Architects, Inc.

seat | seat

spa | DECK

PORCH

SCREENED PORCH
15-4 x 10-0

MASTER BED RM.
16-8 x 15-6

GREAT RM.
17-4 x 19-4
(sloped ceiling)
fireplace

cabinets

balcony above

BRKFST.
10-8 x 9-0

UTILITY
7-8 x 9-4

d | w

KITCHEN
12-8 x 12-8

walk-in closet

lin.

master bath

sto.

cl

bath

DINING
15-0 x 12-4

FOYER
11-8 x 7-0

up

PORCH

up | storage

GARAGE
22-4 x 25-8

covered breezeway

QUOTE ONE®

Cost to build? See page 214
to order complete cost estimate
to build this house in your area!

A wraparound covered porch, an open deck with a spa and seating, arched windows and dormers enhance the already impressive character of this three-bedroom farmhouse. The entrance foyer and great room with sloped ceilings have Palladian window clerestories to allow natural light to enter. All other first-floor spaces have nine-foot ceilings. The spacious great room boasts a fireplace, cabinets and bookshelves. The kitchen, with a cooking island, is conveniently located between a dining room and a breakfast room with an open view of the great room. A generous master bedroom has plenty of closet space as well as an expansive master bath. Bonus room over the garage allows for room to grow.

Design 9632

First Floor: 1,756 square feet
Second Floor: 565 square feet
Total: 2,321 square feet

Design by
Donald A. Gardner,
Architects, Inc.

A wraparound covered porch at the front and sides of this house and an open deck at the back provide plenty of outside living area. The spacious great room features a fireplace, cathedral ceiling and clerestory with an arched window. The island kitchen has an attached, skylit breakfast room complete with a bay window. The first-floor master bedroom contains a generous closet and a master bath with garden tub, double-bowl vanity and shower. The second floor sports two bedrooms and a full bath with double-bowl vanity. An elegant balcony overlooks the great room. Please specify basement or crawlspace foundation when ordering.

QUOTE ONE®

Cost to build? See page 214 to order complete cost estimate to build this house in your area!

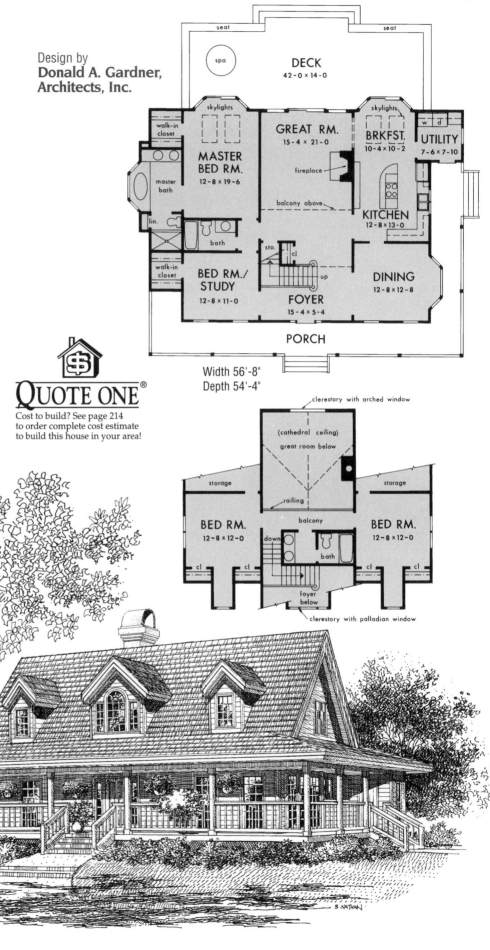

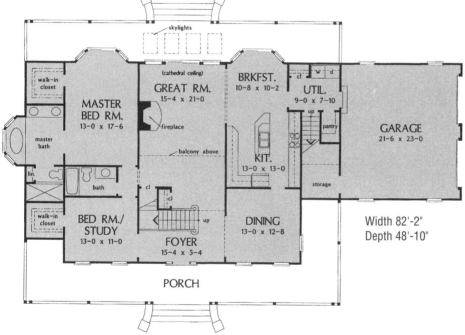

skylights

walk-in closet

MASTER BED RM.
13-0 x 17-6

master bath

lin.

bath

walk-in closet

BED RM./ STUDY
13-0 x 11-0

(cathedral ceiling)

GREAT RM.
15-4 x 21-0

fireplace

balcony above

cl

cl

FOYER
15-4 x 5-4

up

BRKFST.
10-8 x 10-2

UTIL.
9-0 x 7-10

up

w d

a

pantry

KIT.
13-0 x 13-0

DINING
13-0 x 12-8

storage

GARAGE
21-6 x 23-0

PORCH

Width 82'-2"
Depth 48'-10"

great room below

railing

attic storage

BED RM.
12-8 x 12-0

down

bath

BED RM.
12-8 x 12-0

cl

cl

cl

cl

foyer below

attic storage

attic storage

attic storage

BONUS RM.
21-6 x 14-0

down

attic storage

Design 9767

First Floor: 1,829 square feet
Second Floor: 584 square feet
Total: 2,413 square feet

Spaciousness and lots of amenities earmark this design as a family favorite. The front, wraparound porch leads to the foyer where a bedroom/study and dining room open. The central great room presents a warming fireplace, a cathedral ceiling and access to the rear porch. In the kitchen, an abundance of counter and cabinet space are sure to satisfy. An adjacent bayed breakfast nook and a utility room with a pantry round out this side of the plan. In the master bedroom suite, a private bath with a bumped-out tub and a walk-in closet act as enhancements. Upstairs, two bedrooms flank a full bath. A bonus room over the garage allows for future expansion.

Design by
Donald A. Gardner, Architects, Inc.

137

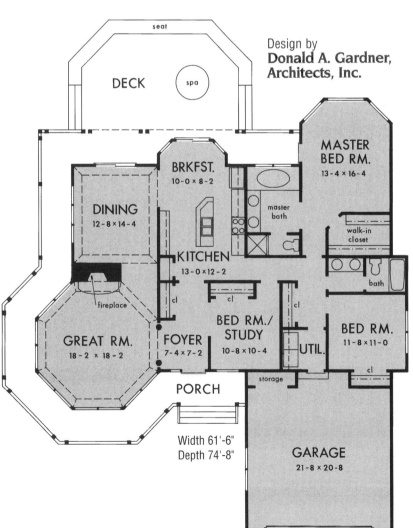

seat

DECK

spa

**Design by
Donald A. Gardner,
Architects, Inc.**

BRKFST.
10-0 × 8-2

MASTER
BED RM.
13-4 × 16-4

DINING
12-8 × 14-4

master
bath

walk-in
closet

KITCHEN
13-0 × 12-2

bath

cl

cl

fireplace

cl

GREAT RM.
18-2 × 18-2

FOYER
7-4 × 7-2

BED RM./
STUDY
10-8 × 10-4

UTIL.

BED RM.
11-8 × 11-0

cl

storage

PORCH

Width 61'-6"
Depth 74'-8"

GARAGE
21-8 × 20-8

Design 9638

Square Footage: 1,865

This Victorian influenced exterior conceals an open, contemporary floor plan. The entrance foyer with round columns offers visual excitement. The octagonal great room has a high tray ceiling and a fireplace. A generous kitchen with an gourmet island counter is centrally located, providing efficient service to the dining room, breakfast room and deck. Note the luxurious master bedroom suite with a large walk-in closet and master bath with double-bowl vanity, shower and garden tub. A fabulous wrap-around porch echoes the shape of the great room and continues on to the rear entertainment deck.

Design 9585

First Floor: 1,337 square feet
Second Floor: 1,025 square feet
Total: 2,362 square feet

An octagonal tower, a wraparound porch and a wealth of amenities combine to give this house its charming Victorian appeal. The tower furnishes more than a pretty face, containing a sunny den on the first floor and a delightful bedroom on the second floor. To the right of the foyer, the formal living room and dining room unite to provide a wonderful place to celebrate special occasions and holidays. A large kitchen featuring an island cooktop easily serves both the formal dining room and the adjoining nook. Here, family members will appreciate the built-in desk for use in meal planning or paying bills. The spacious family room completes the casual living area and supplies easy access to the rear porch. Upstairs, two bedrooms share a full hall bath while the master bedroom revels in its own luxurious private bath. A two-car garage accommodates the family vehicles.

Width 50'-6"
Depth 72'-6"

Design by
**Alan Mascord
Design Associates, Inc.**

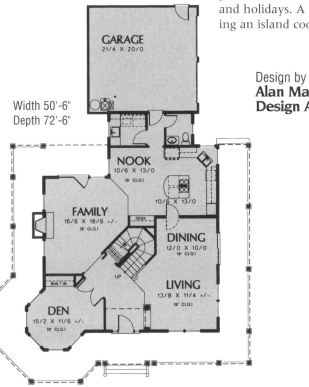

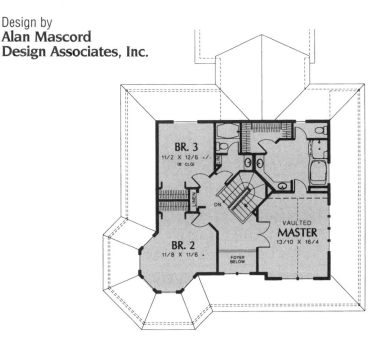

esign 9587

First Floor: 822 square feet
Second Floor: 1,175 square feet
Total: 1,997 square feet

The wraparound porch surrounding this shingled home provides a front row seat to enjoy the soothing sounds of the country—literally. At the entrance to the front porch, a built-in bench has been thoughtfully placed for convenience. Inside, an open floor plan makes the most of the first-floor living area. Enhanced with built-ins, a warming fireplace extends a friendly invitation into the great room. Here, a wall of windows provides plenty of natural light and unobstructed views of the backyard. A bay window fills the adjacent nook with sunlight and brightens the adjoining U-shaped kitchen. Located near the garage for convenience, a laundry room and powder room complete the first floor. The second floor contains a restful master suite, two family bedrooms that share a full bath, and a game room.

Design by
**Alan Mascord
Design Associates, Inc.**

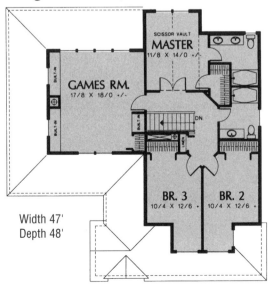

Width 47'
Depth 48'

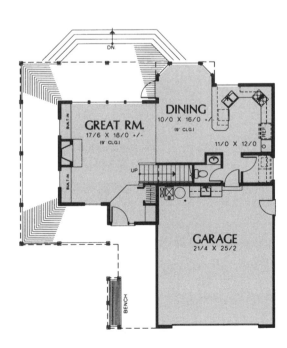

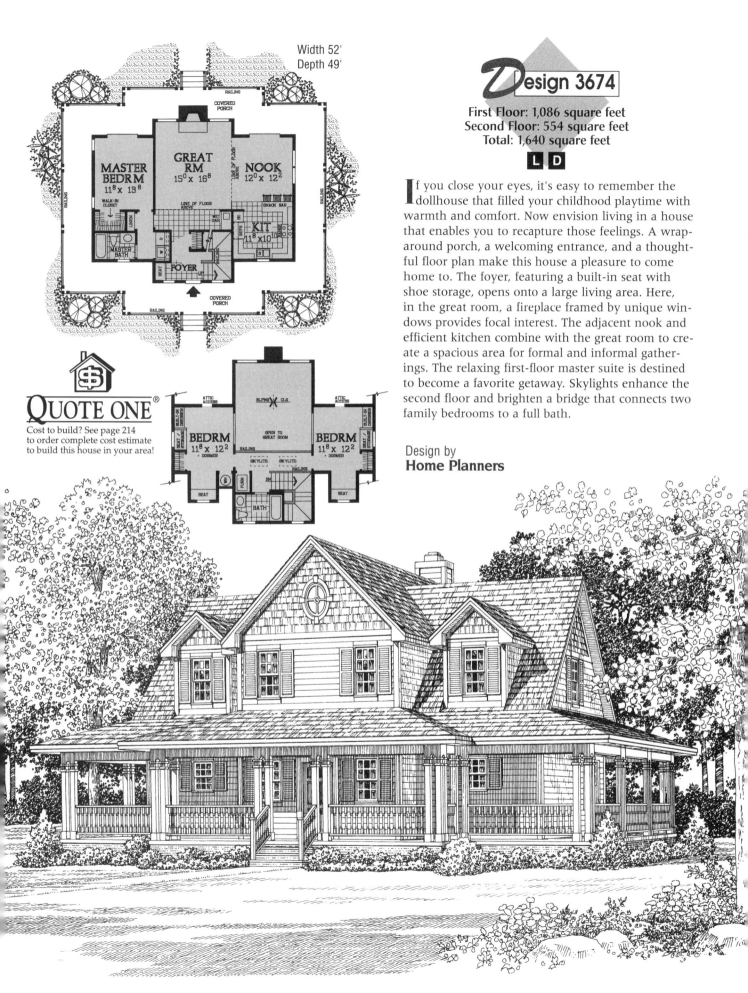

Width 52'
Depth 49'

COVERED PORCH

MASTER BEDRM
11⁸ x 13⁸

GREAT RM
15⁰ x 16⁸

NOOK
12⁰ x 12²

WALK-IN CLOSET

LINEN

LINE OF FLOOR ABOVE

WET BAR

SNACK BAR

KIT
11⁸ x 10⁰

REF'G

MASTER BATH

FOYER

SEAT

COVERED PORCH

RAILING

RAILING

RAILING

ATTIC ACCESS

BUILT-IN DRESSER

SLOPE CLG

ATTIC ACCESS

BUILT-IN DRESSER

SEAT / STORAGE

BEDRM
11⁸ x 12²
+ DORMER

OPEN TO GREAT ROOM

BEDRM
11⁸ x 12²
+ DORMER

SEAT / STORAGE

RAILING

SKYLITE

SKYLITE

RAILING

SEAT

FURN

DN

BATH

SEAT

Design 3674

First Floor: 1,086 square feet
Second Floor: 554 square feet
Total: 1,640 square feet

L D

If you close your eyes, it's easy to remember the dollhouse that filled your childhood playtime with warmth and comfort. Now envision living in a house that enables you to recapture those feelings. A wrap-around porch, a welcoming entrance, and a thoughtful floor plan make this house a pleasure to come home to. The foyer, featuring a built-in seat with shoe storage, opens onto a large living area. Here, in the great room, a fireplace framed by unique windows provides focal interest. The adjacent nook and efficient kitchen combine with the great room to create a spacious area for formal and informal gatherings. The relaxing first-floor master suite is destined to become a favorite getaway. Skylights enhance the second floor and brighten a bridge that connects two family bedrooms to a full bath.

Design by
Home Planners

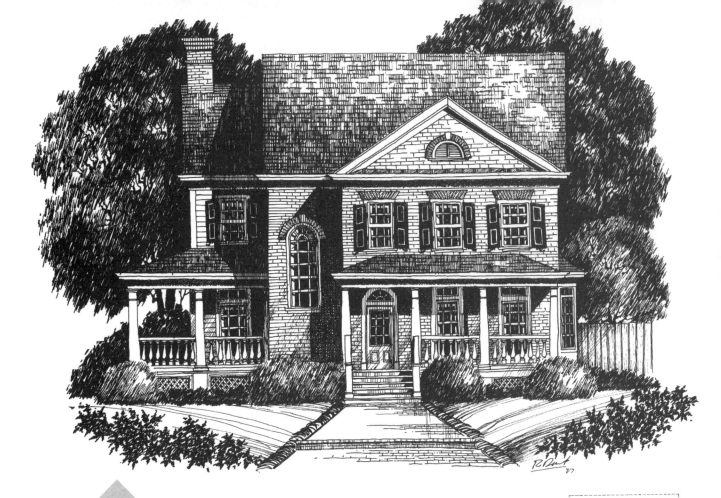

Design 9959

First Floor: 1,440 square feet
Second Floor: 1,339 square feet
Total: 2,779 square feet

Design by
**Stephen Fuller/
Design Traditions**

A front porch and a wrap-around side porch provide plenty of outdoor living space for this lovely colonial home. The great room is warmed by a cozy fireplace and provides dual access to the wraparound porch. The U-shaped kitchen shares space with a breakfast nook—perfect for in-formal meals. The other end of the kitchen adjoins the bay-windowed dining room. The second floor contains the master suite, two secondary bedrooms and a full bath. The spacious master bedroom furnishes angled entry to a luxurious bath with a corner whirlpool tub, a separate shower and a huge walk-in closet. This home is designed with a basement foundation.

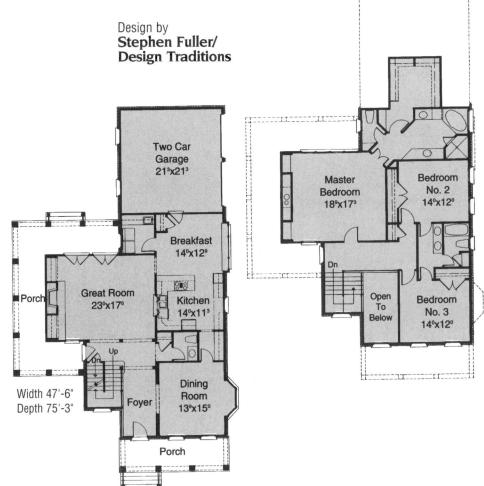

Two Car Garage 21³x21³

Breakfast 14⁰x12⁹

Porch

Great Room 23⁰x17⁶

Kitchen 14⁰x11³

Up

Dn

Foyer

Dining Room 13⁹x15⁰

Width 47'-6"
Depth 75'-3"

Porch

Master Bedroom 18⁰x17³

Bedroom No. 2 14⁰x12⁰

Dn

Open To Below

Bedroom No. 3 14⁰x12⁰

Design by
**Stephen Fuller/
Design Traditions**

Two Car Garage
21^3x21^3

Porch

Breakfast
10^9x12^0

Office
6^0x12^0

Great Room
16^9x18^3

Kitchen
15^3x19^9

Up
Dn

Foyer

Porch

Dining Room
15^0x13^0

Width 52'
Depth 66'

Porch

Master Bedroom
15^6x20^0

Attic Storage

Bedroom No. 2
12^0x12^0

Dn

Open To Below

Bedroom No. 3
13^0x12^0

Design 9965

**First Floor: 1,523 square feet
Second Floor: 1,259 square feet
Total: 2,782 square feet**

This captivating Georgian farmhouse has a columned entry which opens on the right to the formal dining room. A second entry porch, just off the dining room, opens into the large country kitchen with a preparation island. Here a snack bar opens into the breakfast room. The great room has a grand fireplace, doors to the rear porch and stylish built-ins flanking the fireplace. A quiet home office lies just off the breakfast room. Upstairs, a balcony hall joins three bedrooms, including a master suite with a walk-in closet, dual sinks, a separate shower and a garden tub. Two additional bedrooms share a private, compartmented bath. This house is designed with a basement foundation.

143

Design 9956

First Floor: 1,787 square feet
Second Floor: 851 square feet
Total: 2,638 square feet
Bonus Room: 189 square feet

This beautiful brick design displays fine family livability in over 2,600 square feet. The wraparound porch welcomes family and friends to inside living areas. The great room sports an elegant ceiling, a fireplace and built-ins. The kitchen displays good traffic patterning. An island cooktop will please the house gourmet. The dining room features double doors that open out onto the porch. In the master bedroom, a pampering bath includes a whirlpool tub and separate vanities. A walk-in closet is located at the back of the bath. Two family bedrooms upstairs enjoy peace and quiet and a full hall bath with natural illumination. This home is designed with a basement foundation.

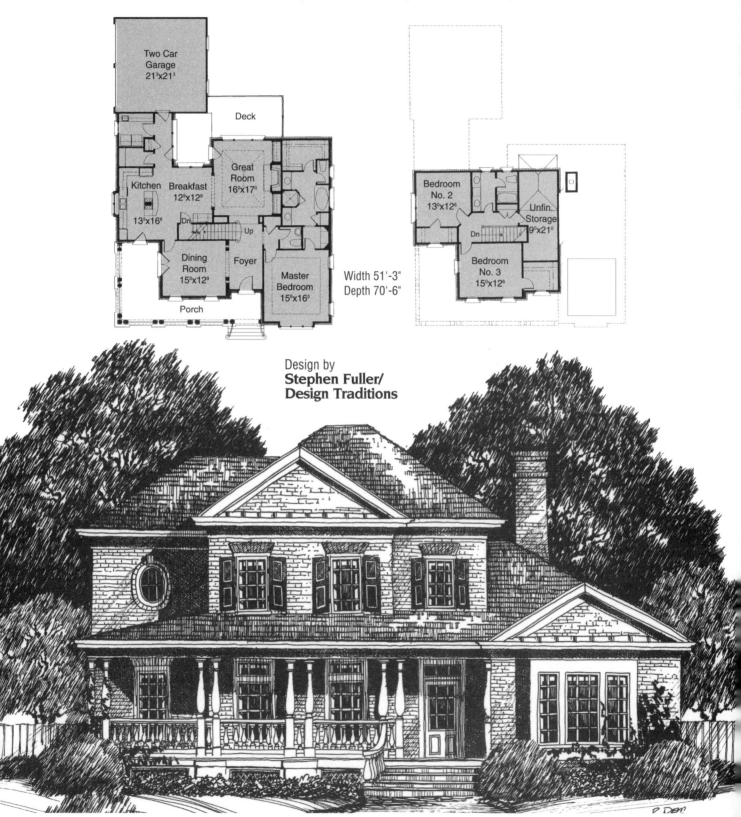

Width 51'-3"
Depth 70'-6"

Design by
Stephen Fuller/
Design Traditions

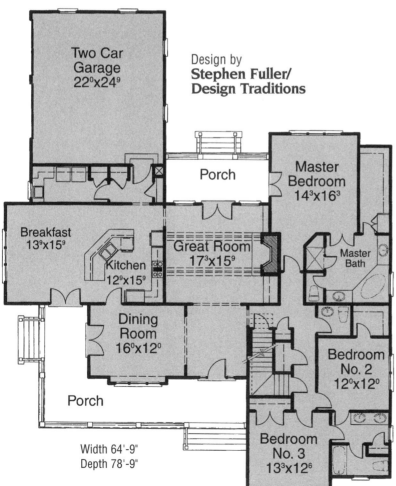

Two Car Garage
22⁰x24⁹

Design by
**Stephen Fuller/
Design Traditions**

Breakfast
13⁹x15⁹

Kitchen
12⁹x15⁹

Porch

Great Room
17³x15⁹

Master Bedroom
14³x16³

Master Bath

Dining Room
16⁰x12⁰

Porch

Bedroom No. 2
12⁰x12⁰

Bedroom No. 3
13³x12⁶

Width 64'-9"
Depth 78'-9"

Design 7807

Square Footage: 2,485

The most inviting amenity of this country plan has to be its extra-wide, side-wrap porch from which three entrances to the home open. The notable great room has a formal ceiling detail, fireplace, built-ins and French doors to the rear porch. Casual entertaining will surely revolve around activity in the open country kitchen. The master bedroom enjoys a lush bath, walk-in closet and private French doors to the rear porch. Two secondary bedrooms share a private bath. A full two-car garage is joined to the rear of the home, out of sight so that the home's curb appeal is not compromised. This house is designed with a basement foundation.

COPYRIGHT LARRY E. BELK

Design 8177

Square Footage: 1,834

Reminiscent of America's farmhouses, this home comes complete with a covered front porch perfect for those hot summer evenings. Inside, the foyer opens to the great room, with a matching pair of double French doors flanking the fireplace and leading out to the rear porch. The dining room adds a formal flair with square columns connected by arched openings. An angled bar design in the kitchen opens the area to the great room and provides a convenient pass-through. The master bedroom features a coffered ceiling and an enormous walk-in closet. Amenities that include a double vanity, a corner whirlpool tub and a shower highlight the master bath. Bedrooms 2 and 3 are located nearby to complete the plan. Please specify crawlspace or slab foundation when ordering.

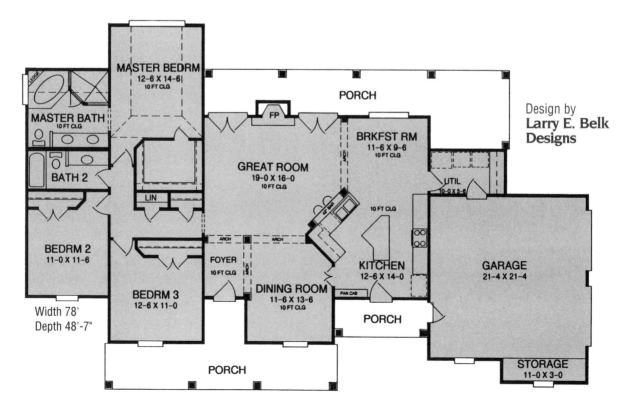

Design by
**Larry E. Belk
Designs**

COPYRIGHT LARRY E. BELK

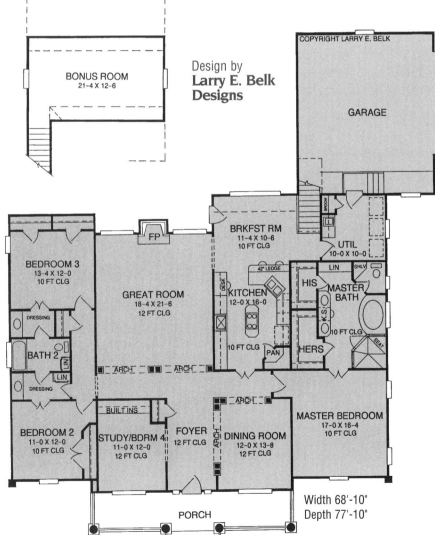

BONUS ROOM
21-4 X 12-6

Design by
**Larry E. Belk
Designs**

COPYRIGHT LARRY E. BELK

GARAGE

FP

BRKFST RM
11-4 X 10-6
10 FT CLG

UTIL
10-0 X 10-0

BEDROOM 3
13-4 X 12-0
10 FT CLG

GREAT ROOM
18-4 X 21-6
12 FT CLG

42" LEDGE

DESK

KITCHEN
12-0 X 16-0

HIS

MASTER
BATH

LIN   SHLV

K.S.

DRESSING

BATH 2

LIN

10 FT CLG

HERS

10 FT CLG

SEAT

PAN

DRESSING

ARCH   ARCH

BUILT INS

ARCH

BEDROOM 2
11-0 X 12-0
10 FT CLG

STUDY/BDRM 4
11-0 X 12-0
12 FT CLG

FOYER
12 FT CLG

DINING ROOM
12-0 X 13-8
12 FT CLG

ARCH

MASTER BEDROOM
17-0 X 16-4
10 FT CLG

Width 68'-10"
Depth 77'-10"

PORCH

Design 8143

Square Footage: 2,648
Bonus Room: 266 square feet

This vintage elevation has all the extras desired by today's homeowners. Inside, twelve-foot ceilings give the study, dining room and great room a lofty, spacious feeling. Graceful arches are flanked by columns to announce the living areas of the home. The kitchen features a cooktop work island, pantry and a snack bar opening into the breakfast room. An optional bonus room over the garage is a great place for a play room on an in-home office. The master suite includes His and Hers closets and an amenity-filled master bath. The two additional bedrooms have roomy closets and share a compartmented bath with private dressing areas. Please specify crawlspace or slab foundation when ordering.

147

Design 3465
Square footage: 1,410

L

An L-shaped veranda employs tapered columns to support a standing seam metal roof. Horizontal siding with brick accents and multi-pane windows all enhance the exterior of this home. Most notable, however, is the metal roof with its various planes. Complementing this is a massive stucco chimney that captures the ambience of the West. A hard-working interior will delight those building within a modest budget. The spacious front room provides plenty of space for both living and family dining activities. A fireplace makes a delightful focal point. The kitchen, set aside, has a handy snack bar and passageway to the garage. To one side is the laundry area, to the other, the stairs to the basement. The centrally located main bath has twin sinks and a nearby linen closet. One of the two secondary bedrooms has direct access to the veranda. The master bedroom is flanked by the master bath and its own private covered porch.

Design by
Home Planners

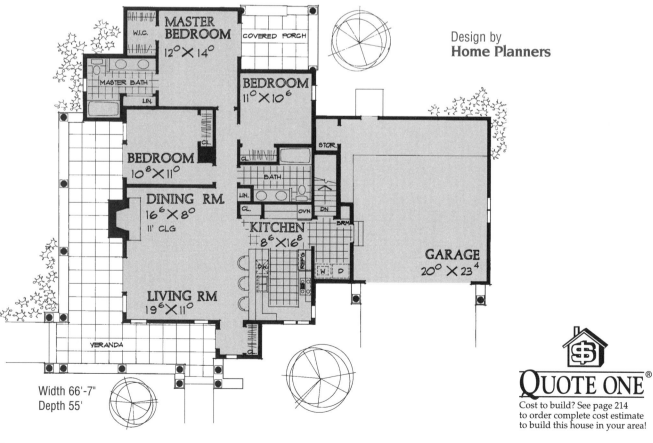

Width 66'-7"
Depth 55'

QUOTE ONE®
Cost to build? See page 214
to order complete cost estimate
to build this house in your area!

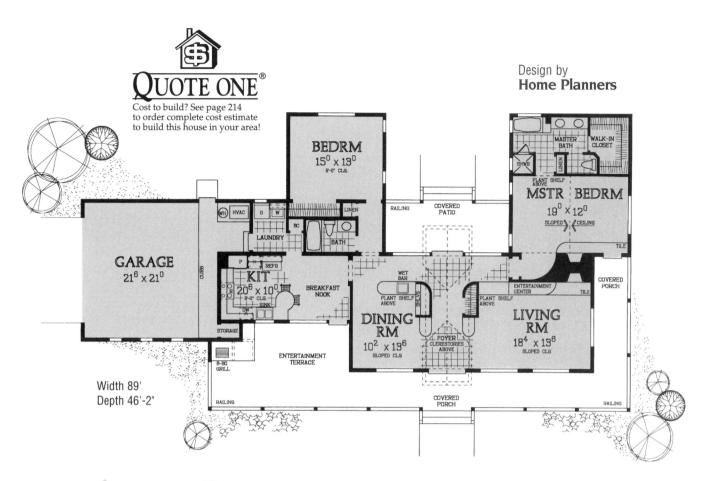

Quote One®

Cost to build? See page 214 to order complete cost estimate to build this house in your area!

Design by
Home Planners

GARAGE
21⁶ x 21⁰

BEDRM
15⁰ x 13⁰
9'-0" CLG.

MASTER BATH

WALK-IN CLOSET

SHWR

LINEN

PLANT SHELF ABOVE

MSTR BEDRM
19⁰ x 12⁰
SLOPED CEILING

COVERED PATIO

RAILING

TILE

WH   **HVAC**   **D**   **W**

LINEN

BC

LAUNDRY

BATH

KIT
20⁶ x 10⁰
9'-0" CLG.

BREAKFAST NOOK

WET BAR

PLANT SHELF ABOVE

SHLVS

ENTERTAINMENT CENTER

PLANT SHELF ABOVE

COVERED PORCH

TILE

P   **REFG**

R   **SINK**

DW

STORAGE

DINING RM
10² x 13⁶
SLOPED CLG

FOYER CLERESTORIES ABOVE

LIVING RM
18⁴ x 13⁶
SLOPED CLG

ENTERTAINMENT TERRACE

B-BQ GRILL

Width 89'
Depth 46'-2"

RAILING

COVERED PORCH

RAILING

Design 3466

Square Footage: 1,800

L D

Small but inviting, this one-story ranch-style farmhouse is the perfect choice for a small family or empty-nesters. It's loaded with amenities even the most particular homeowner can appreciate. For example, the living room and dining room each have plant shelves, sloped ceilings and built-ins to enhance livability. The living room also sports a warming hearth. The master bedroom contains a well-appointed bath with dual vanity and walk-in closet. The additional bedroom has its own bath with linen storage. The kitchen is separated from the breakfast nook by a clever bar area. Access to the two-car garage is through a laundry area with washer/dryer hookup space.

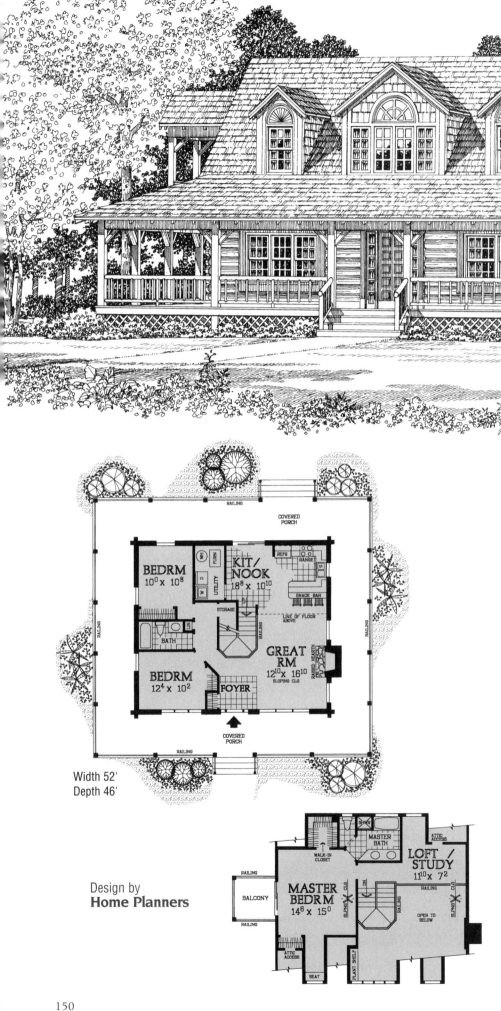

Width 52'
Depth 46'

Design by
Home Planners

Design 3683

First Floor: 1,139 square feet
Second Floor: 576 square feet
Total: 1,715 square feet

L D

Abe Lincoln most likely would have looked upon this log home as a palace. And he would have been correct! A rustically royal welcome extends from the wraparound porch, inviting one and all into a comfortable interior. To the right of the foyer, a two-story great room enhanced by a raised-hearth fireplace sets a spirited country mood. Nearby, a snack bar joins the living area with an efficient, U-shaped kitchen and an attached nook. Two family bedrooms, a full bath and a utility room with space for a washer and dryer complete the first floor. The second-floor master suite features amenities that create a private, restful getaway. Curl up in the window seat with a good book or enjoy fresh air from your own private balcony. The view will enable you to see for miles. A walk-in closet, a soothing master bath and a loft/study for quiet contemplation complete this special retreat.

Live The Sunshine Dream

Sun-Kissed Homes to Romance the Soul

Imagine yourself in a vacation paradise: a warm breeze scented with fragrant flowers wakes you with the morning sun, a delicious fresh fruit breakfast is enjoyed on the shaded patio before a refreshing swim and you plan your day to honor the same easy rhythms of the sun dial in the courtyard. To most, this sounds like a perfect escape from everyday life, but what if this paradise was your everyday?

The simple pursuit of enjoying a sunny life—indoors and out—is a contributing factor in the design of the sun-country home. More than an abundance of windows and cool patios, these homes are designed to offer an ease of living throughout with the floor plans that speak to your romantic side. Living areas are spacious, flowing freely from formal to casual, inside to out on the patio. The easy design of the Santa Fe (Design 3433, page 154) features a massive fireplace that warms the living room, dining room and the rear porch.

Amenities abound in the heart-warming Mission (Design 3660, page 163), where the fabulous master suite is a vacation in itself. The unique use of space creates inviting living spaces that work well together, as well as on their own as zones for media entertainment, relaxing by the fire and outdoor entertaining on the multi-level patio. Bold design and a welcome attention to creature comforts distinguish this collection of sun-country homes—a collection you'll surely warm up to.

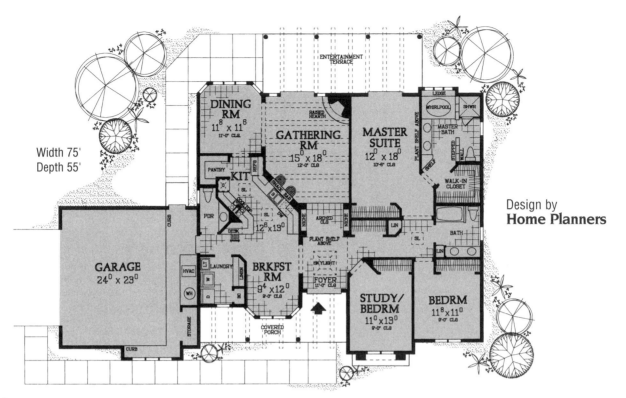

Width 75'
Depth 55'

Design by
Home Planners

Design 3486

Square Footage: 2,000

This classic stucco design provides a cool retreat in any climate. From the covered porch, enter the skylit foyer to find an arched ceiling leading to the central gathering room with its raised-hearth fireplace and terrace access. A connecting corner dining room is conveniently located near the amenity-filled kitchen that features an abundant pantry, a snack bar and a separate breakfast area. The large master bedroom includes terrace access and a master bath with a whirlpool tub, a separate shower and plenty of closet space. A second bedroom and a study that can be converted to a bedroom complete this wonderful plan.

QUOTE ONE®

Cost to build? See page 214
to order complete cost estimate
to build this house in your area!

 Design 3431

Square Footage: 1,907

Design by
Home Planners

Graceful curves welcome you into the courtyard of this Santa Fe home. Inside, a gallery directs traffic to the work zone on the left or the sleeping zone on the right. Straight ahead lies a sunken gathering room with a beam ceiling and a raised-hearth fireplace. A large pantry offers extra storage space for kitchen items. The covered rear porch is accessible from the dining room, gathering room and secluded master bedroom. The master bath has a whirlpool tub, a separate shower, a double vanity and lots of closet space. Two family bedrooms share a compartmented bath.

California Engineered Plans and California Stock Plans are available for this home. Call 1-800-521-6797 for more information.

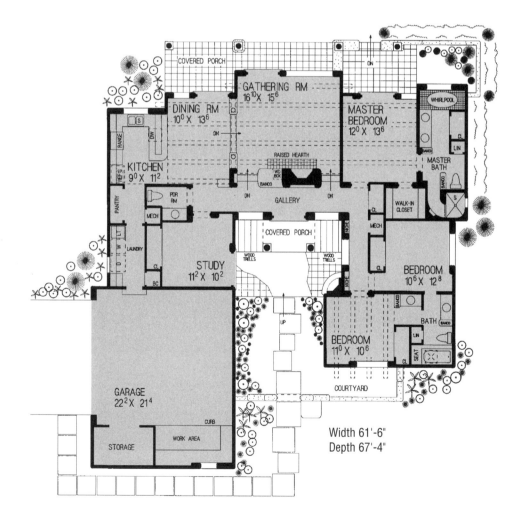

Width 61'-6"
Depth 67'-4"

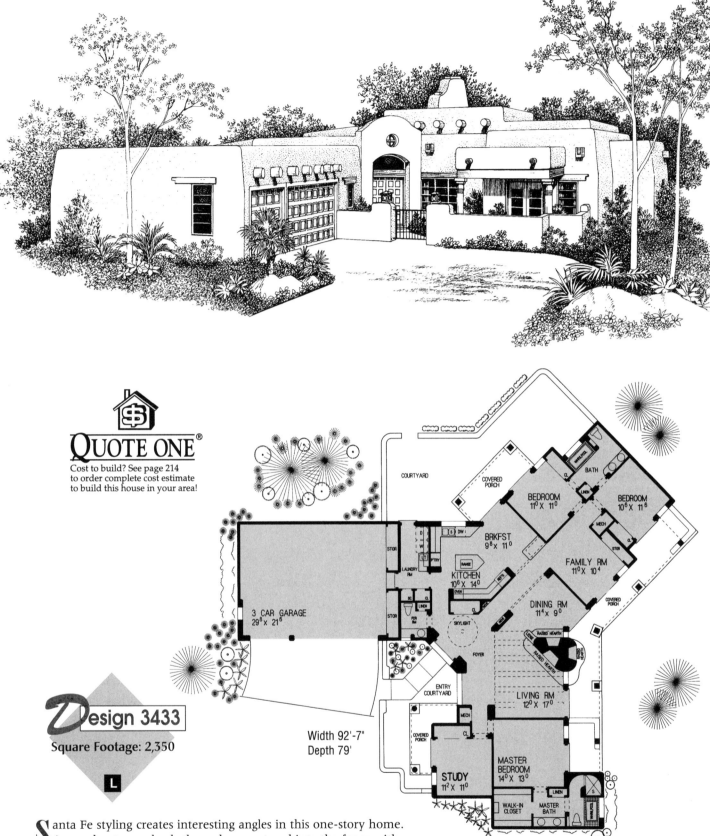

Design 3433

Square Footage: 2,350

L

Width 92'-7"
Depth 79'

CO URTYARD

COVERED PORCH

BEDROOM
11⁰ X 11⁰

BEDROOM
10⁶ X 11⁶

BATH

LINEN

MECH

BRKFST
9⁸ X 11⁰

FAMILY RM
11⁰ X 10⁴

STOR

STOR

LAUNDRY RM

KITCHEN
10⁶ X 14⁰

RANGE

OVEN

DINING RM
11⁴ X 9⁰

COVERED PORCH

3 CAR GARAGE
29⁸ X 21⁶

LINEN

SKYLIGHT

FOYER

RAISED HEARTH

RAISED HEARTH

LIVING RM
12⁰ X 17⁰

ENTRY COURTYARD

COVERED PORCH

MECH

CL

MASTER BEDROOM
14⁰ X 13⁰

STUDY
11² X 11⁰

LINEN

WALK-IN CLOSET

MASTER BATH

Santa Fe styling creates interesting angles in this one-story home. A grand entrance leads through a courtyard into the foyer with a circular skylight, closet space, niches and a convenient powder room. Fireplaces in the living room, dining room and on the covered porch create a warming heart of the home. Make note of the island range in the kitchen and the cozy breakfast room adjacent. The master suite has a privacy wall on the covered porch, a deluxe bath and a study close at hand. Two more family bedrooms are placed quietly in the far wing of the house near a segmented family room. The three-car garage offers extra storage.

Design by
Home Planners

Design 3644

Square Footage: 2,015

This Santa Fe-style home is as warm as a desert breeze and just as comfortable. Outside details are reminiscent of old-style adobe homes, while the interior caters to convenient living. The front covered porch leads to an open foyer. Columns define the formal dining room and the giant great room. The kitchen has an enormous pantry, a snack bar and is connected to a breakfast nook with rear patio access. Two family bedrooms are found on the right side of the plan. They share a full bathroom with twin vanities. The master suite is on the left side of the plan and has a monstrous walk-in closet and a bath with spa tub and separate shower.

Design by
Home Planners

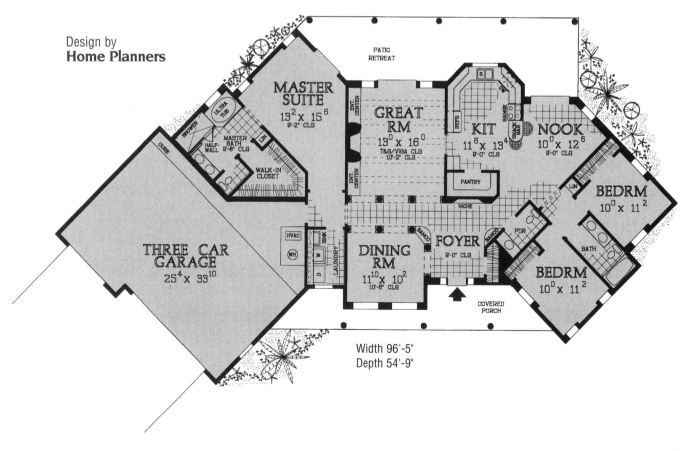

Width 96'-5"
Depth 54'-9"

Design by
Home Planners

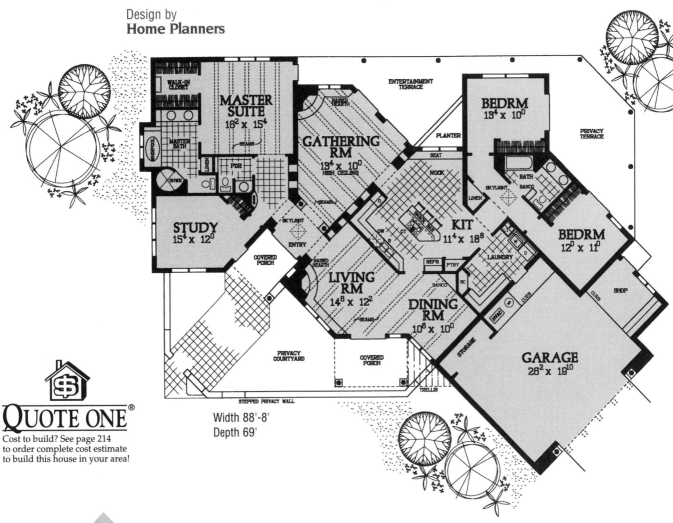

WALK-IN CLOSET

MASTER SUITE
16² x 15⁴

MASTER BATH

WHIRLPOOL

LINEN

PDR

SHWR

STUDY
15⁴ x 12⁰

SKYLIGHT

ENTRY

COVERED PORCH

RAISED HEARTH

LIVING RM
14⁸ x 12²

BEAMS

GATHERING RM
13⁴ x 10⁰
HIGH CEILING

RAISED HEARTH

BEAMS

ENTERTAINMENT TERRACE

BEDRM
13⁴ x 10⁰

PLANTER

SEAT

NOOK

SKYLIGHT

LINEN

BATH

BANCO

PRIVACY TERRACE

KIT
11⁴ x 18⁸

CT

DW

REF'G

PTRY

BANCO

LAUNDRY

BC

D

BEDRM
12⁰ x 11⁰

DINING RM
10⁸ x 10⁰

BEAMS

PRIVACY COURTYARD

COVERED PORCH

STEPPED PRIVACY WALL

TRELLIS

STORAGE

CURB

HVAC

CURB

SHOP

GARAGE
26² x 19¹⁰

Width 88'-8'
Depth 69'

QUOTE ONE®

Cost to build? See page 214
to order complete cost estimate
to build this house in your area!

Design 3406

Square Footage: 2,624

L

Angled living spaces add interest to this already magnificent Santa Fe home. From the offset entry you can travel straight back to the open gathering room—or turn to the right to enter the formal living and dining rooms. The huge kitchen is centralized and features an L-shaped work area with an island. Secondary bedrooms open to a side patio and share a full bath. The master suite is complemented by a warm study and is separated from the secondary bedrooms for privacy.

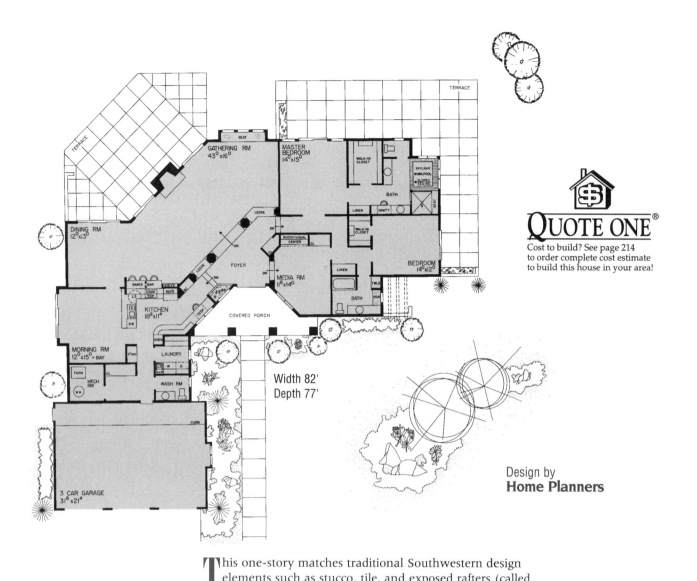

Width 82'
Depth 77'

Design by
Home Planners

Design 2949

Square Footage: 2,922

This one-story matches traditional Southwestern design elements such as stucco, tile, and exposed rafters (called vigas) with an up-to-date floor plan. The 43-foot gathering room provides a dramatic multi-purpose living area. Other unique features include a morning room with a sunny bay and a media room which could serve as a third bedroom. The master bedroom contains a walk-in closet and an amenity-filled bath with a whirlpool tub. An additional bedroom has a walk-in organizer closet and a nearby hall bath. Plenty of room is available in the three-car garage and multi-purpose utility room.

California Engineered Plans and California Stock Plans are available for this home. Call 1-800-521-6797 for more information.

Design by
Home Planners

Width 90'-2"
Depth 69'-10"

QUOTE ONE®

Cost to build? See page 214
to order complete cost estimate
to build this house in your area!

Design 3628

First Floor: 1,731 square feet
Second Floor: 554 square feet
Total: 2,285 square feet

Varying roof planes of colorful tile surfaces helps to make a dramatic statement. Privacy walls add appeal and help form the front courtyard and side private patio. The kitchen has an island cooktop, built-in ovens, a nearby walk-in pantry and direct access to the outdoor covered patio. The living room is impressive with its centered fireplace with long, raised hearth and access through French doors to the rear patio. At the opposite end of the plan is the master bedroom. It has a walk-in closet with shoe storage, twin lavatories in the bath, plus a whirlpool and stall shower. The two secondary bedrooms upstairs have direct access to a bath with twin lavatories. There is also a loft with open rail overlooking the curved stairway.

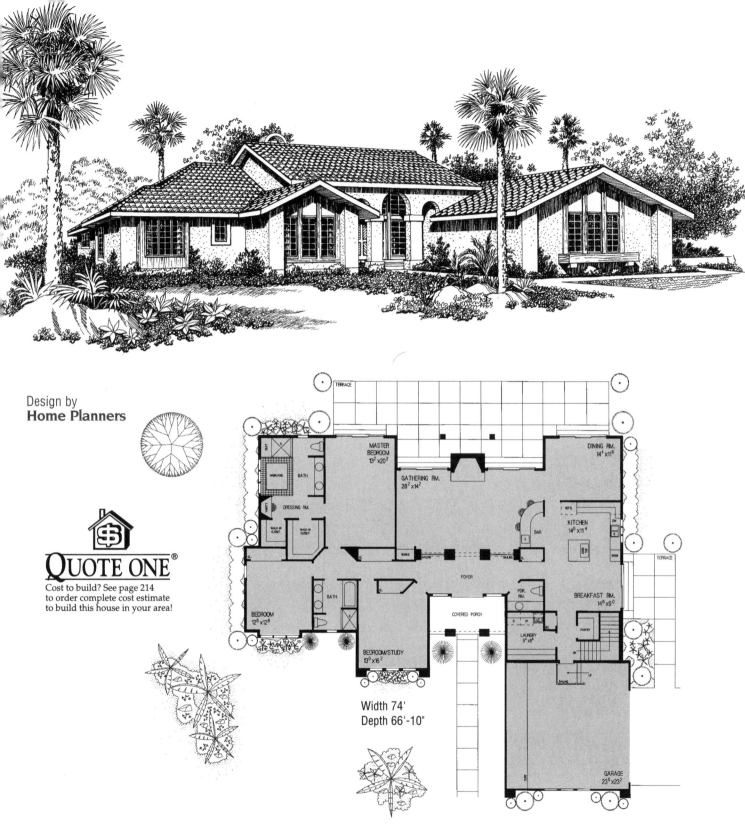

Design by
Home Planners

QUOTE ONE®
Cost to build? See page 214
to order complete cost estimate
to build this house in your area!

TERRACE

MASTER
BEDROOM
13² x20²

BATH

WHIRLPOOL

VANITY

DRESSING RM.

WALK-IN
CLOSET

WALK-IN
CLOSET

GATHERING RM.
28² x14²

DINING RM.
14⁴ x11⁶

REF'S

KITCHEN
14⁶ x11⁴

BAR

OVEN

TERRACE

BOOKS

RAILING

RAILING

FOYER

BEDROOM
12⁶ x12⁸

BATH

CL.

PDR.
RM.

BREAKFAST RM.
14⁶ x9⁰

COVERED PORCH

PANTRY

LAUNDRY
9⁴ x8⁸

BEDROOM/STUDY
13⁰ x16²

Width 74'
Depth 66'-10"

GARAGE
23⁸ x23²

Design 2950

Square Footage: 2,559

A natural desert dweller, this stucco,
tile-roofed beauty is equally comfortable in any clime. Inside, there's a well-
planned design. Common living areas—
gathering room, formal dining room,
and breakfast room—are offset by a
quiet study that could be used as a bedroom or guest room. A lovely hearth
warms the gathering room and complements the snack bar eating area. A master suite features two walk-in closets, a
double vanity, and whirlpool spa. The
two-car garage provides a service
entrance; close by is an adequate laundry area and a pantry.
**California Engineered Plans and
California Stock Plans are available
for this home. Call 1-800-521-6797
for more information.**

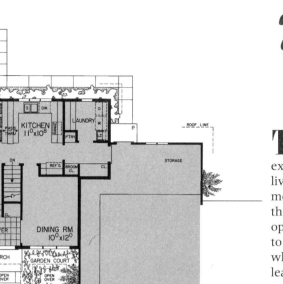

MASTER BEDROOM
12⁴ x 15⁰

WHIRLPOOL

BATH

DRESSING RM.

HER WALK-IN CLOSET

HIS WALK-IN CLOSET

VANITY

BATH

BEDROOM
11⁰ x 13⁴

BEDROOM
10⁰ x 10⁰

SEAT

STUDY
13⁰ x 13⁰

SEAT

PORCH

OPEN OVER

FOYER

SLOPED CEILING

GATHERING RM.
17⁴ x 17⁸

PASS THRU

KITCHEN
11⁰ x 10⁸

LAUNDRY

DN

REF'G

BROOM CL.

CL.

GARDEN COURT

OPEN OVER

GRILLE

DINING RM.
10⁰ x 12⁰

STORAGE

ROOF LINE

GARAGE
21⁴ x 29⁰

CURB

TERRACE

ROOF LINE

SEAT

ROOF LINE

SLOPED CEILING

Width 77'-10"
Depth 46'-4"

Design by
Home Planners

This elegant Spanish design incorporates excellent indoor/outdoor living relationships for modern families who enjoy the sun. Note the overhead openings for rain and sun to fall upon a front garden, while a twin-arched entry leads to the front porch and foyer. Inside, the floor plan features a modern kitchen with pass-through to a large gathering room with fireplace. Other features include a dining room, laundry room, a study off the foyer, plus three bedrooms including a master bedroom with its own whirlpool.

QUOTE ONE®

Cost to build? See page 214 to order complete cost estimate to build this house in your area!

Design 2912

Square Footage: 1,864

Design by
Home Planners

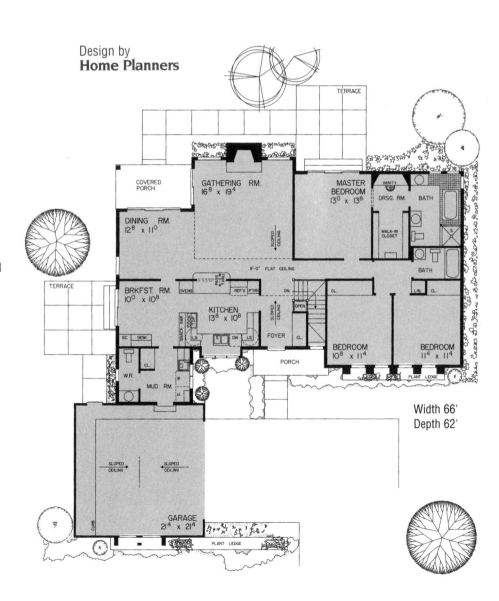

COVERED PORCH

GATHERING RM.
16⁸ x 19⁴

MASTER BEDROOM
13⁰ x 13⁸

VANITY

DRSG. RM.

BATH

DINING RM.
12⁸ x 11⁰

WALK-IN CLOSET

BATH

8'-0" FLAT CEILING

TERRACE

BRKFST. RM.
10⁰ x 10⁸

OVENS

REF'G

PTRY

CL.

LIN.

CL.

DN.

OPEN

KITCHEN
13⁸ x 10⁸

FOYER

BEDROOM
10⁸ x 11⁴

BEDROOM
11⁴ x 11⁴

BC.

DESK

SNACK BAR

PORCH

PLANT LEDGE

CL.

W.R.

MUD RM.

SLOPED CEILING

SLOPED CEILING

GARAGE
21⁴ x 21⁴

PLANT LEDGE

Width 66'
Depth 62'

This modern design with smart Spanish styling incorporates careful zoning by room functions with lifestyle comfort. All three bedrooms, including a master bedroom suite with a large dressing area and lush bath, are isolated at one end of the home. Entry to a breakfast room and kitchen is possible through a mud room off the garage. That's good news for carrying groceries from car to kitchen or slipping off muddy shoes. The modern kitchen includes a snack bar and a convenient cooktop with easy service to the breakfast room, dining room and gathering room. A large rear gathering room features a sloped ceiling and a fireplace. A covered porch just off the dining room furthers living potential.

QUOTE ONE®

Cost to build? See page 214 to order complete cost estimate to build this house in your area!

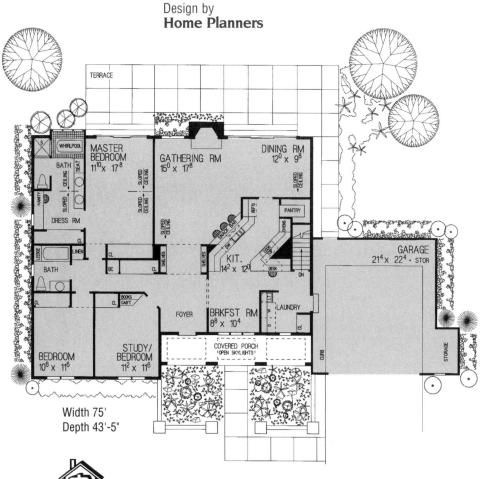

Design 2948

Square Footage: 1,830

Design by
Home Planners

Originally styled for Southwest living, this home is a good choice in any region where casual elegance is desired. Easy living is the focus of the large gathering room apparent in its open relationship to the dining room and kitchen via a snack bar. The long galley kitchen is designed for work efficiency and has a planning desk, service entrance and a beautiful breakfast room framed with windows. The master bedroom and bath have a dramatic sloped ceiling and are joined by a traditional dressing room. Two secondary bedrooms— the front facing one would make a nice study—share a hall bath.

California Engineered Plans and California Stock Plans are available for this home. Call 1-800-521-6797 for more information.

Width 75'
Depth 43'-5"

QUOTE ONE®

Cost to build? See page 214 to order complete cost estimate to build this house in your area!

Design 3660

Square Footage: 2,086

L

This home exhibits wonderful dual-use space in the sunken sitting room and media area. Anchoring each end of this spacious living zone is the raised-hearth fireplace and the entertainment center. The outstanding kitchen has an informal breakfast bay and looks over the snack bar to the family area. To the rear of the plan, a few steps from the kitchen and functioning with the upper patio, is the formal dining room. Through the archway are two children's bedrooms and a bath with a twin vanity. At the far end of the plan is the master suite. It has a sitting area with fine, natural light. A few steps away, French doors open to the covered master patio.

Design by
Home Planners

Quote One®

Cost to build? See page 214 to order complete cost estimate to build this house in your area!

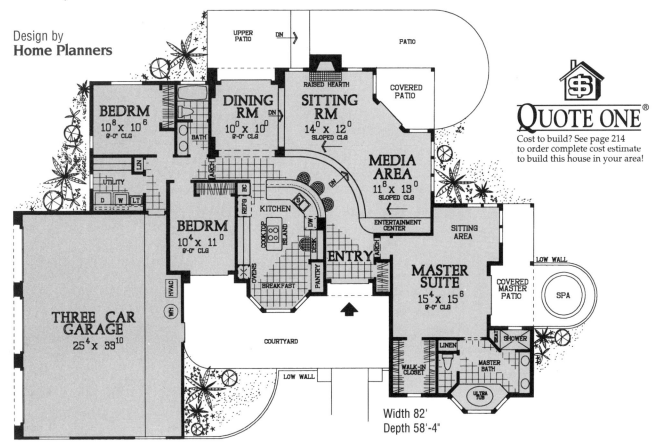

Width 82'
Depth 58'-4"

Design by
Home Planners

QUOTE ONE®
Cost to build? See page 214
to order complete cost estimate
to build this house in your area!

Design 3632
Square Footage: 2,539

L

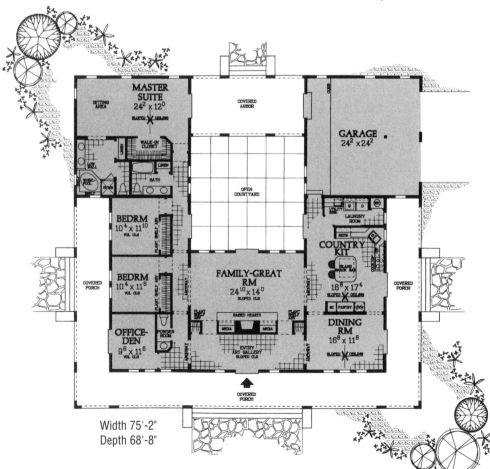

Width 75'-2"
Depth 68'-8"

Exposed rafter tails, arched porch detailing, massive paneled front doors and stucco exterior walls enhance the western character of this ranch house. Double doors open to an elegant art gallery that precedes the spacious great room. The quiet sleeping zone is comprised of an entire wing. The master suite has a generous sitting area, a walk-in closet and a whirlpool. The extra room at the front of this wing may be used for a den or an office. The family dining and kitchen activities are located at the opposite end of the plan. Indoor-outdoor living relationships are outstanding. The large open courtyard is accessible from each of the zones and functions with a covered arbor which looks out over the rear landscape.

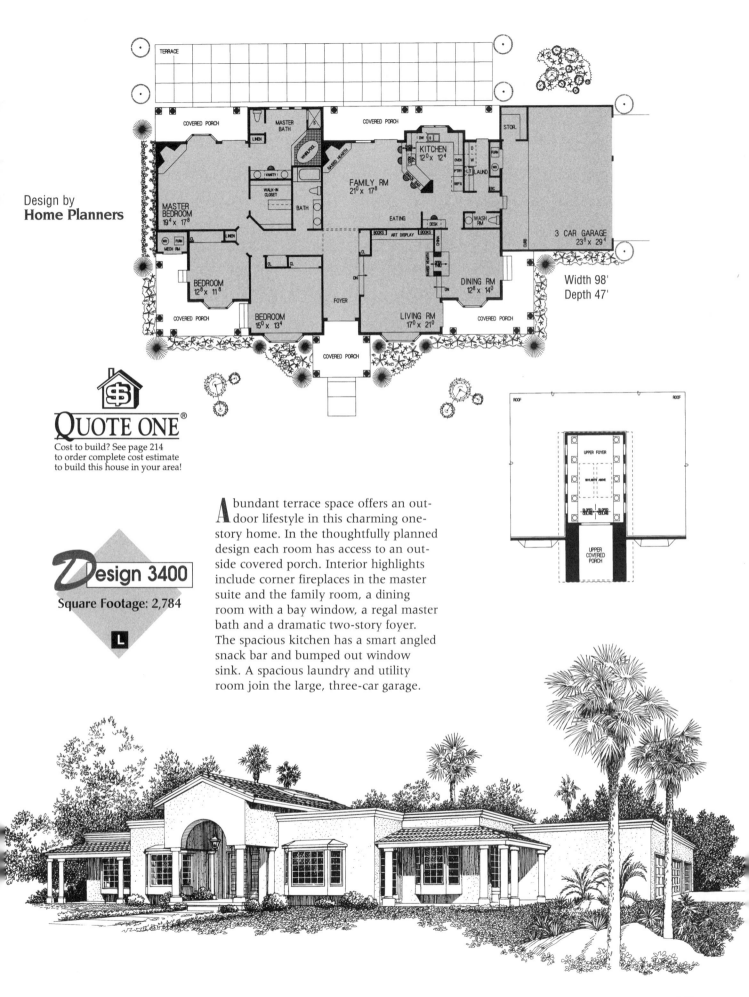

Design by
Home Planners

QUOTE ONE®

Cost to build? See page 214
to order complete cost estimate
to build this house in your area!

Design 3400

Square Footage: 2,784

L

Abundant terrace space offers an out-door lifestyle in this charming one-story home. In the thoughtfully planned design each room has access to an outside covered porch. Interior highlights include corner fireplaces in the master suite and the family room, a dining room with a bay window, a regal master bath and a dramatic two-story foyer. The spacious kitchen has a smart angled snack bar and bumped out window sink. A spacious laundry and utility room join the large, three-car garage.

© The Sater Group, Inc.

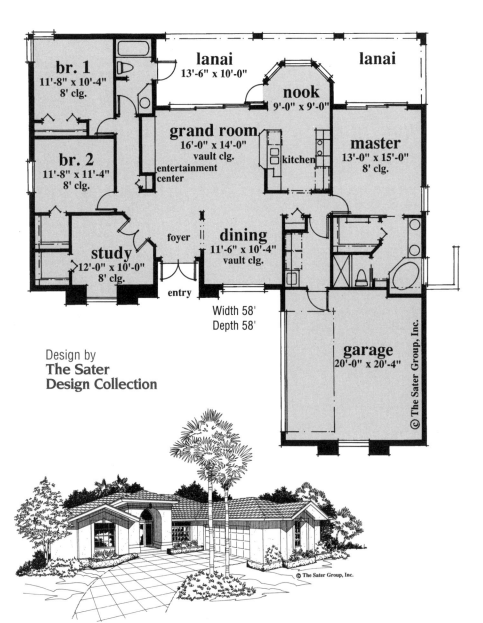

br. 1
11'-8" x 10'-4"
8' clg.

lanai
13'-6" x 10'-0"

lanai

nook
9'-0" x 9'-0"

grand room
16'-0" x 14'-0"
vault clg.

master
13'-0" x 15'-0"
8' clg.

kitchen

br. 2
11'-8" x 11'-4"
8' clg.

entertainment
center

study
12'-0" x 10'-0"
8' clg.

foyer

dining
11'-6" x 10'-4"
vault clg.

entry

Width 58'
Depth 58'

garage
20'-0" x 20'-4"

© The Sater Group, Inc.

Design by
The Sater
Design Collection

© The Sater Group, Inc.

esign **6658**

Square Footage: 1,647

This glorious sun-country cottage gives you the option of two elevations: choose from a hipped or gabled roof at the front entrance. Either way, this plan gives a new look to comfortable resort living. Designed for casual living, the foyer opens to the dining room and grand room while providing great views of the rear lanai and beyond. The grand room has a built-in entertainment center and a snack bar served from the kitchen. The galley kitchen has a gazebo dining nook with a door to the lanai. The master suite is split from the family sleeping wing and features a walk-in closet and a compartmented bath. Two secondary bedrooms, a study and full cabana bath complete this luxurious home.

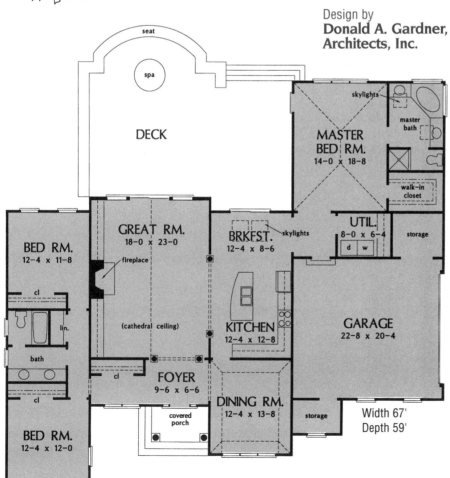

seat

spa

DECK

GREAT RM.
18-0 x 23-0

fireplace

(cathedral ceiling)

BED RM.
12-4 x 11-8

cl

lin.

bath

cl

BED RM.
12-4 x 12-0

cl

FOYER
9-6 x 6-6

covered
porch

DINING RM.
12-4 x 13-8

KITCHEN
12-4 x 12-8

BRKFST.
12-4 x 8-6

skylights

skylights

MASTER
BED RM.
14-0 x 18-8

master
bath

walk-in
closet

UTIL.
8-0 x 6-4

d w

storage

GARAGE
22-8 x 20-4

storage

Width 67'
Depth 59'

Design by
**Donald A. Gardner,
Architects, Inc.**

Design 9744

Square Footage: 2,090

This exciting Southwestern design is enhanced by the use of arched windows and an inviting arched entrance. The large foyer opens to a massive great room with a fireplace and built-in cabinets. The kitchen features an island cooktop and a skylit breakfast area. The master suite has an impressive cathedral ceiling and a walk-in closet as well as a luxurious bath that boasts separate vanities, a corner whirlpool tub and a separate shower. Two additional bedrooms are located at the opposite end of the home for privacy and share a full bath. Please specify crawlspace or slab foundation when ordering.

Design 8630

Square Footage: 1,550

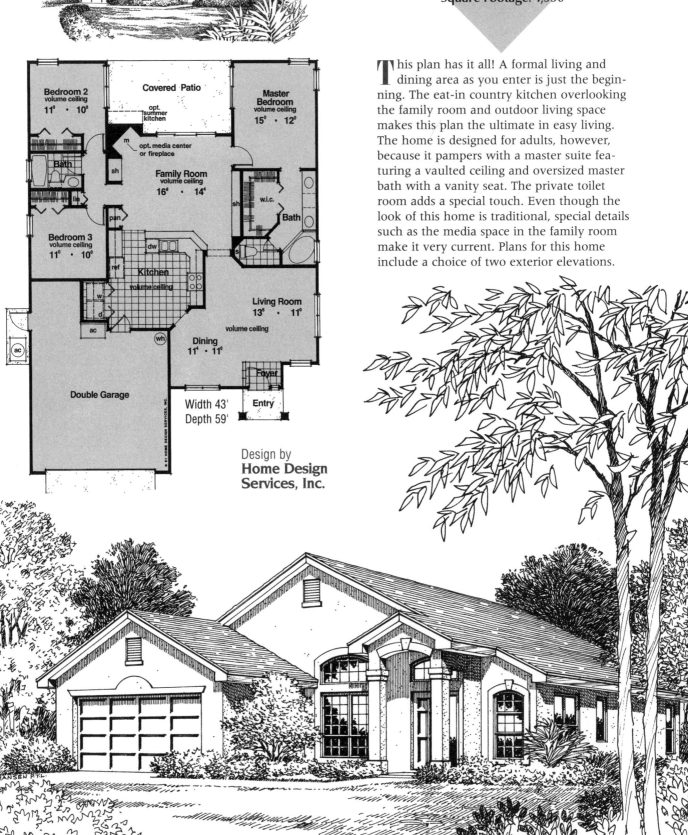

Covered Patio

opt. summer kitchen

Bedroom 2
volume ceiling
11⁰ · 10⁰

Bath

Master Bedroom
volume ceiling
15⁰ · 12⁰

m opt. media center or fireplace

sh

Family Room
volume ceiling
16⁸ · 14⁴

sh w.i.c.

Bath

Bedroom 3
volume ceiling
11⁰ · 10⁰

pan

dw

ref Kitchen
volume ceiling

w

d

ac

ac

wh

Living Room
13⁶ · 11⁰

volume ceiling

Dining
11⁴ · 11⁰

Double Garage

Width 43'
Depth 59'

Foyer

Entry

Design by
Home Design Services, Inc.

This plan has it all! A formal living and dining area as you enter is just the beginning. The eat-in country kitchen overlooking the family room and outdoor living space makes this plan the ultimate in easy living. The home is designed for adults, however, because it pampers with a master suite featuring a vaulted ceiling and oversized master bath with a vanity seat. The private toilet room adds a special touch. Even though the look of this home is traditional, special details such as the media space in the family room make it very current. Plans for this home include a choice of two exterior elevations.

Design 8633

Square Footage: 1,865

This innovative plan takes advantage of an angled entry into the home, maximizing visual impact and making it possible to include many amenities found in larger homes. The joining of the family and dining space makes creative interior decorating possible. The master suite also takes advantage of angles in creating long visual lines. The master bath is designed with all the amenities usually found in much larger homes. The kitchen and breakfast nook overlook the outdoor living space where you can option for an outdoor kitchen area—a great design for entertaining. You can choose between having a front study or extending the double garage to hold three cars.

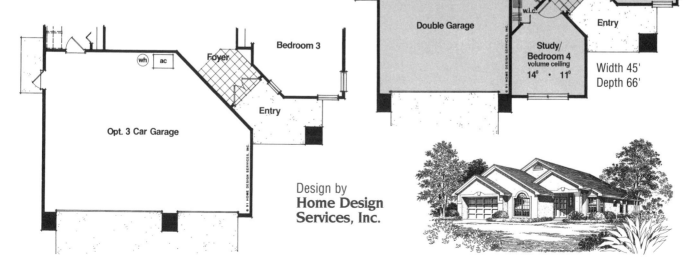

Opt. 3 Car Garage

Foyer
Bedroom 3
Entry

wh | ac

Design by
Home Design
Services, Inc.

---

opt.

Covered Patio

opt. summer kitchen

Master Bedroom
volume ceiling
16⁸ · 12⁰

Bath

Breakfast
volume ceiling

Great Room
15⁸ · 14⁰

w.i.c.

lin

Kitchen
dw
wall to 8'
volume ceiling

opt. media center

m

Bedroom 2
volume ceiling
13⁴ · 10⁰

lin

refl
par.

Bath

Dining
12⁰ · 10¹⁰

Bedroom 3
volume ceiling
13⁴ · 11⁴

opt. sink & stg

Utility
lin

w
d

ac

wh | ac

Foyer

n

Double Garage

w.i.c.

Entry

Study/
Bedroom 4
volume ceiling
14⁰ · 11⁰

Width 45'
Depth 66'

Design 9452

Square Footage: 2,106

With an easy-living, open floor plan and lovely exterior, this Spanish design is a great choice. From the vaulted foyer with skylight, turn left for a formal living and dining room combination with fireplace. Nearby is the kitchen and breakfast nook which opens to the family room that has yet another fireplace. To the right of the foyer is a cozy den that could double as a guest room. A master suite with spa-style bath and walk-in closet is the perfect owner's retreat. The additional bedroom has private entry to the hall bath, making it a perfect guest suite.

Design by
**Alan Mascord
Design Associates, Inc.**

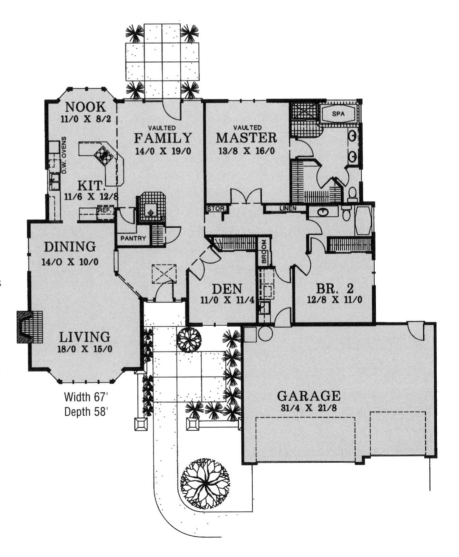

Design 8662

Square Footage: 2,005

A super floor plan makes this sunny volume home that much more attractive. Inside you'll find a formal dining room—defined by columns—to the right and a living room—with an optional fireplace—to the left. Beyond this area is an expansive great room with a vaulted ceiling and openness to the kitchen and breakfast room. A covered patio in the back of the house enhances outdoor livability. Two secondary bedrooms complete the right side of the plan. Each features a volume ceiling, ample closet space and the use of a full hall bath with dual lavatories. The master bedroom enjoys its own bath with a whirlpool tub, separate shower, dual vanity and compartmented toilet.

Width 58'
Depth 60'

Design by
**Home Design
Services, Inc.**

© The Sater Group, Inc.

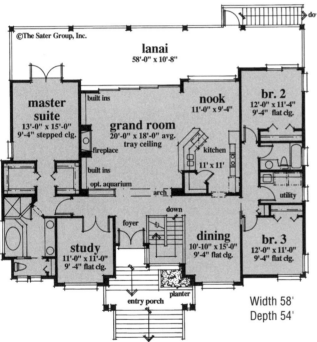

©The Sater Group, Inc.

lanai
58'-0" x 10'-8"

master suite
13'-0" x 15'-0"
9'-4" stepped clg.

built ins

grand room
20'-0" x 18'-0" avg.
tray ceiling

fireplace

built ins

opt. aquarium

nook
11'-0" x 9'-4"

br. 2
12'-0" x 11'-4"
9'-4" flat clg.

kitchen
11' x 11'

arch

utility

down

foyer

study
11'-0" x 11'-0"
9'-4" flat clg.

dining
10'-10" x 15'-0"
9'-4" flat clg.

br. 3
12'-0" x 11'-0"
9'-4" flat clg.

planter

entry porch

Width 58'
Depth 54'

Design 6622
Square Footage: 2,190

Design by
**The Sater
Design Collection**

Quote One®
Cost to build? See page 214
to order complete cost estimate
to build this house in your area!

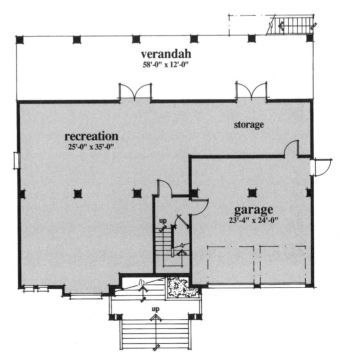

verandah
58'-0" x 12'-0"

recreation
25'-0" x 35'-0"

storage

garage
23'-4" x 24'-0"

up

up

A dramatic set of stairs leads to the entry of this home. The foyer leads to an expansive living room with a fireplace and built-in bookshelves. A lanai opens off this area and will assure outdoor enjoyments. For formal meals, a front-facing dining room offers a bumped-out bay. The kitchen serves this area easily as well as the breakfast room. A study and three bedrooms make up the rest of the floor plan. Two secondary bedrooms share a full hall bath. A utility area is also nearby. In the master suite, two walk-in closets and a full bath are appreciated features. In the bedroom, a set of French doors offers passage to the lanai.

172

Floor Plan Labels

guest 1
14'-8" x 11'-10"
10' flat clg.

master suite
14'-8" x 16'-0"
11' flat clg.

verandah
38'-0" x 15'-0"

leisure
19'-0" x 17'-0"
10' flat clg.

mitered glass

fireplace

dining
12'-0" x 15'-0"
12' flat clg.

living
15'-0" x 16'-0"
14' tray clg.

private garden

nook
9'-0" x 11'-0"

buffet server

kitchen

gallery

15' x 14'

foyer

mitered glass

guest 2
11'-0" x 13'-2"
10' flat clg.

study
11'-8" x 14'-0"
12' flat clg.

garden

entry

utility

garage
23'-0" x 37'-6"

Design by
**The Sater
Design Collection**

Width 70'
Depth 98'

Classic columns, circle-head windows and a bay-windowed study give this stucco home a wonderful street presence. The foyer leads into the formal living and dining areas. An arched buffet server separates these rooms and contributes an open feeling. The kitchen, nook and leisure room are grouped for informal living. A desk/message center in the island kitchen, art niches in the nook and a fireplace with an entertainment center and shelves add custom touches. Two additional suites have private baths and offer full privacy from the master wing—the most gracious guest accommodations. The master suite hosts a private garden area, while the master bath features a walk-in shower that overlooks the garden, and a water closet room with space for books or a television. Large His and Hers walk-in closets complete these private quarters.

Jenkins

Design by
**The Sater
Design Collection**

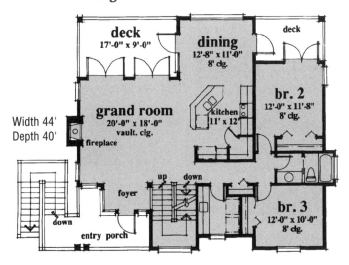

deck
17'-0" x 9'-0"

dining
12'-8" x 11'-0"
8' clg.

deck

grand room
20'-0" x 18'-0"
vault. clg.

kitchen
11' x 12'

br. 2
12'-0" x 11'-8"
8' clg.

Width 44'
Depth 40'

fireplace

up

down

foyer

down

entry porch

br. 3
12'-0" x 10'-0"
8' clg.

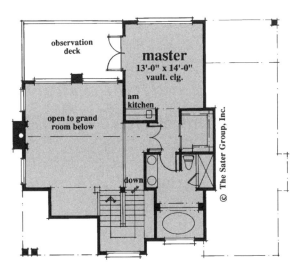

observation
deck

master
13'-0" x 14'-0"
vault. clg.

am
kitchen

open to grand
room below

down

© The Sater Group, Inc.

Design 6654

First Floor: 1,342 square feet
Second Floor: 511 square feet
Total: 1,853 square feet

With influences from homes of the Caribbean, this island home is a perfect seaside residence or primary residence. The main living area is comprised of a grand room with a fireplace and access to a deck. The dining space also accesses this deck plus another that it shares with a secondary bedroom. An L-shaped kitchen with a prep island is open to the living areas. Two bedrooms on this level share a full bath. The master suite dominates the upper level. It has its own balcony and a rewarding bath with dual vanities and a whirlpool tub.

nook
12'-0" x 9'-0"
9' clg.

kitchen
14' x 12'

deck
48'-0" x 9'-0"

grand room
21'-0" x 15'-4"
9' clg.

fireplace

br. 2
13'-0" x 11'-8"
9' clg.

down

down   up

gallery

utility

open to below

dining
13'-0" x 14'-0"
9' clg.

br. 3
13'-0" x 12'-0"
9' clg.

sk al

Width 60'
Depth 44'-6"

deck
28'-0" x 8'-0"

2 view fireplace

master suite
22'-0" x 15'-0"
vault. clg.

down

loft

open to below

am kitchen

deck

reading
13'-0" x 15'-0"
vault. clg.

Design by
**The Sater
Design Collection**

up

verandah
48'-0" x 10'-0"

game room storage
13'-0" x 35'-0"

garage
24'-0" x 28'-0"

planter   up

grand foyer

workshop   entry

Design 6621

Main Floor: 1,642 square feet
Upper Floor: 927 square feet
Total: 2,569 square feet

QUOTE ONE®

Cost to build? See page 214
to order complete cost estimate
to build this house in your area!

Luxury abounds in this Floridian home. A game room just
to the right of the entry gains attention. Up the stairs,
livability takes off with an open living room, a bayed dining
room and a deck that stretches across the back of the plan.
Two bedrooms occupy the right side of this level and share a
full hall bath with dual sinks and a separate tub and shower.
The master retreat on the upper level pleases with its own
library, a morning kitchen, a large walk-in closet and a pampering bath with a double-bowl vanity, a compartmented
toilet and bidet, a whirlpool tub and a shower that opens
outside. A private deck allows outdoor enjoyments.

175

Design 8672

Square footage: 2,397

Low-slung, hipped rooflines and an abundance of glass enhance the unique exterior of this sunny, one-story home. Inside, the use of soffits and tray ceilings heighten the distinctive style of the floor plan. To the left, double doors lead to the private master suite which is bathed in natural light—compliments of an abundant use of glass—and enjoys a garden setting from the corner tub. Convenient planning of the gourmet kitchen places everything at minimum distances and serves the outdoor summer kitchen, breakfast nook and family room with equal ease. Completing the plan are two family bedrooms that share a full bath.

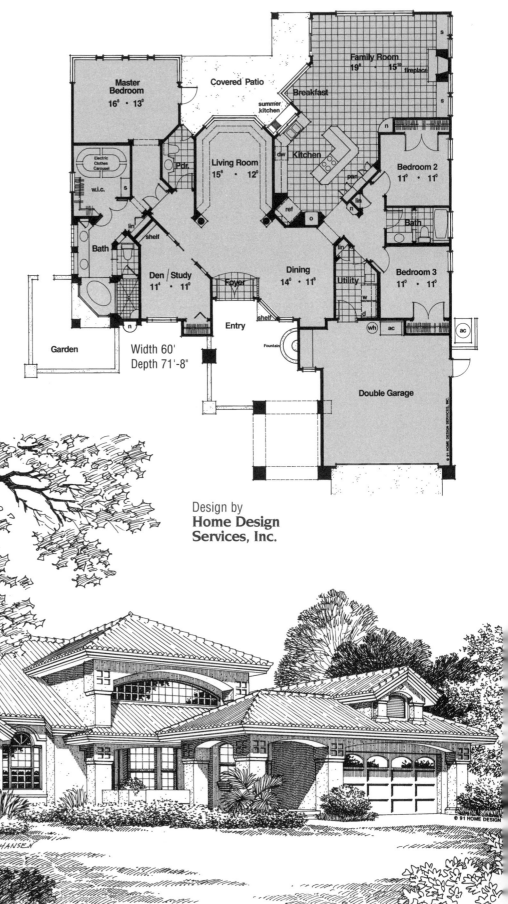

Design by
Home Design Services, Inc.

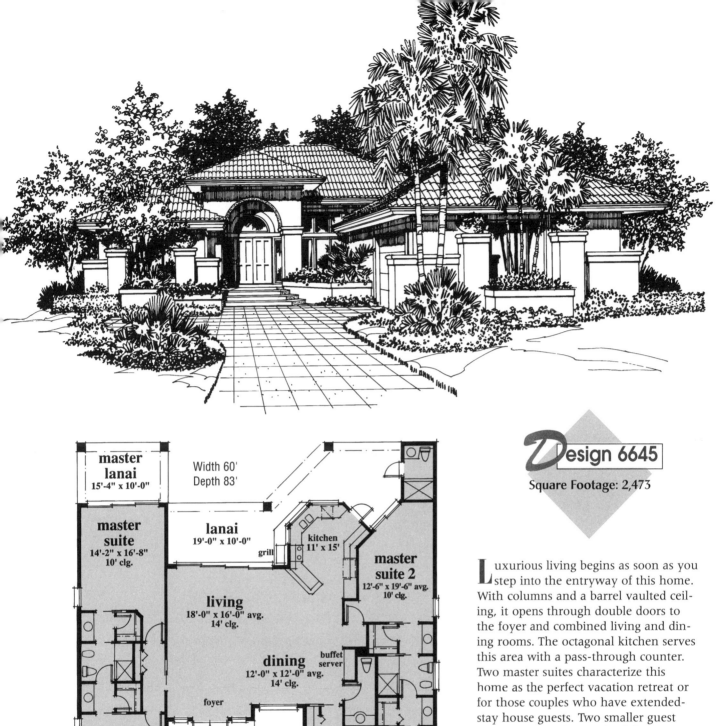

master lanai
15'-4" x 10'-0"

Width 60'
Depth 83'

master suite
14'-2" x 16'-8"
10' clg.

lanai
19'-0" x 10'-0"

grill

kitchen
11' x 15'

master suite 2
12'-6" x 19'-6" avg.
10' clg.

living
18'-0" x 16'-0" avg.
14' clg.

dining
12'-0" x 12'-0" avg.
14' clg.

buffet server

foyer

guest
14'-2" x 13'-0"
10' clg.

plant ledge

plant ledge

planter

entry barrel vault clg.

planter

planter

utility

guest 2
13'-0" x 12'-0"
10' clg.

© The Sater Group, Inc.

garage
21'-0" x 23'-0"

plant ledge

plant ledge

plant ledge

Design by
The Sater Design Collection

Design 6645

Square Footage: 2,473

Luxurious living begins as soon as you step into the entryway of this home. With columns and a barrel vaulted ceiling, it opens through double doors to the foyer and combined living and dining rooms. The octagonal kitchen serves this area with a pass-through counter. Two master suites characterize this home as the perfect vacation retreat or for those couples who have extended-stay house guests. Two smaller guest rooms are joined to each of the master suites via the compartmented bath. Either would make a cozy study or media room. Outdoor living areas include a private lanai off one of the master suites and a larger lanai that stretches across the rear of the house. An outdoor grill and a cabana bath further enhance sunshine living.

Design by
**Home Design
Services, Inc.**

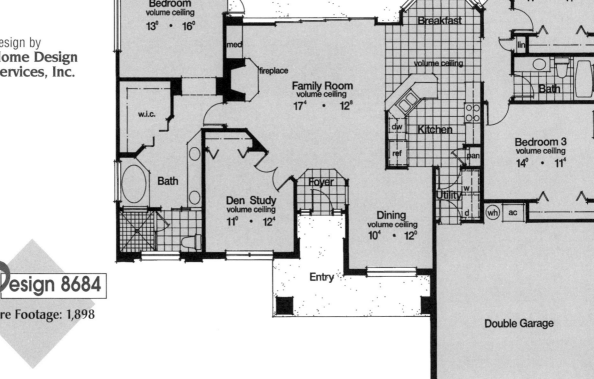

Covered Patio

Master Bedroom
volume ceiling
13⁰ · 16⁰

med

fireplace

Family Room
volume ceiling
17⁴ · 12⁸

Breakfast

volume ceiling

Bedroom 2
volume ceiling
11⁴ · 11⁰

lin

Bath

w.i.c.

dw

Kitchen

ref

pan

Bedroom 3
volume ceiling
14⁰ · 11⁴

Bath

Den Study
volume ceiling
11⁰ · 12⁴

Foyer

w

Utility

d

wh

ac

Dining
volume ceiling
10⁴ · 12⁰

Entry

Double Garage

Design 8684

Square Footage: 1,898

E asy living is at the heart of this brick one-story home inspired by the design of Frank Lloyd Wright. To the left of the foyer, double doors open onto a den/study which easily converts to a media room as well. The master suite is conveniently located nearby. Split away from family bedrooms for privacy, it features a spacious bedroom and a pampering bath with a large walk-in closet, a separate shower and a relaxing tub. Centrally located, the family room, with its cozy fireplace combines well with the kitchen and the bay-windowed breakfast nook for casual family gatherings. The sleeping wing to the right has two secondary bedrooms that share a full bath and patio access.

Width 60'
Depth 59'-4"

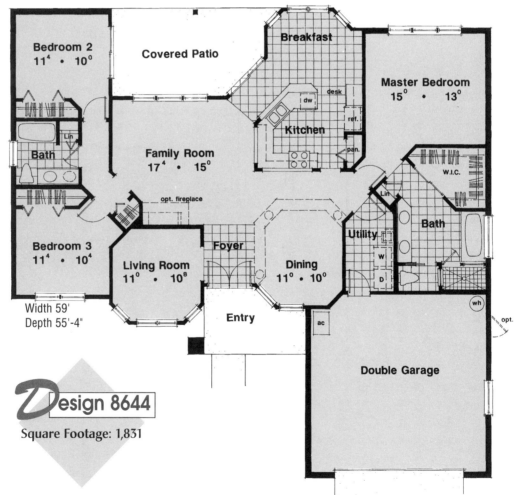

Design by
**Home Design
Services, Inc.**

Bedroom 2
11⁴ • 10⁰

Covered Patio

Breakfast

Master Bedroom
15⁰ • 13⁰

Bath

Lin

Family Room
17⁴ • 15⁰

dw   desk

Kitchen

ref.

pan.

w.i.c.

opt. fireplace

Lin

Bath

Bedroom 3
11⁴ • 10⁴

Living Room
11⁰ • 10⁸

Foyer

Dining
11⁰ • 10⁰

Utility

w
D

Width 59'
Depth 55'-4"

Entry

ac

wh

opt.

Double Garage

esign 8644

Square Footage: 1,831

A two-story entry, varying rooflines and multi-pane windows add to the spectacular street appeal of this three-bedroom home. To the right, off the foyer, is the dining room surrounded by elegant columns. Adjacent is the angular kitchen, which opens to the bayed breakfast nook. The family room includes plans for an optional fireplace and accesses the covered patio. The master bedroom is tucked in the back of the home and features a walk-in closet and full bath with a dual vanity, spa tub and oversized shower. Two additional bedrooms share a full bath.

J.N. HANSEN P.L.

Design by
**Home Design
Services, Inc.**

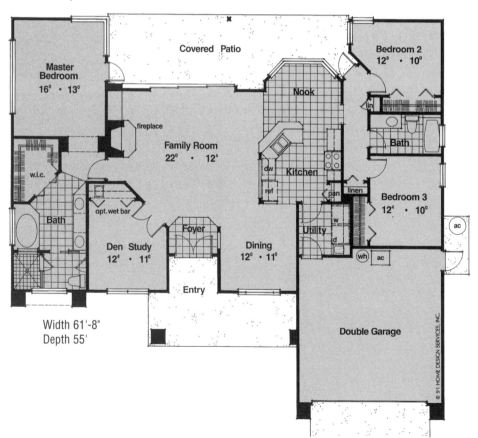

Covered Patio

Master Bedroom
16⁰ · 13⁰

fireplace

Family Room
22⁰ · 12⁴

Nook

w.i.c.

Bath

opt. wet bar

Kitchen
dw
ref

Den Study
12⁴ · 11⁰

Foyer

Dining
12⁰ · 11⁰

Entry

pan
linen

Utility
w
d
wh
ac

Bedroom 2
12⁸ · 10⁰

lin

Bath

Bedroom 3
12⁴ · 10⁰

ac

Double Garage

Width 61'-8"
Depth 55'

© '91 HOME DESIGN SERVICES, INC.

Design 8634

Square Footage: 1,869

This open plan brings indoors and outdoors together beautifully with an undisturbed view of the rear yard. The fireplace and the media center in the family room add fine finishing touches. The open kitchen design allows the cook an open view of the family room and easy service to the breakfast nook and dining room. The secondary bedrooms feature a "kids" door off the hall ideal for bathroom access from the patio area. The super master suite features mitered glass for a great view of the patio area as well as a bath with a walk-in closet, dual lavatories and spa tub. There is even a courtesy door off the toilet area accessing the den/study.

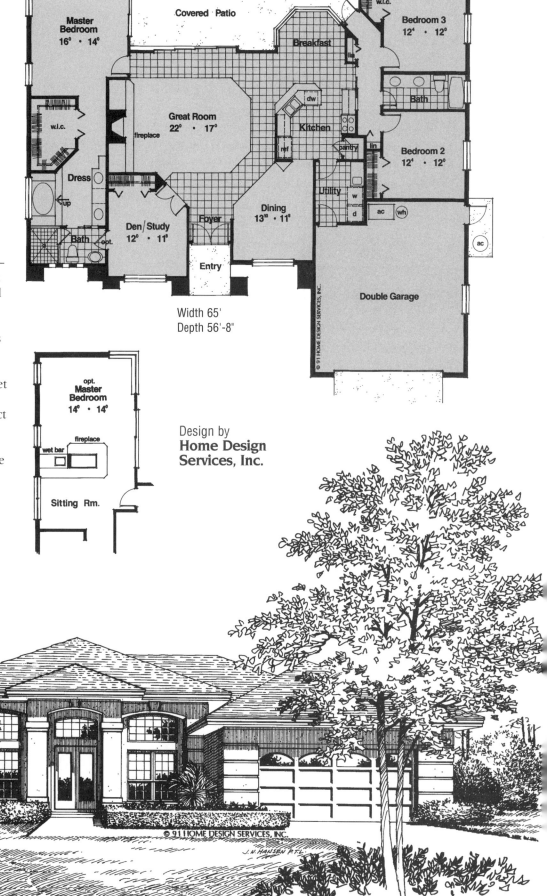

Design 8601

Square Footage: 2,125

A luxurious master suite is yours with this lovely plan— and it comes with two different options—one has a wet bar and fireplace. An oversized great room with a grand fireplace is the heart of casual living in this relaxed plan. A formal dining room lies just off the foyer and offers easy access to the gourmet kitchen. Family bedrooms are split from the living area, perfect for a guest's comfort and privacy. A hall bath is shared by the two bedrooms as is a private door to the covered patio.

Covered Patio

Master Bedroom
16⁰ · 14⁰

w.l.c.

Dress

Bath

opt.

Great Room
22⁰ · 17⁰

fireplace

Den/Study
12⁰ · 11⁸

Foyer

Entry

Breakfast

Kitchen

dw

ref

pantry

lin

Dining
13¹⁰ · 11⁸

Utility

w

d

ac

wh

ac

Bedroom 3
12⁴ · 12⁰

w.l.c.

Bath

Bedroom 2
12⁴ · 12⁰

Double Garage

Width 65'
Depth 56'-8"

© 91 HOME DESIGN SERVICES, INC.

opt.
Master Bedroom
14⁰ · 14⁰

fireplace

wet bar

Sitting Rm.

Design by
Home Design Services, Inc.

© 91 HOME DESIGN SERVICES, INC.

J.H. HANSEN P.T.L.

181

© HOME DESIGN SERVICES, INC.

J.N. HANSEN P.T.C.

Design by
**Home Design
Services, Inc.**

*D*esign 8693

Square Footage: 1,433

A volume entry and open planning give this house a feeling of spaciousness that goes far beyond its modest square footage. The foyer opens onto a large living and dining area that combines for flexible entertaining needs. The kitchen is planned to fulfill a gourmet's dream and merges with the breakfast area for informal dining. Located to the rear for privacy, the master suite opens onto the patio and features a lush bath with a huge walk-in closet. Two secondary bedrooms share a full hall bath. The covered rear patio has a dramatic vaulted ceiling giving an extra touch of elegance to casual living.

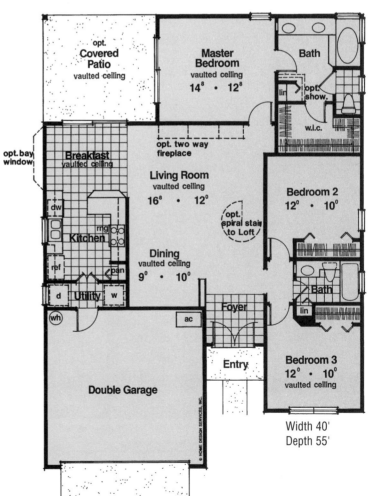

opt.
**Covered
Patio**
vaulted ceiling

**Master
Bedroom**
vaulted ceiling
14⁸ • 12⁸

Bath

lin

opt.
show.

w.i.c.

opt. bay
window

Breakfast
vaulted ceiling

opt. two way
fireplace

Living Room
vaulted ceiling
16⁸ • 12⁰

opt.
spiral stair
to Loft

Bedroom 2
12⁰ • 10⁰

dw

rng

Kitchen

ref

pan

Dining
vaulted ceiling
9⁰ • 10⁰

Bath

lin

d

Utility

w

wh

ac

Foyer

Entry

Double Garage

© HOME DESIGN SERVICES, INC.

Bedroom 3
12⁰ • 10⁰
vaulted ceiling

Width 40'
Depth 55'

You Earned It!

Luxury Homes With a Casual Elegance

The face of the American home building landscape is evolving to include a new class of homeowners that have greater assets to spend on a home. This is largely due to couples having income freed up after their kids are raised or personal advances are made in the professional world. This desire to build a home that better reflects an established couples active lifestyle is realized in homes that offer more luxurious amenities in floor plans that are designed for a single couple.

With less of a need for family bedrooms, Design 2922 (page 185) reallocates its square footage to the living areas that better suit an adult lifestyle. For example, the expansive gathering room has an open relation to the fireplace in the study and the formal dining room. Imagine the entertaining possibilities with the lovely rear terrace and the smashing corner pub!

The exquisite Floridian home on page 189 (Design 6668) makes a grand setting for all sorts of entertaining from elaborate dinners in the formal dining room to afternoon tea on the veranda. House guests will find visiting this gracious home quite comfortable thanks to the private bedrooms and leisure area on the second floor and the secluded guest suite just off the veranda. So far, obtaining your dreams has been a reality. Now comes the hardest part—choosing a home to enjoy them in.

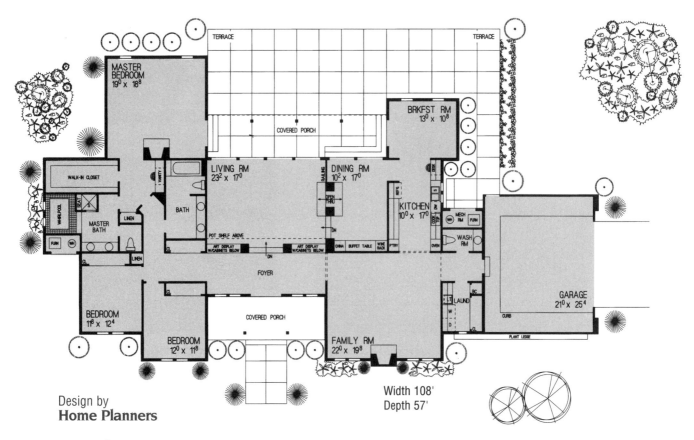

MASTER BEDROOM 19⁰ x 18⁸

TERRACE

TERRACE

COVERED PORCH

BRKFST RM 13⁰ x 10⁸

WALK-IN CLOSET

LIVING RM 23² x 17⁰

DINING RM 10² x 17⁰

KITCHEN 10⁰ x 17⁰

VANITY

BATH

MASTER BATH

WHIRLPOOL

SEAT

LINEN

OPEN THRU

MECH RM

WH

FUN

LINEN

POT SHELF ABOVE

ART DISPLAY W/CABINETS BELOW

ART DISPLAY W/CABINETS BELOW

CHINA

BUFFET TABLE

WINE RACK

PTRY

OVEN

WASH RM

FOYER

BEDROOM 11⁸ x 12⁴

BEDROOM 12⁰ x 11⁸

COVERED PORCH

LAUND

W

D

BC

CURB

GARAGE 21⁰ x 25⁴

PLANT LEDGE

FAMILY RM 22⁰ x 19⁸

Width 108'
Depth 57'

Design by
Home Planners

Design 3402

Square Footage: 3,212

L

This one-story home pairs the customary tile and stucco of Spanish design with an extremely livable floor plan. The sunken living room with its open-hearth fireplace promises to be a cozy gathering place. For more casual occasions, there's a welcoming family room with a fireplace off the entry foyer. The large galley kitchen easily serves the breakfast room and the formal dining room that has a stylish built-in buffet and shares a fireplace with the living room. The master suite has its own fireplace, a dressing area, and lush bath. Two secondary bedrooms share a dual-vanity hall bath.

QUOTE ONE®

Cost to build? See page 214
to order complete cost estimate
to build this house in your area!

Design by
Home Planners

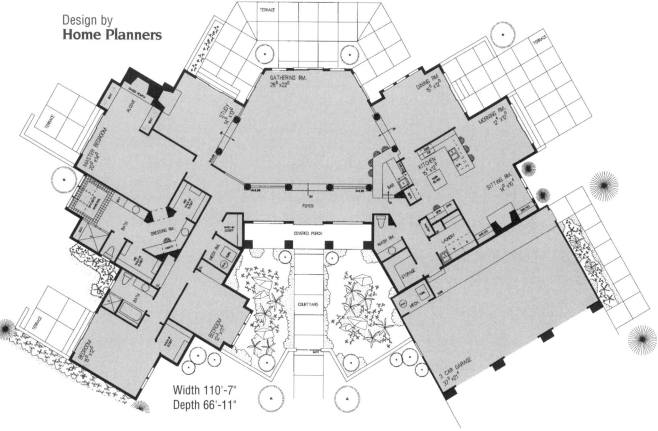

Width 110'-7"
Depth 66'-11"

Design 2922
Square Footage: 3,505

Loaded with custom features, this plan seems to have everything imaginable. It's the perfect home for entertaining—there's an enormous sunken gathering room and cozy study. A full size bar is fashioned to serve the gathering room. The country-style kitchen contains an efficient work area, as well as space for relaxing in the morning room and fireside chats in the sitting room. Two nice-sized bedrooms share a hall bath. The luxurious master suite has a fireplace alcove, and an amenity-rich bath complete with twin walk-in closets, a dressing area, and spa style tub.

California Engineered Plans and California Stock Plans are available for this home. Call 1-800-521-6797 for more information.

Cost to build? See page 214
to order complete cost estimate
to build this house in your area!

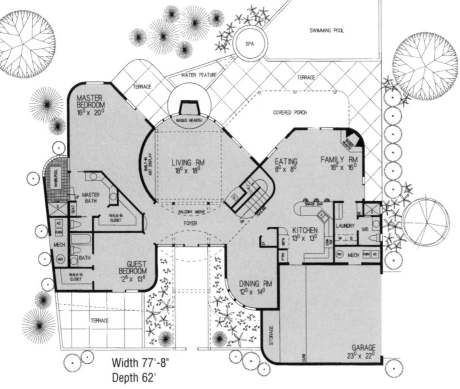

Width 77'-8"
Depth 62'

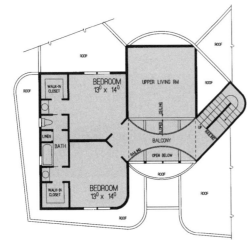

Design by
Home Planners

Design 3403

First Floor: 2,240 square feet
Second Floor: 660 square feet
Total: 2,900 square feet

L

There is no end to the distinctive features in this Southwestern contemporary. Formal living areas are concentrated in the center of the plan, while the kitchen and family room function well together as an informal living area. The optional guest bedroom or den and the master bedroom are located to the left of the plan. The second floor holds two bedrooms that share a compartmented full bath.

California Engineered Plans and California Stock Plans are available for this home. Call 1-800-521-6797 for more information.

QUOTE ONE®

Cost to build? See page 214 to order complete cost estimate to build this house in your area!

Design by
Home Planners

GATHERING RM
29⁸ X 19⁵

DINING RM
15⁶ X 12⁰

BEDROOM
16⁶ X 11⁸

BEDROOM
15⁴ X 11⁸

MASTER
BATH

WHIRLPOOL

WALK-IN
CLOSET

LINEN MECH

A/C

BATH

BATH

PANTRY

LINEN

FAMILY
KITCHEN

LAUNDRY

A/C

WH

RAISED HEARTH

WB

DN

DN

UP

FOYER

MASTER
BEDROOM
22⁰ X 16⁶

GUEST/
STUDY
18⁸ X 12²

COVERED
PORCH

COVERED
PORCH

KITCHEN
10⁸ X 14⁰

SITTING
10⁰ X 14⁸

COOK
TOP

TERRACE

3 CAR
GARAGE
35⁴ X 21⁰

UP

Width 139'-10"
Depth 63'-8"

In classic Santa Fe style, this home strikes a beautiful combination of historic exterior detailing and open floor planning on the inside. A covered porch running the width of the facade leads to an entry foyer that connects to a huge gathering room with a fireplace and a formal dining room. The family kitchen allows special space for casual gatherings. The right wing of the home holds two family bedrooms and a full bath. The left wing is devoted to the master suite and a guest room or a study.

California Engineered Plans and California Stock Plans are available for this home. Call 1-800-521-6797 for more information.

Design 3405

Square Footage: 3,144

L

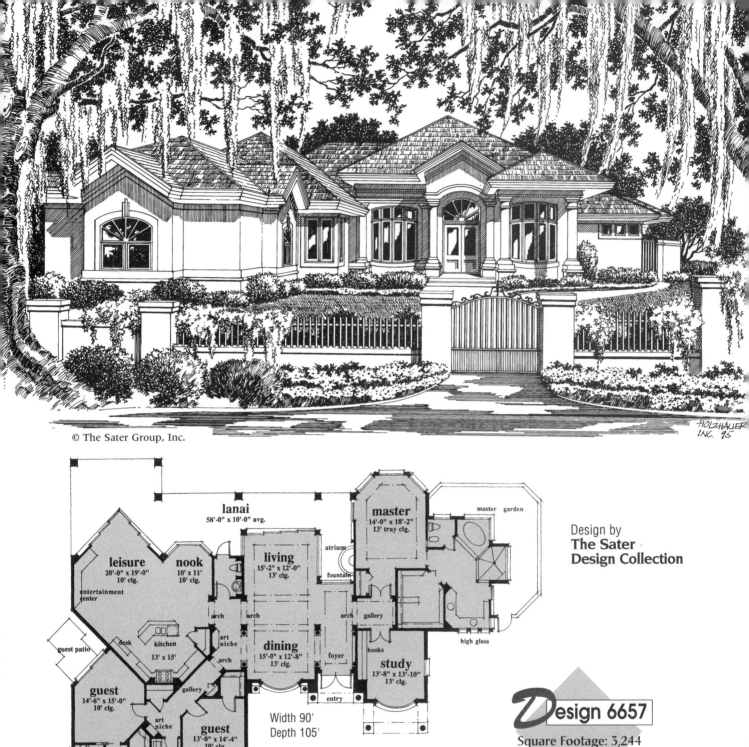

© The Sater Group, Inc.

lanai
58'-0" x 10'-0" avg.

master
14'-0" x 18'-2"
13' tray clg.

master garden

Design by
**The Sater
Design Collection**

leisure
20'-0" x 19'-0"
10' clg.

nook
10' x 11'
10' clg.

living
15'-2" x 12'-0"
13' clg.

atrium

fountain

entertainment center

guest patio

desk

kitchen
13' x 15'

art niche

arch

arch

arch

dining
15'-0" x 12'-8"
13' clg.

arch

gallery

foyer

study
13'-8" x 13'-10"
13' clg.

books

high glass

guest
14'-6" x 15'-0"
10' clg.

art niche

gallery

guest
13'-0" x 14'-4"
10' clg.

entry

Width 90'
Depth 105'

garden

util.

Design 6657

Square Footage: 3,244

garage
22'-0" x 32'-0"

© The Sater Group, Inc.

A high, hipped roof and contemporary fanlight windows set the tone for this elegant master plan. The grand foyer opens to the formal dining and living rooms that are set apart with arches, highlighted with art niches and framed with walls of windows. Discreetly removed from the entertaining area is the leisure room, where casual living takes precedence. Featuring a gourmet kitchen, breakfast nook and leisure room with built-in entertainment center, this area has full view and access to the lanai. Secondary bedrooms are privately situated through a gallery hall and both have private baths and walk-in closets. The master wing is preceded with a gallery hall and houses a full study and master suite with a private garden. An oversized closet and spa-style bath complete this luxurious retreat.

188

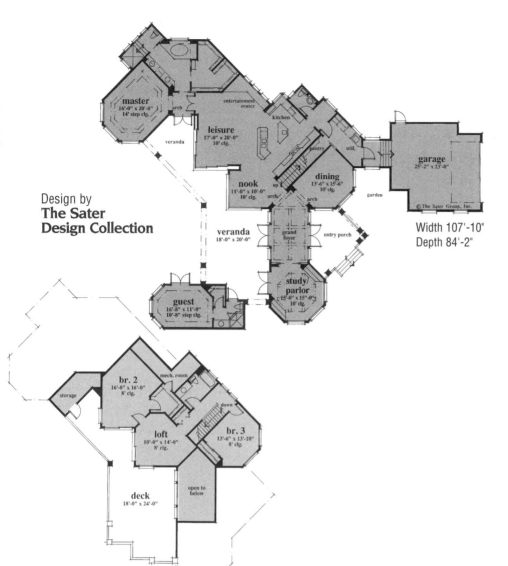

master
16'-0" x 20'-0"
14' step clg.

veranda

arch

leisure
17'-0" x 20'-0"
10' clg.

entertainment center

kitchen

pantry

util.

garage
25'-2" x 23'-0"

nook
11'-0" x 10'-0"
10' clg.

up

arch

dining
13'-6" x 15'-6"
10' clg.

garden

© The Sater Group, Inc.

Design by
**The Sater
Design Collection**

veranda
18'-0" x 20'-0"

grand foyer

entry porch

Width 107'-10"
Depth 84'-2"

study/parlor
15'-0" x 15'-0"
10' clg.

guest
16'-8" x 11'-0"
10'-8" step clg.

storage

br. 2
16'-0" x 16'-0"
8' clg.

mech. room

down

loft
10'-0" x 14'-0"
8' clg.

br. 3
13'-6" x 13'-10"
8' clg.

deck
18'-0" x 24'-0"

open to below

Design 6668

**First Floor: 2,397 square feet
Second Floor: 887 square feet
Guest suite: 291 square feet
Total: 3,575 square feet**

This stunning home is a gracious representation of the owner's own hospitality, from the elegant receiving rooms to the quaint guest quarters. Enter the grand foyer that opens straight through onto the expansive veranda, and proceed to the left to the parlor, and to the right into the formal dining room. The casual area centers around the oversized, gourmet kitchen. A breakfast nook offers a casual place to dine while the leisure room with built-in entertainment center is the perfect family gathering place. The master suite is secluded at the rear of the plan and is fashioned with veranda doors, detailed ceiling, spa-style bath and a huge, walk-in closet. At the top of the stairs, a loft open to the grand foyer gives access to the deck. Two large family bedrooms share a full hall bath. Joined to the main house by the veranda is a lovely guest suite.

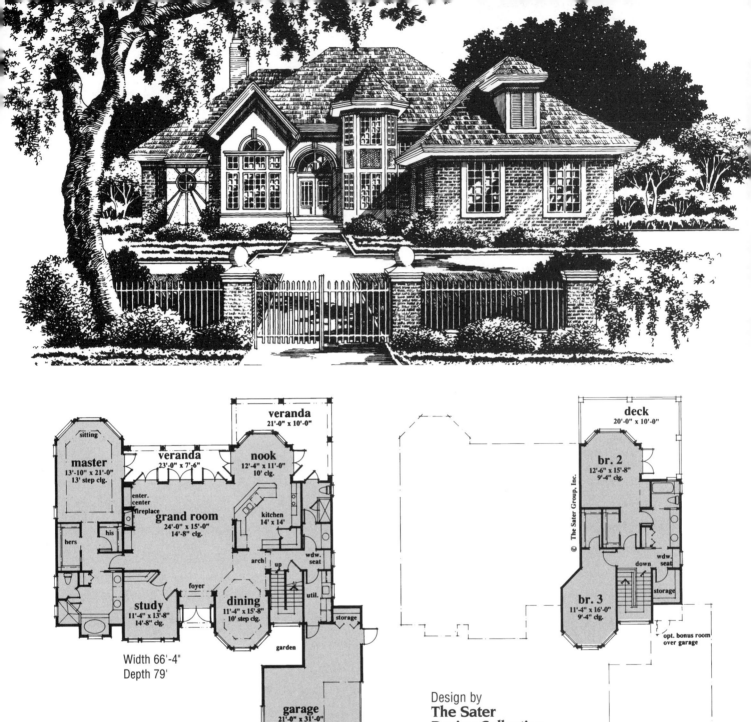

veranda
21'-0" x 10'-0"

veranda
23'-0" x 7'-6"

nook
12'-4" x 11'-0"
10' clg.

master
13'-10" x 21'-0"
13' step clg.

sitting

enter.
center
fireplace

his

hers

grand room
24'-0" x 15'-0"
14'-8" clg.

kitchen
14' x 14'

arch

up

wdw.
seat

study
11'-4" x 13'-8"
14'-8" clg.

foyer

dining
11'-4" x 15'-8"
10' step clg.

util.

storage

garden

Width 66'-4"
Depth 79'

garage
21'-0" x 31'-0"

deck
20'-0" x 10'-0"

br. 2
12'-6" x 15'-8"
9'-4" clg.

down

wdw.
seat

storage

br. 3
11'-4" x 16'-0"
9'-4" clg.

opt. bonus room
over garage

© The Sater Group, Inc.

Design by
**The Sater
Design Collection**

Design 6652

First Floor: 2,181 square feet
Second Floor: 710 square feet
Total: 2,891 square feet

An arched, covered porch presents fine double doors leading to a spacious foyer in this decidedly European home. A two-story tower contains an elegant formal dining room on the first floor and a spacious bedroom on the second floor. The grand room is aptly named with a fireplace, a built-in entertainment center, three sets of doors opening onto the veranda. A large kitchen is ready to please the gourmet of the family with a big walk-in pantry and a sunny, bay-windowed eating nook. The secluded master suite is luxury in itself. A bay-windowed sitting area, access to the rear veranda, His and Hers walk-in closets and a lavish bath are all set to pamper you. Upstairs, two bedrooms, both with walk-in closets, share a full hall bath with twin vanities. Please specify basement or slab foundation when ordering.

MASTER
14/2 X 16/0
(13' CLG)

SPA

FAMILY RM.
17/6 X 16/0
TWO STORY

NOOK
10/8 X 13/4
(9' CLG)

SHELVES SHELVES

STORAGE

DINING
12/2 X 11/10

UP

PANTRY DESK

15/8 X 17/0 +/-

REF.

D.W.

DEN
12/0 X 11/4
(11'-4" CLG)

LIVING
14/0 X 15/6
TWO STORY

GARAGE
32/0 X 25/4

Width 84'-9"
Depth 76'-2"

OPTIONAL
BR. 4
OR
ATTIC
STORAGE

FAMILY RM.
BELOW

BR. 2
11/10 X 13/4

SHELVES SHELVES

LINEN

DN.

NICHE

BR. 3
11/6 X 13/0 +/-

FOYER
BELOW

LIVING RM.
BELOW

BONUS RM.
32/0 X 12/4 +/-

Design 9498

First Floor: 2,270 square feet
Second Floor: 788 square feet
Total: 3,058 square feet

This spectacular plan offers a recessed entry, double rows of multi-pane windows and two dormers over the three-car garage. On the inside, formal living and dining areas reside to the right of the foyer and are designated by stately columns. A private den opens through double French doors from the foyer. The family room with an inviting fireplace soars a full two stories and is overlooked by an upstairs loft. The oversized kitchen has a cooktop island and a breakfast nook that is open to the family room. The master suite is privately located on the first floor through double French doors. Two additional bedrooms share a private bath, and another bath is just down the hall from the large bonus room over the garage.

Design by
**Alan Mascord
Design Associates, Inc.**

Design 7805

First Floor: 1,888 square feet
Second Floor: 1,374 square feet
Total: 3,262 square feet

This gracious Colonial home speaks of a more gracious era with the first step up its lovely columned porch. A formal living room with a bay window detail and cozy fireplace joins the formal dining room with pairs of stately columns. Stra-tegically located between formal and casual living areas is the gourmet kitchen with a uniquely angled cooktop island and breakfast area. The two-story great room is appointed with a lofty fireplace, a media corner and a rear staircase. Upstairs, tray ceilings grace the master suite and lush bath with a fireplace highlighting the bedroom. Two additional bedrooms and a full bath complete the sleeping quarters. This house is designed with a basement foundation.

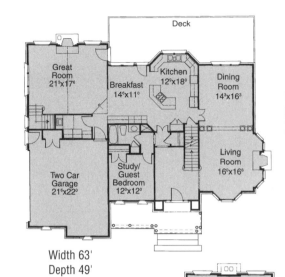

Width 63'
Depth 49'

Design by
**Stephen Fuller/
Design Traditions**

Design 7814

First Floor: 1,621 square feet
Second Floor: 1,766 square feet
Total: 3,387 square feet

Design by
**Stephen Fuller/
Design Traditions**

An All-American charm springs from the true Colonial style of this distinguished home. Formal living areas are set off from the entrance foyer with pairs of columns. Double French doors partition the casual region of the home, headlined with the comfortable family room and its lovely fireplace. The oversized kitchen features a cooktop island and a work counter that's open to the breakfast and family rooms. A guest room is located behind the kitchen area, making it a perfect maid's or nurse's room. The master suite has a private study, fireplace and an amenity-laden bath with extended walk-in closet. Two additional bedrooms share a private, compartmented bath. This home is designed with a basement foundation.

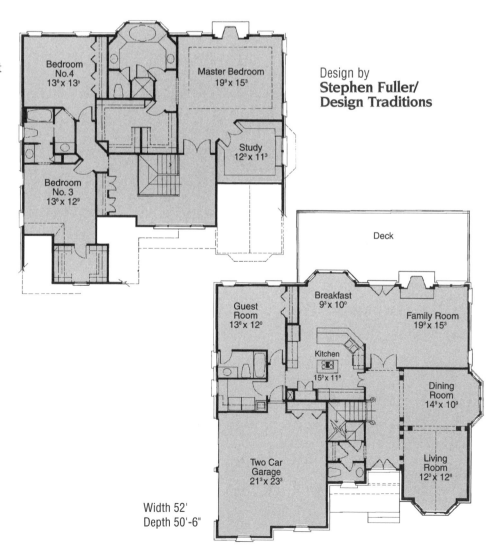

Bedroom No.4
13⁶ x 13⁰

Master Bedroom
19⁹ x 15³

Study
12³ x 11³

Bedroom No. 3
13⁶ x 12⁹

Deck

Guest Room
13⁶ x 12⁰

Breakfast
9³ x 10⁰

Family Room
19⁹ x 15³

Kitchen
15⁰ x 11⁹

Dining Room
14⁹ x 10⁹

Two Car Garage
21³ x 23³

Living Room
12³ x 12⁶

Width 52'
Depth 50'-6"

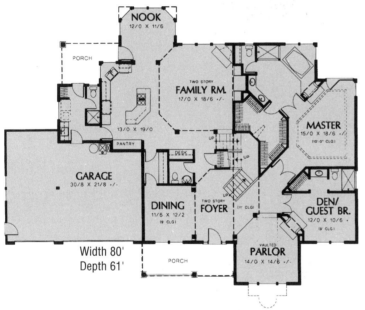

NOOK
12/0 X 11/6

PORCH

TWO STORY
FAMILY RM.
17/0 X 18/6 +/-

13/0 X 19/0

PANTRY

MASTER
15/0 X 18/6 +/-
(10'-0" CLG)

GARAGE
30/8 X 21/8 +/-

DESK

DINING
11/6 X 12/2
(9' CLG)

TWO STORY
FOYER
(11' CLG)

UP

DEN/
GUEST BR.
12/0 X 10/6
(9' CLG)

Width 80'
Depth 61'

PORCH

VAULTED
PARLOR
14/0 X 14/6 +/-

Design by
Alan Mascord
Design Associates, Inc.

BR. 2
12/6 X 11/0
(9' CLG)

FAMILY RM.
BELOW

ATTIC
STORAGE

BONUS RM.
18/6 X 10/0 +/-

LINEN

DN

DN

FOYER
BELOW

BR. 3
11/2 X 12/0

Design 7403

First Floor: 2,642 square feet
Second Floor: 603 square feet
Total: 3,245 square feet
Bonus: 255 square feet

This lovely country estate is the perfect blend of refinement and home-spun comfort. It's more than a farm-house with the dramatic split staircase and decidedly elegant columns that frame the dining room, parlor and family room. Casual living areas are comfortably situated in the rear of the home. The open kitchen with a cook-top island has welcome interaction with the family room and casual dining area. The master suite is set off the living area for privacy with a den serving as a buffer. The master bath is pure fantasy with a full size spa-tub, dressing area and an expanded walk-in closet. Upstairs, two additional bedrooms and a bonus room share a compartmented hall bath.

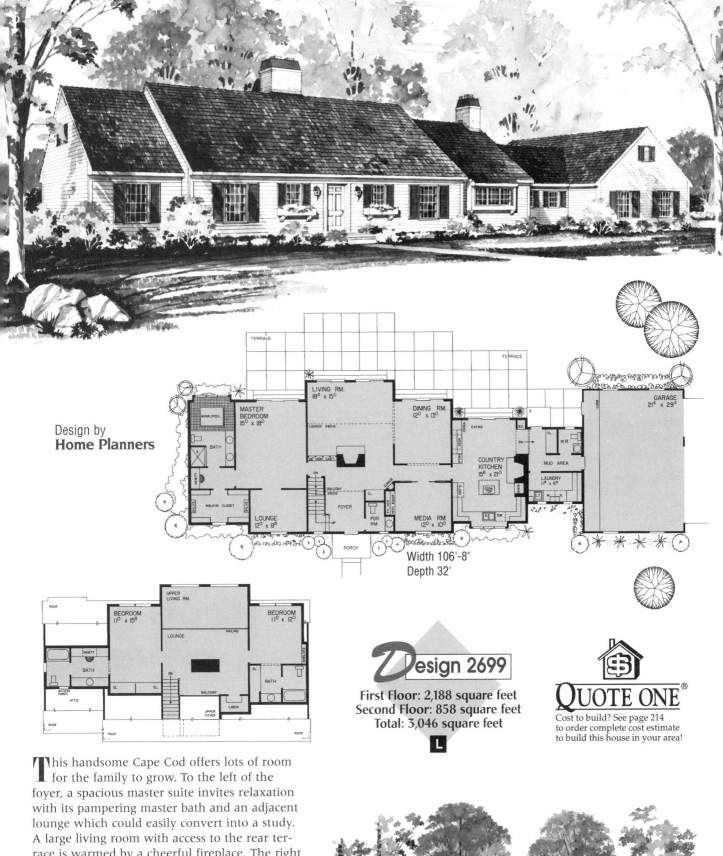

Design by
Home Planners

TERRACE

TERRACE

WHIRLPOOL

MASTER BEDROOM
15⁰ x 18⁰

LIVING RM.
18⁴ x 15⁰

LOUNGE ABOVE

36" HIGH CAB'T

DINING RM.
12⁰ x 13⁰

GARAGE
21⁴ x 29⁴

EATING

COUNTRY KITCHEN
15⁸ x 21⁰

COOK TOP

MUD AREA

LAUNDRY
11⁸ x 6⁰

BATH

VANITY

SHLVS.

WALK-IN CLOSET

SHLVS.

DN

BALCONY ABOVE

CL.

FOYER

POR. RM.

TV/VCR
HI-FI EQUP.

MEDIA RM.
12⁰ x 10⁰

LOUNGE
12⁰ x 8⁸

UP

PORCH

Width 106'-8"
Depth 32'

ROOF

BEDROOM
11⁰ x 15⁸

UPPER LIVING RM.

BEDROOM
11⁰ x 12⁰

VANITY

LOUNGE

RAILING

BATH

DN

CL.

CL.

BALCONY

BATH

SHELVES

ACCESS PANEL

ATTIC

UPPER FOYER

LINEN

ROOF

ROOF

ROOF

Design 2699

First Floor: 2,188 square feet
Second Floor: 858 square feet
Total: 3,046 square feet

L

QUOTE ONE®

Cost to build? See page 214
to order complete cost estimate
to build this house in your area!

This handsome Cape Cod offers lots of room for the family to grow. To the left of the foyer, a spacious master suite invites relaxation with its pampering master bath and an adjacent lounge which could easily convert into a study. A large living room with access to the rear terrace is warmed by a cheerful fireplace. The right side of the plan is comprised of a media room, a dining room and a country kitchen that is a cook's delight. A conveniently located mud room and laundry room complete the first floor. The second floor contains two secondary bedrooms, each with their own full baths, and a spacious lounge.

Design 9969

Square Footage: 2,987

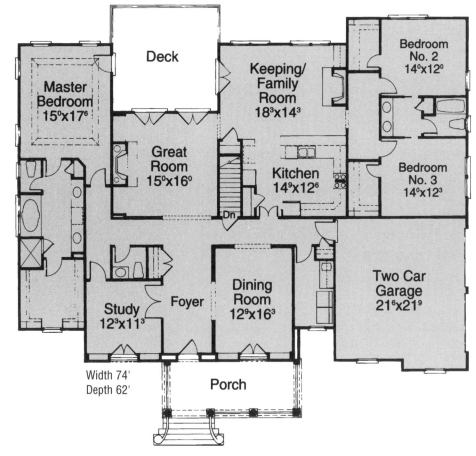

R eaching back through the centuries for its inspiration, this home reflects the grandeur that was ancient Rome...as it looked to newly independent Americans in the 1700's. The entry portico provides a classic twist: the balustrade that would have marched across the roof line of a typical Revival home trims to form the balcony outside the French doors of the study. Inside, the foyer opens on the left to a quiet study, on the right to the formal dining room, and straight ahead to a welcoming great room warmed by a fireplace. The left wing is given over to a private master suite with a master bath that offers the ultimate in luxury and a large walk-in closet. On the right side of the house, two additional bedrooms share a full bath. Separating the sleeping wings is the kitchen, with its nearby keeping room/family room. This home is designed with a basement foundation.

Deck

Master Bedroom 15⁰x17⁶

Keeping/Family Room 18³x14³

Bedroom No. 2 14⁰x12⁰

Great Room 15⁰x16⁰

Kitchen 14⁹x12⁶

Bedroom No. 3 14⁰x12³

Dn

Study 12³x11³

Foyer

Dining Room 12⁹x16³

Two Car Garage 21⁶x21⁹

Width 74'
Depth 62'

Porch

Design by
**Stephen Fuller/
Design Traditions**

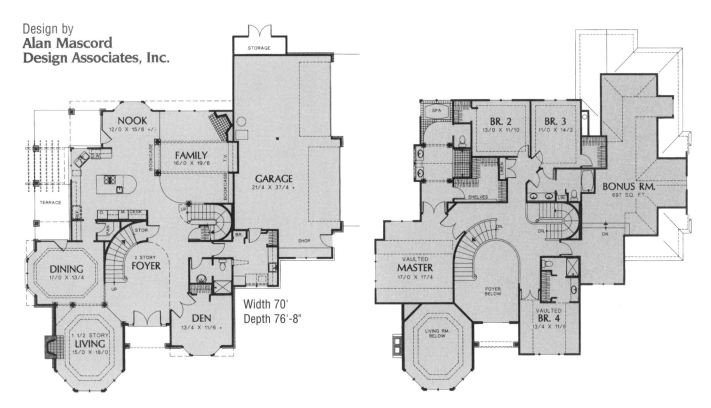

Design by
**Alan Mascord
Design Associates, Inc.**

**Width 70'
Depth 76'-8"**

Design 9596

**First Floor: 2,190 square feet
Second Floor: 1,680 square feet
Total: 3,870 square feet
Bonus Room: 697 square feet**

This lovely Tudor home displays a formal flair, yet reflects the charm and comfort of an English country house. A dramatic entry with a graceful curved staircase is a fitting introduction to the formal dining and living rooms. Here, the mood is set with a detailed tray ceiling and fireplace, and spectacular transom windows. The large island kitchen serves the formal and informal dining areas with equal ease. A second fireplace adds charm to the family room which is further accented with built-in bookcases and a media center. The master suite is fashioned for luxurious relaxation with a vaulted ceiling and an expanded bath. Three additional bedrooms and two full baths complete the upstairs in addition to a large bonus room over the garage.

Photo by Dave Rowland

Design by
Home Planners

There is much more to this design than meets the eye. While it may look like a modest 1½-story plan, bonus recreation and hobby space in the walk-out basement adds almost 1,000 square feet. The first floor features the main living area of the home. The large gathering room shares a two-way fireplace with the media room and has open views to the formal dining room.

The comfortable kitchen has a handy snack bar opening to the breakfast room. The master bedroom opens to both the foyer and to the media room and is appointed with a walk-in closet and a compartmented bath. Two family bedrooms on the second floor are connected by a balcony that overlooks the gathering room below.

Design 3366

Main Level: 1,638 square feet
Upper Level: 650 square feet
Lower Level: 934 square feet
Total: 3,222 square feet

L

Width 57'
Depth 51'-8"

QUOTE ONE®

Cost to build? See page 214 to order complete cost estimate to build this house in your area!

Outside Possibilities

Garages, Potting Sheds, and More

As you consider building and moving into a new home with a more modest square footage, questions of where to find storage space and recreation areas will arise. While you may have relied upon a somewhat cramped spare bedroom to house your model train or sewing machine, now you can plan for your hobbies and outside interests in a space designed with your tastes in mind.

Our great combination garages (pages 201-205) work overtime to meet your specific needs. Not only a stylish shelter for the family fleet, these structures may also house: a fully-equipped workshop that will take any project start to finish; a delightfully posh pool house that's sure to keep the patio party going; a smart studio or one-bedroom apartment—a perfect compromise for a college bound student or a home office.

When younger relatives come to visit, they'll love the special "kids only" playhouse (Design R126, page 206) just as much as you will appreciate the sunny solitude of the garden cottage on page 207 (Design G109). Wherever your interests or aspirations take you, you're sure to find the perfect auxiliary structure to serve your needs—perhaps even a stable for the trusty steed you'll gallop into the sunset.

Design G294

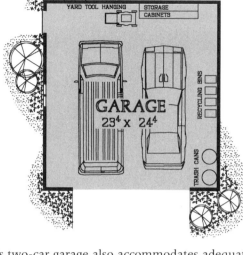

Design G295

This two-car garage also accommodates adequate storage areas for tools, yard and gardening equipment, and recycling and trash bins. A 16'x7' garage door provides safe passage for vehicles, and an exterior door at the back of the side wall offers easy access to the storage areas. Four different exterior elevations are available ensuring a perfect blend of style with the main house structure.

Design G297

Width 24'
Depth 25'

Design by
Home Planners

Design G296

Design G282

Design G283

Design G284

Design G285

Width 36'
Depth 25'

Design by
Home Planners

This well-thought-out floor plan is the perfect solution for a home office addition. A single 16'x7' garage door provides shelter for two cars, plus out-of-sight storage areas for yard and garden equipment, garbage cans, and recycling bins. A four-column porch provides entry to the compact apartment or office area. A mini-kitchen (or make this extra work area) and a bath with a shower provide added convenience. The bedroom at the back could also be used for additional storage. Four different exterior elevations are available.

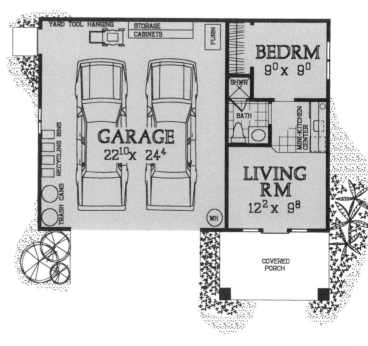

Behind what looks like another garage door is just what you've always wanted—a fully equipped workshop. Accessed through an 8'x7' garage door, or from an interior door within the garage itself, is 300 square feet of workshop area. It contains plenty of room for your favorite power tools, work table, storage cabinets, counter space and overhead racks for lumber. On the garage side of this multi-use structure is a two-car garage with a 16'x7' door. It allows space for yard and garden equipment, plus a convenient area for recycling bins and garbage cans. Four different exterior elevations are available.

Design G279

Width 36'
Depth 25'

Design by
Home Planners

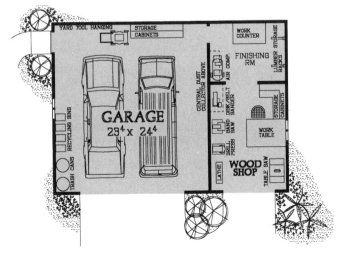

Design G280

Design G281

Design G278

Design G274

Design G275

Design G276

Design by
Home Planners

Design G277

Width 36'
Depth 25'

Locate this roomy structure near the pool and provide security for two cars, plus a spacious pool house with a changing room and an outdoor patio/lounge area shaded by a generous room extension. The garage area provides plenty of space to store yard and garden equipment and other necessities like garbage cans and recycling bins. Natural light enters the interior of the changing area through two skylights over the bath and shower area. Built-in benches and countertops, plus storage and linen closets, offer lots of convenience. The kitchenette is cooled by a ceiling fan and French doors leading to the patio. Four different exterior elevations are available.

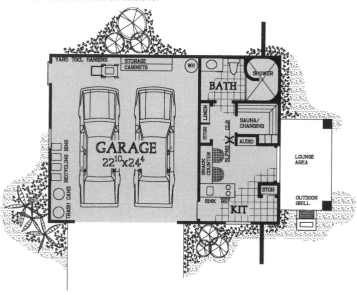

Design G206

Width 34'-4"
Depth 24'

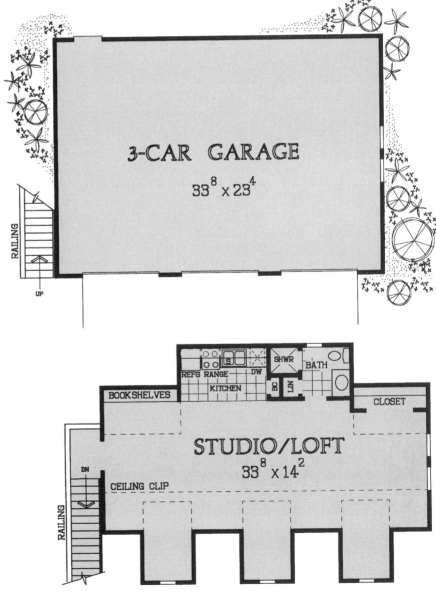

3-CAR GARAGE
33^8 x 23^4

BOOKSHELVES   REFG RANGE   KITCHEN   DW   SHWR   BATH   CLOSET

STUDIO/LOFT
33^8 x 14^2

CEILING CLIP

RAILING   DN

Attractive and functional, this impressive structure has room for three cars in the garage section and 670 square feet of living area—complete with kitchen, bathroom, bookshelves and closet—to use as a studio or a hideaway loft for guests. The treatment of the steeply pitched gable roof is repeated in three gabled dormers, each with tall narrow windows framed with shutters. Access to the second-floor loft area is by a railed exterior stairway which leads to a small landing with its own covered roof supported by wooden columns. The clipped corners of the trim around each of the three car bays lend country charm. Four wrought-iron coach lights complete the effect.

Design by
Home Planners

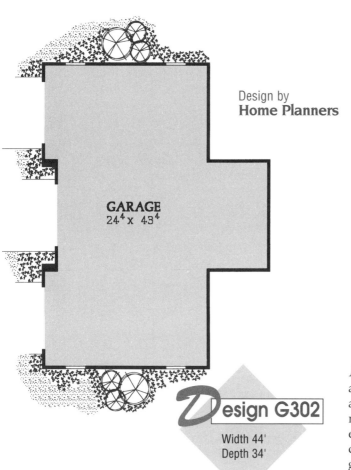

Design by
Home Planners

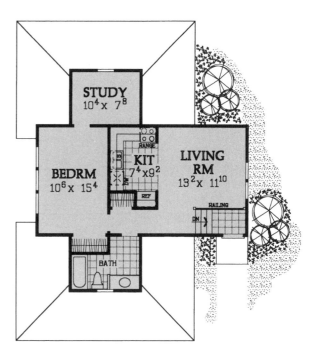

STUDY
10⁴ x 7⁸

BEDRM
10⁶ x 15⁴

KIT
7⁴ x 9²

LIVING
RM
13² x 11¹⁰

BATH

RANGE

REF

RAILING

DN

Design G302

Width 44'
Depth 34'

Almost too grand to be a mere garage, this design provides enough space for three vehicles, plus a handy work area at the garage level. The second-floor apartment weighs in at a sizable 1,241 square feet and allows for a large living room, a serviceable kitchen, a bedroom with a full bath and even a study. Use it for frequent guests, a mother-in-law, college student or even as a home office. The exterior of this garage fits nicely with almost any style of home, but will work especially well with European, Southwestern, or Mediterranean designs.

GARAGE
24⁴ x 43⁴

Design by
Home Planners

Design R126

Width 16'
Depth 22'

Lucky are the kids who stake claim to this private retreat! The overall size of 352 square feet provides plenty of space for study, TV or just hangin' out. Special features include a raised, carpeted platform in the TV lounge; a comfy window seat for reading, a separate niche for electronic games; and a unique, brightly painted graffiti wall in the entryway. It's wired for sound, and the bright colors and windows in a variety of shapes mark this specially designed, free-standing building as kid territory.

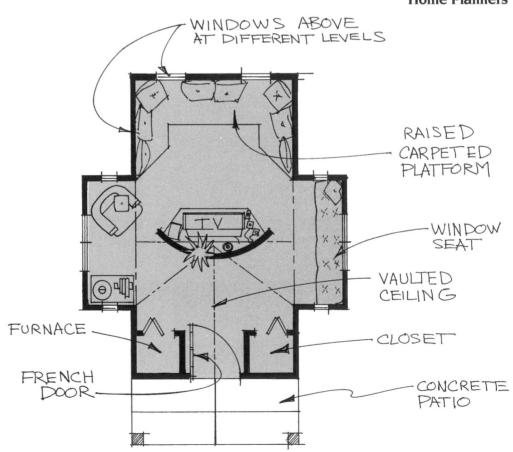

WINDOWS ABOVE
AT DIFFERENT LEVELS

RAISED
CARPETED
PLATFORM

WINDOW
SEAT

VAULTED
CEILING

CLOSET

CONCRETE
PATIO

FURNACE

FRENCH
DOOR

TV

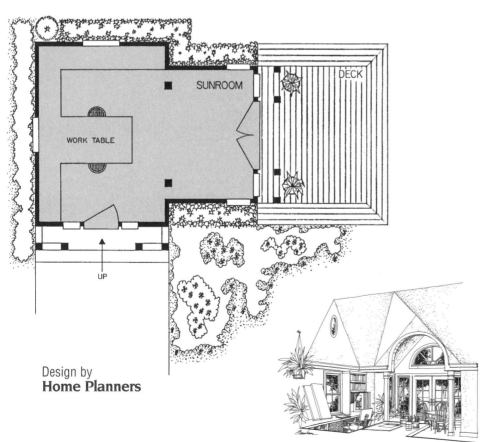

WORK TABLE

SUNROOM

DECK

UP

Design by
Home Planners

Design G109

Width 20'
Depth 16'

Sunshine and fresh air pour into all 320 square feet of this functional garden cottage through the arched roofline above the support columns and the fanlights above the French doors and tall double-hung windows. Enjoy the sunshine outside on the deck, or inside in the bright and cheerful sunroom. Work, if you must, at a built-in table with an ample counter stretching out on either side. This is the perfect place to spread out all the pieces of a sewing or craft project or to exercise an artistic talent at the easel.

207

Design G247

Width 12'
Depth 6'

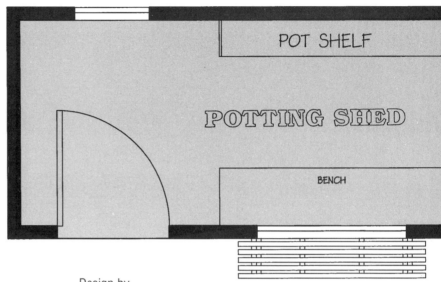

POT SHELF

POTTING SHED

BENCH

Design by
Home Planners

Designed to blend into the garden surrounding, this cozy little building keeps all your garden tools and supplies at your fingertips. You can vary the materials to create the appearance best suited to your site. This 72 square foot structure is large enough to accommodate a potting bench, shelves and an area for garden tools. The window above the potting bench allows ample light, but electricity could be added easily. Although the house is designed to be built on a concrete slab, you could use treated lumber for the floor joists, and set it right on the ground. To convert this shed design to a playhouse, simply change the window shelf into a planter and add a step with a handrail at the door.

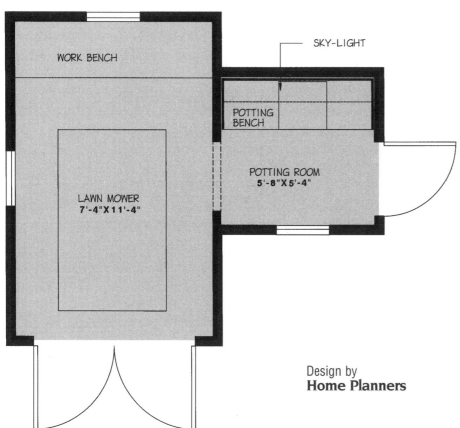

WORK BENCH

SKY-LIGHT

POTTING
BENCH

POTTING ROOM
5'-8" X 5'-4"

LAWN MOWER
7'-4" X 11'-4"

Design by
Home Planners

Design G222

Width 14'
Depth 12'

Open the double doors of this multi-purpose structure and it's a mini-garage for garden tools. Enter by the single door, and it's a potting shed. The tool-shed section is large enough to house the largest lawn tractor, with room to spare for other garden equipment such as shovels, rakes, lawn trimmers and hoses. With windows on all sides and a skylight above the potting bench, the interior has plenty of natural light—the addition of electrical wiring would make this structure even more practical. The design is shown in a Victorian style, but can be modified to match any gable-roof home design. Total of 168 square feet

Design by
Home Planners

Design G293

Width 24'
Depth 24'

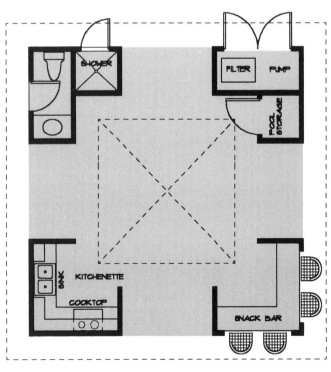

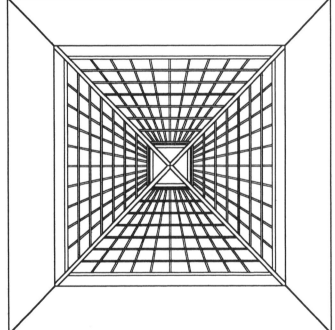

ROOF PLAN

Entertain the possibilities for pool-side parties with this smart, multi-functional ramada. Four corner units are united by open-air walkways and are almost literally tied together by a trellis roof. Pull up a chair to the outside bar in one corner for a refreshing drink or snack. Across the walkway is an efficiency kitchenette to make the goodies. In the next corner is a restroom and a shower, each with a separate entrance. The final corner hides all the pool essentials with double doors leading to the filter and pump room and a separate storage room for other pool equipment and toys. Total of 516 square feet under ramada.

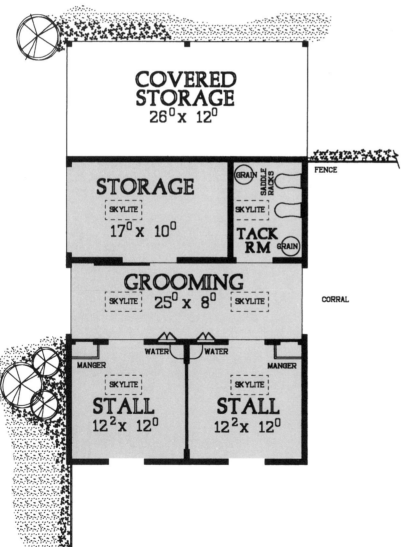

COVERED
STORAGE
26⁰ x 12⁰

STORAGE
SKYLITE
17⁰ x 10⁰

GRAIN

SADDLE RACKS

SKYLITE

TACK RM

GRAIN

FENCE

GROOMING
SKYLITE 25⁰ x 8⁰ SKYLITE

CORRAL

WATER   WATER

MANGER   MANGER

SKYLITE   SKYLITE

STALL
12²x 12⁰

STALL
12²x 12⁰

Design G291

Width 26'
Depth 44'

With 1,144 square feet under roof, this expanded structure will be home to your prize stock. Outside, a 26' x 12' covered area with a concrete floor provides storage and parking for tractors and other equipment. Inside, six sky-lights illuminate the interior of three major areas: 1) two 12'-2" x 12' stalls with dirt floors, each with built-in feed-ers, fresh-water hook-ups and Dutch doors leading to an outside pen; 2) a covered grooming area with a slightly sloped, grooved concrete flooring and maximum access though double doors at each end; and 3) a 17' x 10' storage area with concrete floors for feed and a 7'-6" x 10' secured tack room with built-in saddle racks.

Design by
Home Planners

When You're Ready To Order . . .

Let Us Show You Our Home Blueprint Package.

Building a home? Planning a home? Our Blueprint Package has nearly everything you need to get the job done right, whether you're working on your own or with help from an architect, designer, builder or subcontractors. Each Blueprint Package is the result of many hours of work by licensed architects or professional designers.

QUALITY

Hundreds of hours of painstaking effort have gone into the development of your blueprint set. Each home has been quality-checked by professionals to insure accuracy and buildability.

VALUE

Because we sell in volume, you can buy professional-quality blueprints at a fraction of their development cost. With our plans, your dream home design costs only a few hundred dollars, not the thousands of dollars that custom architects charge.

SERVICE

Once you've chosen your favorite home plan, you'll receive fast, efficient service whether you choose to mail or fax your order to us or call us toll free at 1-800-521-6797.

SATISFACTION

Over 50 years of service to satisfied home plan buyers provide us unparalleled experience and knowledge in producing quality blueprints. What this means to you is satisfaction with our product and performance.

ORDER TOLL FREE 1-800-521-6797

After you've looked over our Blueprint Package and Important Extras on the following pages, simply mail the order form on page 221 or call toll free on our Blueprint Hotline: 1-800-521-6797. We're ready and eager to serve you.

. . . .

Each set of blueprints is an interrelated collection of detail sheets which includes components such as floor plans, interior and exterior elevations, dimensions, cross-sections, diagrams and notations. These sheets show exactly how your house is to be built.

Among the sheets included may be:

Frontal Sheet
This artist's sketch of the exterior of the house gives you an idea of how the house will look when built and landscaped. Large ink-line floor plans show all levels of the house and provide an overview of your new home's livability, as well as a handy reference for deciding on furniture placement.

Foundation Plan
This sheet shows the foundation layout includ-

SAMPLE PACKAGE

ing support walls, excavated and unexcavated areas, if any, and foundation notes. If slab construction rather than basement, the plan shows footings and details for a monolithic slab. This page, or another in the set, may include a sample plot plan for locating your house on a building site.

Detailed Floor Plans

These plans show the layout of each floor of the house. Rooms and interior spaces are carefully dimensioned and keys are given for cross-section details provided later in the plans. The positions of electrical outlets and switches are shown.

House Cross-Sections

Large-scale views show sections or cut-aways of the foundation, interior walls, exterior walls, floors, stairways and roof details. Additional cross-sections may show important changes in floor, ceiling or roof heights or the relationship of one level to another. Extremely valuable for construction, these sections show exactly how the various parts of the house fit together.

Interior Elevations

Many of our drawings show the design and placement of kitchen and bathroom cabinets, laundry areas, fireplaces, bookcases and other built-ins. Little "extras," such as mantelpiece and wainscoting drawings, plus moulding sections, provide details that give your home that custom touch.

Exterior Elevations

These drawings show the front, rear and sides of your house and give necessary notes on exterior materials and finishes. Particular attention is given to cornice detail, brick and stone accents or other finish items that make your home unique.

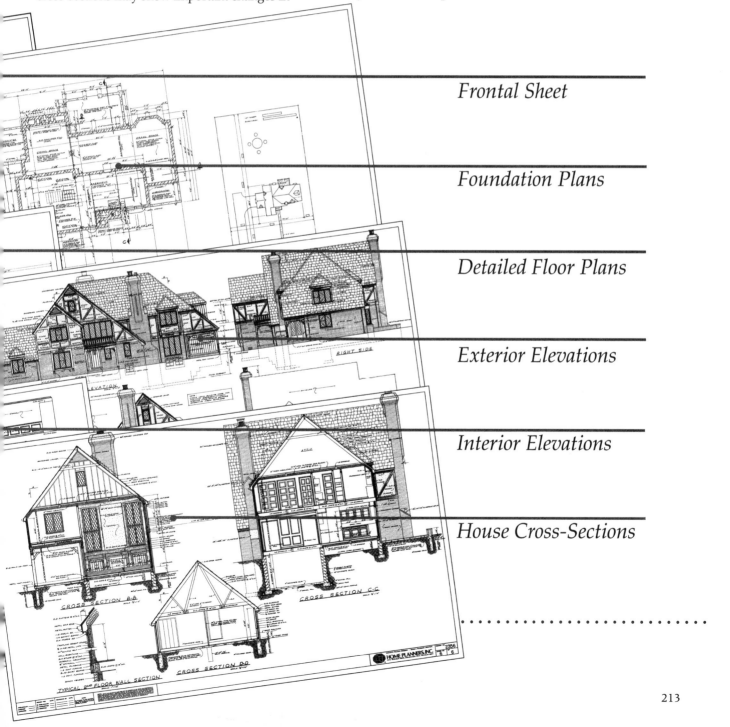

Frontal Sheet

Foundation Plans

Detailed Floor Plans

Exterior Elevations

Interior Elevations

House Cross-Sections

*I*ntroducing nine important planning and construction aids

NEW

CUSTOM ENGINEERING

Our Custom Engineering Service Package provides an engineering seal for the structural elements of any Home Planners plan. This new Package provides complete calculations (except foundation engineering) from a registered professional, and offers many options invaluable to anyone planning to build. The Package includes: Structural framing plans for each horizontal framing area; Individual, certified truss designs; Specifications for all framing members; Calculation sheets detailing engineering problems and solutions concerning shear, bending, and deflections for all key framing members; Structural details for all key situations; Hanger and special connections specifications; Load and geometry information that may be used by a foundation design engineer and a Registered Professional Engineer's Seal for all of the above services. Home Planners also offers 3 Optional Engineering Services: Lateral load calculations and specifications for both wind and seismic considerations; Secondary Framing information for roofs, floors and walls; Light-gauge steel framing, providing details and cost comparisons for steel and wood.

SPECIFICATION OUTLINE

This valuable 16-page document is critical to building your house correctly. Designed to be filled in by you or your builder, this book lists 166 stages or items crucial to the building process. It provides a comprehensive review of the construction process and helps in making choices of materials. When combined with the blueprints, a signed contract, and a schedule, it becomes a legal document and record for the building of your home.

MATERIALS LIST

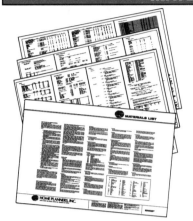

(Note: Because of the diversity of local building codes, our Materials List does not include mechanical materials.)

For many of the designs in our portfolio, we offer a customized materials take-off that is invaluable in planning and estimating the cost of your new home. This Materials List outlines the quantity, type and size of materials needed to build your house (with the exception of mechanical system items). Included are framing lumber, windows and doors, kitchen and bath cabinetry, rough and finish hardware, and much more. This handy list helps you or your builder cost out materials and serves as a reference sheet when you're compiling bids.

QUOTE ONE®

Summary Cost Report / Materials Cost Report

A new service for estimating the cost of building select designs, the Quote One® system is available in two separate stages: The Summary Cost Report and the Materials Cost Report.

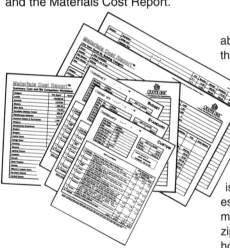

The Summary Cost Report is the first stage in the package and shows the total cost per square foot for your chosen home in your zip-code area and then breaks that cost down into ten categories showing the costs for building materials, labor and installation. The total cost for the report (which includes three grades: Budget, Standard and Custom) is just $19.95 for one home, and additionals are only $14.95. These reports allow you to evaluate your building budget and compare the costs of building a variety of homes in your area.

Make even more informed decisions about your home-building project with the second phase of our package, our Materials Cost Report. This tool is invaluable in planning and estimating the cost of your new home. The material and installation (labor and equipment) cost is shown for each of over 1,000 line items provided in the Materials List (Standard grade) which is included when you purchase this estimating tool. It allows you to determine building costs for your specific zip-code area and for your chosen home design. Space is allowed for additional estimates from contractors and subcontractors, such as for mechanical materials, which are not included in our packages. This invaluable tool is available for a price of $110 ($120 for a Schedule E plan) which includes a Materials List.

To order these invaluable reports, use the order form on page 221 or call 1-800-521-6797.

CONSTRUCTION INFORMATION

If you want to know more about techniques—and deal more confidently with subcontractors we offer these useful sheets. Each set is an excellent tool that will add to your understanding of these technical subjects.

Plan-A-Home®

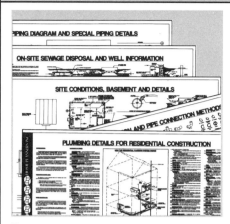

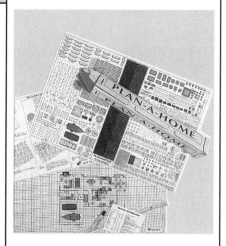

PLUMBING

The Blueprint Package includes locations for all the plumbing fixtures in your new house, including sinks, lavatories, tubs, showers, toilets, laundry trays and water heaters. However, if you want to know more about the complete plumbing system, these 24x36-inch detail sheets will prove very useful. Prepared to meet requirements of the National Plumbing Code, these six fact-filled sheets give general information on pipe schedules, fittings, sump-pump details, water-softener hookups, septic system details and much more. Color-coded sheets include a glossary of terms.

ELECTRICAL

The locations for every electrical switch, plug and outlet are shown in your Blueprint Package. However, these Electrical Details go further to take the mystery out of household electrical systems. Prepared to meet requirements of the National Electrical Code, these comprehensive 24x36-inch drawings come packed with helpful information, including wire sizing, switch-installation schematics, cable-routing details, appliance wattage, door-bell hook-ups, typical service panel circuitry and much more. Six sheets are bound together and color-coded for easy reference. A glossary of terms is also included.

Plan-A-Home® is an easy-to-use tool that helps you design a new home, arrange furniture in a new or existing home, or plan a remodeling project. Each package contains:

- **More than 700 reusable peel-off planning symbols** on a self-stick vinyl sheet, including walls, windows, doors, all types of furniture, kitchen components, bath fixtures and many more.

- **A reusable, transparent, 1/4-inch scale planning grid** that matches the scale of actual working drawings (1/4-inch equals 1 foot). This grid provides the basis for house layouts of up to 140x92 feet.

- **Tracing paper** and a protective sheet for copying or transferring your completed plan.

- **A felt-tip pen,** with water-soluble ink that wipes away quickly.

Plan-A-Home® lets you lay out areas as large as a 7,500 square foot, six-bedroom, seven-bath house.

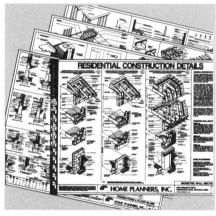

CONSTRUCTION

The Blueprint Package contains everything an experienced builder needs to construct a particular house. However, it doesn't show all the ways that houses can be built, nor does it explain alternate construction methods. To help you understand how your house will be built—and offer additional techniques—this set of drawings depicts the materials and methods used to build foundations, fireplaces, walls, floors and roofs. Where appropriate, the drawings show acceptable alternatives. These six sheets will answer questions for the advanced do-it-yourselfer or home planner.

MECHANICAL

This package contains fundamental principles and useful data that will help you make informed decisions and communicate with subcontractors about heating and cooling systems. The 24x36-inch drawings contain instructions and samples that allow you to make simple load calculations and preliminary sizing and costing analysis. Covered are today's most commonly used systems from heat pumps to solar fuel systems. The package is packed full of illustrations and diagrams to help you visualize components and how they relate to one another.

To Order, Call Toll Free 1-800-521-6797

To add these important extras to your Blueprint Package, simply indicate your choices on the order form on page 221 or call us Toll Free 1-800-521-6797 and we'll tell you more about these exciting products.

▣ *The Deck Blueprint Package*

Many of the homes in this book can be enhanced with a professionally designed Home Planners' Deck Plan. Those home plans highlighted with a ▣ have a matching or corresponding deck plan available which includes a Deck Plan Frontal Sheet, Deck Framing and Floor Plans, Deck Elevations and a Deck Materials List. A Standard Deck Details Package, also available, provides all the how-to information necessary for building *any* deck. Our Complete Deck Building Package contains 1 set of Custom Deck Plans of your choice, plus 1 set of Standard Deck Building Details all for one low price. Our plans and details are carefully prepared in an easy-to-understand format that will guide you through every stage of your deck-building project. This page contains a sampling of 12 of the 25 different Deck layouts to match your favorite house. See page 218 for prices and ordering information.

SPLIT-LEVEL SUN DECK
Deck Plan D100

BI-LEVEL DECK WITH COVERED DINING
Deck Plan D101

WRAP-AROUND FAMILY DECK
Deck Plan D104

DECK FOR DINING AND VIEWS
Deck Plan D107

TREND SETTER DECK
Deck Plan D110

TURN-OF-THE-CENTURY DECK
Deck Plan D111

WEEKEND ENTERTAINER DECK
Deck Plan D112

CENTER-VIEW DECK
Deck Plan D114

KITCHEN-EXTENDER DECK
Deck Plan D115

SPLIT-LEVEL ACTIVITY DECK
Deck Plan D117

TRI-LEVEL DECK WITH GRILL
Deck Plan D119

CONTEMPORARY LEISURE DECK
Deck Plan D120

L The Landscape Blueprint Package

For the homes marked with an L in this book, Home Planners has created a front-yard landscape plan that matches or is complementary in design to the house plan. These comprehensive blueprint packages include a Frontal Sheet, Plan View, Regionalized Plant & Materials List, a sheet on Planting and Maintaining Your Landscape, Zone Maps and Plant Size and Description Guide. These plans will help you achieve professional results, adding value and enjoyment to your property for years to come. Each set of blueprints is a full 18" x 24" in size with clear, complete instructions and easy-to-read type. Six of the forty front yard Landscape Plans to match your favorite house are shown below.

Regional Order Map

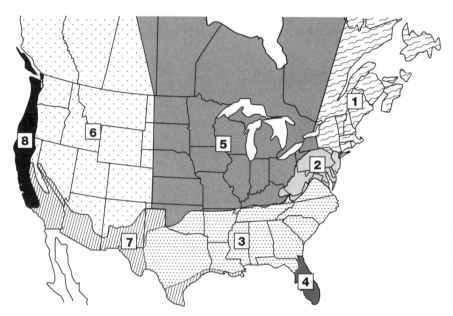

Most of the Landscape Plans shown on these pages are available with a Plant & Materials List adapted by horticultural experts to 8 different regions of the country. Please specify Geographic Region when ordering your plan. See page 218 for prices, ordering information and regional availability.

Region	1	Northeast
Region	2	Mid-Atlantic
Region	3	Deep South
Region	4	Florida & Gulf Coast
Region	5	Midwest
Region	6	Rocky Mountains
Region	7	Southern California & Desert Southwest
Region	8	Northern California & Pacific Northwest

CAPE COD COTTAGE
Landscape Plan L202

GAMBREL-ROOF COLONIAL
Landscape Plan L203

CENTER-HALL COLONIAL
Landscape Plan L204

CLASSIC NEW ENGLAND COLONIAL
Landscape Plan L205

COUNTRY-STYLE FARMHOUSE
Landscape Plan L207

TRADITIONAL SPLIT-LEVEL
Landscape Plan L228

Price Schedule & Plans Index

House Blueprint Price Schedule
(Prices guaranteed through December 31, 1998)

Tier	1-set Study Package	4-set Building Package	8-set Building Package	1-set Reproducible Sepias	Home Customizer® Package
A	$350	$395	$455	$555	$605
B	$390	$435	$495	$615	$665
C	$430	$475	$535	$675	$725
D	$470	$515	$575	$735	$785
E	$590	$635	$695	$795	$845

Prices for 4- or 8-set Building Packages honored only at time of original order.

Additional Identical Blueprints in same order ....$50 per set
Reverse Blueprints (mirror image).................................$50 per set
Specification Outlines ....$10 each
Materials Lists (available only from those designers listed below):
  ▲ Home Planners Designs $50
  † Design Basics Designs $75
  ✳ Alan Mascord Designs $50
  ◆ Donald Gardner Designs $50
  ■ Design Traditions Designs $50
  ● The Sater Design Collection $50
  ✱ Larry Garnett Designs $50

Materials Lists for "E" price plans are an additional $10.

Deck Plans Price Schedule

CUSTOM DECK PLANS

Price Group	Q	R	S
1 Set Custom Plans	$25	$30	$35
Additional identical sets		$10 each	
Reverse sets (mirror image)		$10 each	

STANDARD DECK DETAILS
1 Set Generic Construction Details ....$14.95 each

COMPLETE DECK BUILDING PACKAGE

Price Group	Q	R	S
1 Set Custom Plans, plus 1 Set Standard Deck Details	$35	$40	$45

Landscape Plans Price Schedule

Price Group	X	Y	Z
1 set	$35	$45	$55
3 sets	$50	$60	$70
6 sets	$65	$75	$85

Additional Identical Sets...................................$10 each
Reverse Sets (mirror image)..............................$10 each

Index

To use the Index below, refer to the design number listed in numerical order (a helpful page reference is also given). Note the price index letter and refer to the House Blueprint Price Schedule above for the cost of one, four or eight sets of blueprints or the cost of a reproducible sepia. Additional prices are shown for identical and reverse blueprint sets, as well as a very useful Materials List for some of the plans. Also note in the Index below those plans that have matching or complementary Deck Plans or Landscape Plans. Refer to the schedules above for prices of these plans. All Home Planners' plans can be customized with Home Planners' Home Customizer® Package. These plans are indicated below with this symbol: 🏠. See page 221 for information. Some plans are also part of our Quote One® estimating service and are indicated by this symbol 🏠. See page 214 for more information.

To Order: Fill in and send the order form on page 221—or call toll free 1-800-521-6797 or 520-297-8200.

DESIGN	PRICE	PAGE	CUSTOMIZABLE	QUOTE ONE®	DECK	DECK PRICE	LANDSCAPE	LANDSCAPE PRICE	REGIONS
▲2488	A	57	🏠	🏠	D102	Q			
▲2490	A	59	🏠	🏠					
▲2563	B	24	🏠	🏠	D114	R	L201	Y	1-3,5,6,8
▲2571	A	23	🏠		D114	R	L202	X	1-3,5,6,8
▲2597	B	22	🏠	🏠	D114	R	L226	X	1-8
▲2661	B	21	🏠	🏠	D113	R	L202	X	1-3,5,6,8
▲2671	B	53	🏠	🏠	D114	R	L234	Y	1-8
▲2682	A	20	🏠	🏠	D115	Q	L200	X	1-3,5,6,8
▲2699	C	195	🏠	🏠			L211	Y	1-8
▲2707	A	106	🏠	🏠	D117	S	L226	X	1-8
▲2777	B	26	🏠	🏠	D101	R	L221	X	1-3,5,6,8
▲2802	B	103	🏠	🏠	D118	R	L220	Y	1-3,5,6,8
▲2805	B	107	🏠	🏠	D113	R	L220	Y	1-3,5,6,8
▲2871	B	58	🏠	🏠	D117	S			
▲2875	B	160	🏠	🏠	D113	R	L236	Z	3,4,7
▲2878	B	34	🏠	🏠	D112	R	L200	X	1-3,5,6,8
▲2880	C	27	🏠	🏠	D114	R	L212	Z	1-8
▲2912	B	161	🏠	🏠					
▲2913	B	55	🏠	🏠	D124	S			
▲2918	B	52	🏠	🏠	D124	S			
▲2922	D	185		🏠					
▲2947	B	112	🏠	🏠	D112	R	L200	X	1-3,5,6,8
▲2948	B	162	🏠	🏠					
▲2949	C	157	🏠	🏠					
▲2950	C	159	🏠	🏠					
▲2962	B	104	🏠	🏠					
▲2964	B	102	🏠	🏠					
▲2067	B	105	🏠				L217	Y	1-8
▲3314	B	46	🏠	🏠			L200	X	1-3,5,6,8
▲3316	A	47	🏠	🏠			L202	X	1-3,5,6,8
▲3321	C	48	🏠	🏠	D116	R	L209	Y	1-8
▲3331	A	97	🏠	🏠			L203	Y	1-3,5,6,8
▲3332	B	29	🏠	🏠			L200	X	1-3,5,6,8
▲3340	B	35	🏠	🏠			L224	Y	1-3,5,6,8
▲3355	A	31	🏠	🏠	D117	S	L220	Y	1-3,5,6,8
▲3366	D	198	🏠	🏠			L220	Y	1-3,5,6,8
▲3368	C	61	🏠	🏠	D104	S	L220	Y	1-3,5,6,8
▲3376	B	108	🏠	🏠	D114	R	L205	Y	1-3,5,6,8
▲3400	C	165	🏠	🏠			L236	Z	3,4,7
▲3402	D	184	🏠	🏠			L236	Z	3,4,7
▲3403	B	87	🏠	🏠			L237	Y	7
▲3405	D	187	🏠	🏠			L236	Z	3,4,7
▲3406	C	156	🏠	🏠			L232	Y	4,7
▲3431	B	153	🏠	🏠					
▲3433	C	154	🏠	🏠			L213	Z	1-8
▲3442	A	64	🏠	🏠	D115	Q	L200	X	1-3,5,6,8
▲3453	A	63	🏠	🏠			L238	Y	3,4,7,8
▲3465	A	148	🏠	🏠			L205	Y	1-3,5,6,8

DESIGN	PRICE	PAGE	CUSTOMIZABLE	QUOTE ONE®	DECK	DECK PRICE	LANDSCAPE	LANDSCAPE PRICE	REGIONS
▲ 3466	B	149	●	🏠	D110	R	L207	Z	1-8
▲ 3486	B	152	●	🏠					
▲ 3487	B	36	●	🏠					
▲ 3491	B	37	●	🏠	D111	S	L209	Y	1-6,8
▲ 3497	B	49	●	🏠			L215	Z	1-6,8
▲ 3519	C	25	●	🏠					
▲ 3622	C	101	●	🏠			L282	X	1-8
▲ 3628	C	158	●	🏠			L224	Y	1-3,5,6,8
▲ 3632	C	164	●	🏠			L237	Y	7
▲ 3644	B	155	●	🏠					
▲ 3652	B	54	●	🏠	D105	R	L220	Y	1-3,5,6,8
▲ 3656	A	30	●	🏠			L205	Y	1-3,5,6,8
▲ 3659	B	33	●	🏠			L290	Y	1-8
▲ 3660	B	163	●	🏠			L236	Z	3,4,7
▲ 3674	B	141	●	🏠	D110	R	L292	X	1-8
▲ 3679	B	132	●	🏠	D111	S	L282	X	1-8
▲ 3683	B	150	●		D111	S	L292	X	1-8
6602	D	173							
• 6621	D	175		🏠					
• 6622	C	172		🏠					
6645	C	177							
6652	E	190							
6654	D	174							
6657	E	188							
6658	C	166							
6668	E	189							
† 7220	C	96							
† 7221	C	66							
† 7226	B	18							
† 7291	C	113							
† 7292	C	122							
† 7293	D	127							
† 7299	D	124							
7403	E	194							
7601	C	118							
7800	B	78							
7805	E	192							
7806	C	82							
7807	D	145							
7814	E	193							
7818	C	81							
7820	C	83							
8064	B	8							
8143	D	147							
8158	C	13							
8164	C	91							
8165	C	9							
8166	B	12							
8168	B	16							
8169	A	15							
8174	A	14							
8175	A	115							
8177	B	146							
8183	B	90							
8224	C	92							
8229	B	28							
8601	B	181							
8630	B	168							
8633	B	169							
8634	B	180							
8644	B	179							
8662	B	171							
8672	C	176							
8684	B	178							
8693	A	182							
8894	A	56							
8923	D	99		🏠					
8956	C	4							
8992	D	121							
8997	C	133							
8998	C	126							
✷ 9055	D	93		🏠					
✷ 9063	D	95		🏠					
✷ 9055	D	100		🏠					
✷ 9131	C	7		🏠					
9164	C	5							
9185	C	50							
9186	C	6							
9187	C	32							
† 9200	C	71		🏠					
† 9202	C	65							
† 9204	D	74		🏠					
† 9237	C	70							
† 9238	C	10		🏠					

DESIGN	PRICE	PAGE	CUSTOMIZABLE	QUOTE ONE®	DECK	DECK PRICE	LANDSCAPE	LANDSCAPE PRICE	REGIONS
† 9250	C	72		🏠					
† 9265	C	11		🏠					
† 9323	D	17							
† 9361	C	88							
✷ 9422	A	62							
✷ 9430	B	42							
✷ 9432	C	73							
✷ 9452	B	170							
✷ 9459	B	60							
✷ 9483	C	69							
✷ 9498	E	191							
✷ 9502	B	67							
✷ 9529	A	51							
✷ 9530	A	51							
✷ 9531	A	51							
✷ 9578	C	68		🏠					
✷ 9585	C	139							
✷ 9587	C	140							
✷ 9588	C	130							
✷ 9596	E	197							
◆ 9605	D	134							
◆ 9621	C	131		🏠					
◆ 9632	D	136		🏠					
◆ 9634	D	98							
◆ 9638	C	138							
◆ 9645	C	94		🏠					
◆ 9660	D	89							
◆ 9661	C	44		🏠					
◆ 9664	B	119		🏠					
◆ 9679	C	43							
◆ 9702	D	135		🏠					
◆ 9705	D	40							
◆ 9726	B	114							
◆ 9728	C	19							
◆ 9734	C	39		🏠					
◆ 9736	D	41							
◆ 9738	D	129		🏠					
◆ 9742	C	123							
◆ 9744	D	167							
◆ 9747	C	116							
◆ 9749	C	110							
◆ 9753	B	111							
◆ 9757	D	80							
◆ 9760	B	38							
◆ 9763	C	120							
◆ 9764	C	117		🏠					
◆ 9767	D	137							
◆ 9771	C	125							
◆ 9783	C	128							
■ 9831	C	76		🏠					
■ 9853	B	79		🏠					
■ 9862	C	77		🏠					
■ 9884	C	86		🏠					
■ 9885	C	84		🏠					
■ 9904	B	87		🏠					
9949	B	85							
9956	C	144							
9959	C	142							
9965	C	143							
9969	D	196							
▲ G109		207							
▲ G206		204							
▲ G222		209							
▲ G247		208							
▲ G274		203							
▲ G275		203							
▲ G276		203							
▲ G277		203							
▲ G278		202							
▲ G279		202							
▲ G280		202							
▲ G281		202							
▲ G282		201							
▲ G283		201							
▲ G284		201							
▲ G285		201							
▲ G291		211							
▲ G293		210							
▲ G294		200							
▲ G295		200							
▲ G296		200							
▲ G297		200							
▲ G302		205							
R126		206							

Before You Order . . .

Before filling out the coupon at right or calling us on our Toll-Free Blueprint Hotline, you may want to learn more about our services and products. Here's some information you will find helpful.

Quick Turnaround

We process and ship every blueprint order from our office within 48 hours. Because of this quick turnaround, we won't send a formal notice acknowledging receipt of your order.

Our Exchange Policy

Since blueprints are printed in response to your order, we cannot honor requests for refunds. However, we will exchange your entire first order for an equal number of blueprints at a price of $50 for the first set and $10 for each additional set; $70 total exchange fee for 4 sets; $100 total exchange fee for 8 sets . . . *plus* the difference in cost if exchanging for a design in a higher price bracket or *less* the difference in cost if exchanging for a design in lower price bracket. One exchange is allowed within a year of purchase date. **(Sepias are not exchangeable.)** All sets from the first order must be returned before the exchange can take place. Please add $18 for postage and handling via ground service; $30 via Second Day Air; $40 via Next Day Air.

About Reverse Blueprints

If you want to build in reverse of the plan as shown, we will include an extra set of reverse blueprints (mirror image) for an additional fee of $50. Although lettering and dimensions will appear backward, reverses will be a useful aid if you decide to flop the plan.

Revising, Modifying and Customizing Plans

The wide variety of designs available in this publication allows you to select ideas and concepts for a home to fit your building site and match your family's needs, wants and budget. Like many homeowners who buy these plans, you and your builder, architect or engineer may want to make changes to them. Some minor changes may be made by your builder, but we recommend that most changes be made by a licensed architect or engineer. If you need to make alterations to a design that is customizable, you need only order our Home Customizer® Package to get you started. As set forth below, we cannot assume any responsibility for blueprints which have been changed, whether by you, your builder or by professionals selected by you or referred to you by us, because such individuals are outside our supervision and control.

Architectural and Engineering Seals

Some cities and states are now requiring that a licensed architect or engineer review and "seal" a blueprint, or officially approve it, prior to construction due to concerns over energy costs, safety and other factors. Prior to application for a building permit or the start of actual construction, we strongly advise that you consult your local building official who can tell you if such a review is required.

About the Designers

The architects and designers whose work appears in this publication are among America's leading residential designers. Each plan was designed to meet the requirements of a nationally recognized model building code in effect at the time and place the plan was drawn. Because national building codes change from time to time, plans may not comply with any such code at the time they are sold to a customer. In addition, building officials may not accept these plans as final construction documents of record as the plans may need to be modified and additional drawings and details added to suit local conditions and requirements. We strongly advise that purchasers consult a licensed architect or engineer, and their local building official, before starting any construction related to these plans.

Local Building Codes and Zoning Requirements

At the time of creation, our plans are drawn to specifications published by the Building Officials and Code Administrators (BOCA) International, Inc.; the Southern Building Code Congress (SBCCI) International, Inc.; the International Conference of Building Officials; or the Council of American Building Officials (CABO). Our plans are designed to meet or exceed national building standards. Because of the great differences in geography and climate throughout the United States and Canada, each state, county and municipality has its own building codes, zone requirements, ordinances and building regulations. Your plan may need to be modified to comply with local requirements regarding snow loads, energy codes, soil and seismic conditions and a wide range of other matters. In addition, you may need to obtain permits or inspections from local governments before and in the course of construction. Prior to using blueprints ordered from us, we strongly advise that you consult a licensed architect or engineer—and speak with your local building official—before applying for any permit or beginning construction. We authorize the use of our blueprints on the express condition that you strictly comply with all local building codes, zoning requirements and other applicable laws, regulations, ordinances and requirements. **Notice:** Plans for homes to be built in Nevada must be re-drawn by a Nevada-registered professional. Consult your building official for more information on this subject.

Foundation and Exterior Wall Changes

Most of our plans are drawn with either a full or partial basement foundation. Depending on your specific climate or regional building practices, you may wish to change this basement to a slab or crawlspace. Most professional contractors and builders can easily adapt your plans to alternate foundation types. Likewise, most can easily change 2x4 wall construction to 2x6, or vice versa.

Disclaimer

We and the designers we work with have put substantial care and effort into the creation of our blueprints. However, because we cannot provide on-site consultation, supervision and control over actual construction, and because of the great variance in local building requirements, building practices and soil, seismic, weather and other conditions, WE CANNOT MAKE ANY WARRANTY, EXPRESS OR IMPLIED, WITH RESPECT TO THE CONTENT OR USE OF OUR BLUEPRINTS, INCLUDING BUT NOT LIMITED TO ANY WARRANTY OF MERCHANTABILITY OR OF FITNESS FOR A PARTICULAR PURPOSE.

Terms and Conditions

The terms and conditions governing our license of blueprints to you are set forth in the material accompanying the blueprints. This material tells you how to return the blueprints if you do not agree to these terms and conditions.

How Many Blueprints Do You Need?

A single set of blueprints is sufficient to study a home in greater detail. However, if you are planning to obtain cost estimates from a contractor or subcontractors—or if you are planning to build immediately—you will need more sets. Because additional sets are cheaper when ordered in quantity with the original order, make sure you order enough blueprints to satisfy all requirements. The following checklist will help you determine how many you need:

____ Owner

____ Builder (generally requires at least three sets; one as a legal document, one to use during inspections, and at least one to give to subcontractors)

____ Local Building Department (often requires two sets)

____ Mortgage Lender (usually one set for a conventional loan; three sets for FHA or VA loans)

____ TOTAL NUMBER OF SETS

Have You Seen Our Newest Designs?

Home Planners is one of the country's most active home design firms, creating nearly 100 new plans each year. At least 50 of our latest creations are featured in each edition of our New Design Portfolio. You may have received a copy with your latest purchase by mail. If not, or if you purchased this book from a local retailer, just return the coupon below for your FREE copy. Make sure you consider the very latest of what Home Planners has to offer.

Yes! Please send my FREE copy of your latest New Design Portfolio.

Offer good to U.S. shipping address only.

Name _____

Address _____

City_____State_____Zip _____

HOME PLANNERS, A Division of
Hanley-Wood, Inc.
3275 WEST INA ROAD, SUITE 110
TUCSON, ARIZONA 85741

Order Form Key

| TB47 |

Toll Free 1-800-521-6797

Regular Office Hours:
8:00 a.m. to 8:00 p.m. Eastern Time, Monday through Friday
Our staff will gladly answer any questions during regular office hours. Our answering service can place orders after hours or on weekends.

If we receive your order by 4:00 p.m. Eastern Time, Monday through Friday, we'll process it and ship within 48 hours. When ordering by phone, please have your charge card ready. We'll also ask you for the Order Form Key Number at the bottom of the coupon.

By FAX: Copy the Order Form on the next page and send it on our FAX line: 1-800-224-6699 or 1-520-544-3086.

Canadian Customers
Order Toll-Free 1-800-561-4169

For faster service and plans that are modified for building in Canada, customers may now call in orders directly to our Canadian supplier of plans and charge the purchase to a charge card. Or, you may complete the order form at right, adding 40% to all prices and mail in Canadian funds to:

The Plan Centre 60 Baffin Place
Unit 5
Waterloo, Ontario N2V 1Z7

OR: Copy the Order Form and send it via our Canadian FAX line: 1-800-719-3291.

The Home Customizer®

"This house is perfect...if only the family room were two feet wider." Sound familiar? In response to the numerous requests for this type of modification, Home Planners has developed **The Home Customizer® Package**. This exclusive package offers our top-of-the-line materials to make it easy for anyone, anywhere to customize any Home Planners design to fit their needs. Check the index on page 218 for those plans which are customizable.

Some of the changes you can make to any of our plans include:

- exterior elevation changes
- kitchen and bath modifications
- roof, wall and foundation changes
- room additions and more!

The Home Customizer® Package includes everything you'll need to make the necessary changes to your favorite Home Planners design. The package includes:

- instruction book with examples
- architectural scale and clear work film
- erasable red marker and removable correction tape
- ¼"-scale furniture cutouts
- 1 set reproducible, erasable Sepias
- 1 set study blueprints for communicating changes to your design professional
- a copyright release letter so you can make copies as you need them
- referral letter with the name, address and telephone number of the professional in your region who is trained in modifying Home Planners designs efficiently and inexpensively.

The price of the **Home Customizer® Package** ranges from $555 to $795, depending on the price schedule of the design you have chosen. **The Home Customizer® Package** will not only save you 25% to 75% of the cost of drawing the plans from scratch with a custom architect or engineer, it will also give you the flexibility to have your changes and modifications made by our referral network or by the professional of your choice. Now it's even easier and more affordable to have the custom home you've always wanted.

New Custom Engineering Service

Through this exciting new service, you can now obtain an engineering seal for the structural elements of any Home Planners plan including complete calculations (minus foundation engineering) from a competent, registered professional. You'll receive a detailed analysis and engineering seal that will assist with the permit process, even in areas that normally require very specific calculations. For more complete information about this service, see page 214.

 For information about any of the above services or to order call 1-800-521-6797.

| **BLUEPRINTS ARE NOT RETURNABLE** |

ORDER FORM

HOME PLANNERS, A Division of Hanley-Wood, Inc.
SUITE 110, TUCSON, ARIZONA 85741

THE BASIC BLUEPRINT PACKAGE
Rush me the following (please refer to the Plans Index and Price Schedule in this section):

_____	Set(s) of blueprints for plan number(s) _____.	$_____
_____	Set(s) of sepias for plan number(s) _____.	$_____
_____	Home Customizer® Package for plan(s)_____.	$_____
_____	Additional identical blueprints in same order @ $50 per set.	$_____
_____	Reverse blueprints @ $50 per set.	$_____
_____	Custom Engineering Service for plan _____.	$_____
	_____ Lateral Load Calculations (add 25%)	$_____
	_____ Roof, Floors and Walls Framing (add 25%)	$_____
	_____ Steel Framing Options (add 50%)	$_____

IMPORTANT EXTRAS
Rush me the following:

_____	Materials List: $50	
	$75 Design Basics. Add $10 for a Schedule E plan Materials List.	$_____
_____	**Quote One®** Summary Cost Report @ $19.95 for 1, $14.95 for each additional, for plans _____	$_____
	Building location: City _____ Zip Code _____	
_____	**Quote One®** Materials Cost Report @ $110 Schedule A-D; $120 Schedule E for plan_____	$_____
	(Must be purchased with Blueprints set.)	
	Building location: City _____ Zip Code _____	
_____	Specification Outlines @ $10 each.	$_____
_____	Detail Sets @ $14.95 each; any two for $22.95; any three for $29.95; all four for $39.95 (save $19.85).	$_____
	❏ Plumbing ❏ Electrical ❏ Construction ❏ Mechanical (These helpful details provide general construction advice and are not specific to any single plan.)	
_____	Plan-A-Home® @ $29.95 each.	$_____

DECK BLUEPRINTS

_____	Set(s) of Deck Plan _____.	$_____
_____	Additional identical blueprints in same order @ $10 per set.	$_____
_____	Reverse blueprints @ $10 per set.	$_____
_____	Set of Standard Deck Details @ $14.95 per set.	$_____
_____	Set of Complete Building Package (Best Buy!) Includes Custom Deck Plan _____. (See Index and Price Schedule) Plus Standard Deck Details	$_____

LANDSCAPE BLUEPRINTS

_____	Set(s) of Landscape Plan _____.	$_____
_____	Additional identical blueprints in same order @ $10 per set.	$_____
_____	Reverse blueprints @ $10 per set.	$_____

Please indicate the appropriate region of the country for
Plant & Material List. (See Map on page 217): Region _____

POSTAGE AND HANDLING

	1-3 sets	4+ sets
DELIVERY (Requires street address - No P.O. Boxes)		
•Regular Service (Allow 4-6 days delivery)	❏ $15.00	❏ $18.00
•2nd Day Air (Allow 2-3 days delivery)	❏ $20.00	❏ $30.00
•Next Day Air (Allow 1 day delivery)	❏ $30.00	❏ $40.00
CERTIFIED MAIL (Requires signature) If no street address available. (Allow 4-6 days delivery)	❏ $20.00	❏ $30.00
OVERSEAS DELIVERY Note: All delivery times are from date Blueprint Package is shipped.	fax, phone or mail for quote	

POSTAGE (From box above)	$_____
SUB-TOTAL	$_____
SALES TAX (AZ 5%, CA & NY 8.25%, DC 5.75%, IL 6.25%, MI 6%, MN 6.5%)	$_____
TOTAL (Sub-total and tax)	$_____

YOUR ADDRESS (please print)

Name _____

Street _____

City _____ State_____ Zip _____

Daytime telephone number (_____) _____

FOR CREDIT CARD ORDERS ONLY
Please fill in the information below:
Credit card number _____
Exp. Date: Month / Year _____
Check one ❏ Visa ❏ MasterCard ❏ Discover Card

Signature _____

Please check appropriate box: ❏ Licensed Builder-Contractor *End of week*
❏ Homeowner

 ORDER TOLL FREE!
1-800-521-6797 or 520-297-8200

Order Form Key
| TB47 |

Heather X 8165

221

Helpful Books & Software

Home Planners wants your building experience to be as pleasant and trouble-free as possible. That's why we've expanded our library of Do-It-Yourself titles to help you along. In addition to our beautiful plans books, we've added books to guide you through specific projects as well as the construction process. In fact, these are titles that will be as useful after your dream home is built as they are right now.

COUNTRY

1 200 country designs from classic to contemporary by 7 winning designers. 224 pages $8.95

BUDGET-SMART

2 200 efficient plans from 7 top designers, that you can really afford to build! 224 pages $8.95

MOVE-UP

3 200 stylish designs for today's growing families from 9 hot designers. 224 pages $8.95 NEW!

NARROW-LOT

4 200 unique homes less than 60' wide from 7 designers. Up to 3,000 square feet. 224 pages $8.95

REGIONAL BEST

5 200 beautiful homes from across America by 7 regional designers. 224 pages $8.95 NEW!

EXPANDABLES

6 200 flexible plans that expand with your needs from 7 top designers. 240 pages $8.95 NEW!

BEST SELLERS

7 NEW! Our 50th Anniversary book with 200 of our very best designs in full color! 224 page $12.95

NEW ENGLAND

8 260 of the best in Colonial home design. Special interior design sections, too. 384 pages $14.95

AFFORDABLE

9 430 cost-saving plans specially selected for modest to medium building budgets. 320 pages $9.95

LUXURY

10 154 fine luxury plans-loaded with luscious amenities! 192 pages $14.95

ONE-STORY

11 448 designs for all lifestyles. 860 to 5,400 square feet. 384 pages $9.95 NEW!

TWO-STORY

12 460 designs for one-and-a-half and two stories. 1,245 to 7,275 square feet. 384 pages $9.95

VACATION

13 345 designs for recreation, retirement and leisure. 312 pages $8.95 NEW!

MULTI-LEVEL

14 312 designs for split-levels, bi-levels, multi-levels and walkouts. 224 pages $8.95 NEW!

OUTDOOR

15 42 unique outdoor projects. Gazebos, strombellas, bridges, sheds, playsets and more! 96 pages $7.95 NEW!

DECKS
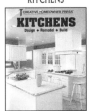
16 25 outstanding single-, double- and multi-level decks you can build. 112 pages $7.95

ENCYCLOPEDIA

17 500 exceptional plans for all styles and budgets—the best book of its kind! 352 pages $9.95

MODERN & CLASSIC

18 341 impressive homes featuring the latest in contemporary design. 304 pages $9.95

TRADITIONAL

19 403 designs of classic beauty and elegance. 304 pages $9.95

VICTORIAN

20 160 striking Victorian and Farmhouse designs from three leading designers. 192 pages $12.95

SOUTHERN

21 207 homes rich in Southern styling and comfort. 240 pages $8.95 NEW!

WESTERN

22 215 designs that capture the spirit and diversity of the Western lifestyle. 208 pages $9.95

EMPTY-NESTER
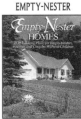
23 200 exciting plans for empty-nesters, retirees and childless couples. 224 pages $8.95

STARTER

24 200 easy-to-build plans for starter and low-budget houses. 224 pages $8.95

Landscape Designs

FRONT & BACK

25 The first book of do-it-yourself landscapes. 40 front, 15 backyards. 208 pages $14.95

BACKYARDS

26 40 designs focused solely on creating your own specially themed backyard oasis. 160 pages $14.95

EASY CARE

27 NEW! 41 special landscapes designed for beauty and low maintenance. 160 pages $14.95

Design Software

BOOK & CD ROM

28 NEW! Both the Home Planners Gold book and matching Windows™ CD ROM with 3D floor-plans. $24.95

3D HOME DESIGNER

29 Take home design to the next level. Windows™ compatible program automatically creates 3D views of any floor plan you draw. Includes bonus CD of 500 Designs. $49.95

Interior Design

HOME DECORATING

30 Special effects and creative ideas for all surfaces. Includes simple step-by-step diagrams. 96 pages $9.95

BATHROOMS

31 An innovative guide to organizing, remodeling and decorating your bathroom. 96 pages $8.95

KITCHENS
32 An imaginative guide to designing the perfect kitchen. Chock full of bright ideas to make your job easier. 176 pages $14 .95

Planning Books & Quick Guides

TRIM & MOLDING 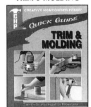	**PAINTING** 	**ROOFING** 	**WALLS & MORE** 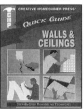

33 Step-by-step instructions for installing baseboards, window and door casings and more. 80 pages $7.95

34 Tips from the pros on everything from preparation to clean-up. 80 pages $7.95

35 Information on the latest tools, materials and techniques for roof installation or repair. 80 pages $7.95

36 A clear and concise guide to repairing or remodeling walls and ceilings. 80 pages $7.95

FLOORS 	**PATIOS & WALKS** 	**WINDOWS & DOORS** 	**PLUMBING** 

37 All the information you need for repairing, replacing or installing floors in any home. 80 pages $7.95

38 Clear step-by-step instructions take you from the basic design stages to the finished project. 80 pages $7.95

39 Installation techniques and tips that make your project easier and more professional looking. 80 pages $7.95

40 Tackle any plumbing installation or repair as quickly and efficiently as a professional. 160 pages $12.95

ADDING SPACE 	**HOME REPAIR** 	**TILE**	**WALLPAPERING** 

41 Convert attics, basements and bonus rooms to useful living space. 160 pages $14.95

42 An owner's manual for your home. Sound advice on home maintenance and improvements. 256 pages $9.95

43 Every kind of tile for every kind of application. Includes tips on use installation and repair. 176 pages $12.95

44 Use the book the pros use. Covers tools and techniques for every type of wallcovering. 136 pages $12.95

BASIC WIRING 	**HOUSE CONTRACTING** 	**VISUAL HANDBOOK** 	**CONTRACTING GUIDE**

45 A straight forward guide to one of the most misunderstood systems in the home. 160 pages $12.95

46 Everything you need to know to act as your own general contractor...and save up to 25% off building costs. 134 pages $12.95

47 A plain-talk guide to the construction process; financing to final walk-through, this book covers it all. 498 pages $19.95

48 Loaded with information to make you more confident in dealing with contractors and subcontractors. 287 pages $18.95

FRAMING

49 For those who want to take a more-hands on approach to their dream. 319 pages $19.95

Additional Books Order Form

To order your books, just check the box of the book numbered below and complete the coupon. We will process your order and ship it from our office within 48 hours. Send coupon and check (in U.S. funds).

YES! Please send me the books I've indicated:

☐ 1:FH $8.95	☐ 26:BYL $14.95
☐ 2:BS $8.95	☐ 27:ECL $14.95
☐ 3:MU $8.95	☐ 28:HPGC $24.95
☐ 4:NL $8.95	☐ 29:PLAN3D $49.95
☐ 5:AA $8.95	☐ 30:CDP $9.95
☐ 6:EX $8.95	☐ 31:CDB $8.95
☐ 7:HPG $12.95	☐ 32:CKI $14.95
☐ 8:NES $14.95	☐ 33:CGT $7.95
☐ 9:AH $9.95	☐ 34:CGP $7.95
☐ 10:LD2 . . . . $14.95	☐ 35:CGR $7.95
☐ 11:VO $9.95	☐ 36:CGC $7.95
☐ 12:VT $9.95	☐ 37:CGF $7.95
☐ 13:VH $8.95	☐ 38:CGW $7.95
☐ 14:VS $8.95	☐ 39:CGD $7.95
☐ 15:YG $7.95	☐ 40:CMP $12.95
☐ 16:DP $7.95	☐ 41:CAS $14.95
☐ 17:EN $9.95	☐ 42:CHR $9.95
☐ 18:EC $9.95	☐ 43:CWT $12.95
☐ 19:ET $9.95	☐ 44:CW $12.95
☐ 20:VDH $12.95	☐ 45:CBW $12.95
☐ 21:SH $8.95	☐ 46:SBC $12.95
☐ 22:WH $9.95	☐ 47:RVH $19.95
☐ 23:EP $8.95	☐ 48:BCC $18.95
☐ 24:ST $8.95	☐ 49:SRF $19.95
☐ 25:HL $14.95	

Canadian Customers
Order Toll-Free 1-800-561-4169

Additional Books Sub-Total $_____
ADD Postage and Handling $ 3.00
Sales Tax: (AZ 5%, CA & NY 8.25%, DC 5.75%,
IL 6.25%, MI 6%, MN 6.5%) $_____
YOUR TOTAL (Sub-Total, Postage/Handling, Tax) $_____

YOUR ADDRESS (Please print)

Name _____

Street _____

City _____State_____Zip _____

Phone (_____) _____—_____

YOUR PAYMENT
Check one: ☐ Check ☐ Visa ☐ MasterCard ☐ Discover Card
Required credit card information:

Credit Card Number_____

Expiration Date (Month/Year) _____/ _____

Signature Required _____

 Home Planners, A Division of Hanley-Wood, Inc.
3275 W Ina Road, Suite 110, Dept. BK, Tucson, AZ 85741

TB47

ABOUT THE DESIGNERS

The Blue Ribbon Designer Series™ is a collection of books featuring the home plans of a diverse group of outstanding home designers and architects known as the Blue Ribbon Network of Designers. This group of companies is dedicated to creating and marketing the finest possible plans for home construction on a regional and national basis. Each of the companies exhibits superior work and integrity in all phases of the stock-plan business including modern, trendsetting floor planning, a professionally executed blueprint package and a strong sense of service and commitment to the consumer.

Design Basics, Inc.

For nearly a decade, Design Basics, a nationally recognized home design service located in Omaha, has been developing plans for custom home builders. Since 1987, the firm has consistently appeared in *Builder* magazine, the official magazine of the National Association of Home Builders, as the top-selling designer. The company's plans also regularly appear in numerous other shelter magazines such as *Better Homes and Gardens, House Beautiful* and *Home Planner.*

Stephen Fuller/Design Traditions

Design Traditions was established by Stephen S. Fuller with the tenets of innovation, quality, originality and uncompromising architectural techniques in traditional and European homes. Especially popular throughout the Southeast, Design Traditions' plans are known for their extensive detail and thoughtful design. They are widely published in such shelter magazines as *Southern Living* magazine and *Better Homes and Gardens.*

Alan Mascord Design Associates, Inc.

Founded in 1983 as a local supplier to the building community, Mascord Design Associates of Portland, Oregon began to successfully publish plans nationally in 1985. With plans now drawn exclusively on computer, Mascord Design Associates quickly received a reputation for homes that are easy to build yet meet the rigorous demands of the buyers' market, winning local and national awards. The company's trademark is creating floor plans that work well and exhibit excellent traffic patterns. Their motto is: "Drawn to build, designed to sell."

Larry E. Belk Designs

Through the years, Larry E. Belk has worked with individuals and builders alike to provide a quality product. After listening to over 4,000 dreams and watching them become reality all across America, Larry's design philosophy today combines traditional exteriors with upscale interiors designed for contemporary lifestyles. Flowing, open spaces and interesting angles define his interiors. Great emphasis is placed on providing views that showcase the natural environment. Dynamic exteriors reflect Larry's extensive home construction experience, painstaking research and talent as a fine artist.

Larry W. Garnett & Associates, Inc.

Starting as a designer of homes for Houston-area residents, Garnett & Associates has been marketing designs nationally for the past ten years. A well-respected design firm, the company's plans are regularly featured in *House Beautiful, Country Living, Home* and *Professional Builder.* Numerous accolades, including several from the Texas Institute of Building Design and the American Institute of Building Design, have been awarded to the company for excellence in architecture.

Home Planners

Headquartered in Tucson, Arizona, with additional offices in Detroit, Home Planners is one of the longest-running and most successful home design firms in the United States. With over 2,500 designs in its portfolio, the company provides a wide range of styles, sizes and types of homes for the residential builder. All of Home Planners' designs are created with the care and professional expertise that fifty years of experience in the home-planning business affords. Their homes are designed to be built, lived in and enjoyed for years to come.

Donald A. Gardner, Architects, Inc.

The South Carolina firm of Donald A. Gardner was established in response to a growing demand for residential designs that reflect constantly changing lifestyles. The company's specialty is providing homes with refined, custom-style details and unique features such as passive-solar designs and open floor plans. Computer-aided design and drafting technology resulting in trouble-free construction documents places the firm at the leading edge of the home plan industry.

The Sater Design Collection

The Sater Design Collection has a long established tradition of providing South Florida's most diverse and extraordinary custom designed homes. Their goal is to fulfill each client's particular need for an exciting approach to design by merging creative vision with elements that satisfy a desire for a distinctive lifestyle. This philosophy is proven, as exemplified by over 50 national design awards, numerous magazine features and, most important, satisfied clients. The result is an elegant statement of lasting beauty and value.

Home Design Services, Inc.

For the past fifteen years, Home Design Services of Longwood, Florida, has been formulating plans for the sun-country lifestyle. At the forefront of design innovation and imagination, the company has developed award-winning designs that are consistently praised for their highly detailed, free-flowing floor plans, imaginative and exciting interior architecture and elevations which have gained international appeal.